Love, motherhood and the African heritage

The legacy of Flora Nwapa

Femi Nzegwu

African
Renaissance

First published in Great Britain and Senegal in 2001 by
African Renaissance
B.P. 5336,
Dakar,
Senegal,
West Africa.

A catalogue record for this book is available from the British Library.

ISBN 1-903625-09-2

500749196

920 NWAP

African Renaissance is a member of the Praxis
publishing co-operative.

www.nursingpraxis.com

Printed and bound in Great Britain by
RPM Reprographics, Chichester, West Sussex.

This book is dedicated to four people, who collectively represent two generations of my family. It is a tribute to my mother Felicia Aina Nzegwu, and father Theophilus Enwezor Nzegwu. To my mother, who literally worked herself to the bone to ensure that my siblings and I had a headstart in life after she lost Daddy, a wonderful man and beloved friend and partner whose precious life was senselessly terminated in July 1966 in the mayhem that was, and is, the Nigerian state. I honour you for your ideals, your courage, your honesty, your faith, your integrity which both your lives have represented to all who knew you. Thank you mama and daddy for all that you ever did for me. I also dedicate this book to my sons Nnamdi Nzegwu Ekwe-Ekwe and Chidi Nzegwu Ekwe-Ekwe that they may always know from whence they came, and that they may one day see the true Africa of their heritage fully actualised.

The systematic looting of language can be recognized by the tendency of its users to forgo its nuanced, complex, mid-wifery properties, replacing them with menace and subjugation. Oppressive language does more than represent violence; it is violence; does more than represent the limits of knowledge; it limits knowledge. Whether it is obscuring state language or the faux language of mindless media; whether it is the proud but calcified language of the academy or the commodity-driven language of law-without ethics, or language designed for the estrangement of minorities, hiding its racist plunder in its literary cheek - it must be rejected, altered and exposed.

Toni Morrison, *The Nobel Lecture in Literature*, 1993

Contents

Acknowledgements

First of all I wish to thank God and my *chi* for the opportunity to have written this book. This study first started life as a PhD thesis and I warmly acknowledge the steadfast support given to me throughout the research by my then supervisor, Professor Lyn Innes of the University of Canterbury, Kent. I would like to thank my parents the late Mrs Felicia Aina Lakeson-Nzegwu and Major Theophilus Nzegwu for ensuring that I recognised, valued and enjoyed my dual Igbo/Yoruba heritages originating from two extremely progressive and advanced civilisations. I most sincerely thank my husband Herbert Ekwe-Ekwe without whose support this book simply would never have been written. My husband, in his support, epitomises the Igbo dual-sex complementarity of relationships. To my children Nnamdi and Chidi I give thanks for being perpetual reminders of the beautiful possibilities and inevitabilities of Africa. I also remember with great warmth two very beautiful young people Bidiak and Arit Amana, who prepared me so well for the joys of motherhood! I gratefully acknowledge and salute all those scholars and social critics/activists both at home in Africa and in the diaspora - those now resting in peace with the ancestors, and those still amongst us who have given valued meaning to being an African and thus to my life and work: in particular, the Igbo women who waged the 1929 Women's War against the British conquest and occupation of their homeland, Funmilayo Ransome-Kuti, Flora Nwapa, Olaudah Equiano, Marcus Garvey, George Washington Carver, Patrice Lumumba, Okot p'Bitek, David Diop, Amilcar Cabral, Duke Ellington, Walter Rodney, Cheikh Anta Diop, Chancellor Williams, Fela Anikulapo-Kuti; and Chinua Achebe, Kamene Okonjo, Nelson Mandela, Adiele Afigbo, Toni Morrison, Herbert Ekwe-Ekwe, Ifi Amadiume, Oprah Winfrey, Nina Mba, Elizabeth Isichei, Chinweizu, Chimalum Nwankwo, Kimani Nehusi, Gani Fawehinmi. To all I say *e se pupo, unu dalu o!*

Femi Nzegwu
Reading & Dakar, 8 December 2000

1
Introduction:
foreshadowing a renaissance

In recent years, following the success of the liberation of South Africa from centuries of European-minority rule, there has been an intensification of a major debate amongst Africans both at home and in the diaspora on their history, their reality, their future, and the means by which total self-determination and control over their destinies may be reasserted. This intellectual movement has as one of its purposes a critical examination of the *essences* of those components that define the totality of the African community/society to function optimally. The process of examining these varied facets of African cultural life has occurred at a time of immense challenges in the African World which have arisen despite the spectacular successes of territorial liberation. Thanks to the unprecedented, breath-taking phenomenal struggles and breakthroughs of the African resistance particularly during the course of the last 50 years, Africa begins a new decade, indeed a new century, and definitely a new millennium without having to contend with the formal, juridico-political, territorial occupation of any of its lands by a foreign aggressor state. This development is an incredible geo-political liberatory feat which must not be lost on the serious observer however depressing the overall socio-economic condition of contemporary Africa is, as we demonstrate in this study. This is why 40 years after liberation, with the virtual collapse of the nation-state as a result of artificially-constructed multi-nationalities, corrupt leaderships, bankrupt economies, incessant wars and the HIV/AIDS epidemic, Africans are literally asking themselves: 'What went wrong? When did the rain begin to beat us?' The current African debate is indeed an occasion for a profound re-examination of African social existence and the formulation of a strategy to embark on a much-needed programme for the restructuring and rehabilitation of the humanity of this continent. Africa and its peoples urgently require the dignity, spirit and sense of value that is necessary for a transformation of the conditions of existence and long-term progress. It is perhaps the coalescing of this set of multi-dimensional inquiries into the way forward for Africa that we see in the current African renaissance movement articulated by President Thabo Mbeki of South Africa.

In Flora Nwapa we find an African woman novelist whose writings during this 40-year period of African liberation continuously touch on a crucial feature of African existence that must be centrally placed in the current thinking on African renaissance: women. Nwapa concentrates on women in her society, both in the definition of themselves and their roles, as well as in relation to the totality of their social and cultural existence, thus opening up an entirely new, extremely innovative, women-centred front on the concerted African anti-colonial discourse of the late 1950s-1970s. Her contribution was aimed at restoring to the African experience the 'dual-gender' complementarity that defined independent, pre-conquest social relations and which had been dislocated and marginalised by both the European occupation and the emerging (post-conquest) African state. For Nwapa, the role of motherhood, family, relationship with spouse and all that defines the spouse (family, occupation, friends, interests), and the impact that these have on a range of economic and social factors in society are fundamental to an understanding of the contemporary African female experience. In Nwapa's contribution to this renaissance, we witness a historical bridging of the African woman's experience defined in the context of her political, social and economic existence that is anchored in the overwhelmingly vital institution of motherhood. This bridge is fundamental to identifying the medium through which those invaluable spheres and shades of African culture that require preservation and transmission to subsequent generations can occur. The overall aim of this research, therefore, is to demonstrate how Nwapa defined and contributed, long before the 'popularisation' of the intellectual movement known presently as 'African renaissance' or 'Afrocentrism', to the debate on the essence and dynamics of the African heritage, especially as it centres on women and motherhood.

Flora Nwapa, the first daughter of six children was born in Ugwuta in 1931 into a prominent and wealthy family. She attended primary and secondary school in Ugwuta, Elelenwa and Lagos and later gained admission to study English, History and Geography at University College, Ibadan from where she graduated in 1957. In 1958 she attended the University of Edinburgh where she obtained a Diploma in Education. Following her return from Scotland, she became an education officer in Calabar in 1958 and then proceeded to teach at Queen's School, Enugu in 1959. From 1962 to 1967 she held the position of assistant registrar at the University of Lagos and it was during this period of her life that her literary career was launched with the publication of her first novel *Efuru* by Heinemann in 1966. This was the same year that Nwapa fled her post in Lagos for Igboland following the Igbo massacres in northern Nigeria, which led the Igbo to declare their independence from the Nigeria federal state. In response to this development Nigeria declared war on Biafra which raged from 1967-1970. With the end of war in January 1970, Nwapa was appointed minister of health and social welfare in a government of reconstruction in Enugu. She is credited with performing the monumental task of locating and reuniting children placed in numerous orphanages set up in Biafra during the war with their families. She extended this rehabilitation feat by supervising the safe return to their families of those Biafran children who had been evacuated to Gabon and Cote d'Ivoire at the height of the war. A year later, Nwapa was appointed minister for land, survey, urban development and establishment, a position she held until 1975, and during which she switched her role from the task of children's rehabilitation to the rehabilitation of battered towns and cities. During her political career from 1970 to 1975 she published two novels, *Idu* (1970) and *Never Again* (1975), a collection of short stories, *This is Lagos and Other Stories* (1971) and her first children's book, *Emeka-Driver's Guard* (1972).

Flora Nwapa's next line of career would be in publishing. She and her husband Gogo Nwakuche founded Flora Nwapa and Co. and Tana Press in 1976 and opened for business in 1977. From its inception Nwapa confronted monumental difficulties in the running of her publishing house. In spite of the sentiments expressed in the country about the need for indigenously produced texts (novels and other learning material), Nwapa found this, in reality, to be mostly rhetoric. She noted a decided lack of interest and encouragement by the Nigerian government and its state-controlled education system towards indigenous publishers such as herself: '[Y]ou have to lobby for the school system to accept your books despite the high level of its relevance or appropriateness. There are some of us who cannot lobby so we just sell our books[W]e do not have orders from educational ministries.'[1] The financial outlays were considerable as Nwapa herself acknowledges: 'The publisher invests her money on the writer. Publishing is not a charitable organisationWe have published about twenty children's books (in 1988) but out of those only two are selling fairly well. Not one has been accepted to be used in schools'[2] In addition 'she [the publisher] must show the writer that she is fair. She must pay

---

[1]Quoted in Ezenwa-Ohaeto, 'Breaking Through: The Publishing Enterprise of Flora Nwapa,' in Marie Umeh, ed., *Emerging Perspectives on Flora Nwapa: Critical and Theoretical Essays* (Trenton and Asmara: Africa World, 1998), p. 194.
[2]Quoted in ibid, p. 195.

the writer whatever it is that is due her as royalty and must be prompt. The publisher must not give the writer the impression that the latter has been cheated of her royalties.'[3] It is to this problem that Chinua Achebe made reference almost a decade earlier: 'Literary gossip travels very far and very fast and a publisher who is [perceived to be] a shoddy business [person] will soon find no worthwhile manuscripts coming to him[/her].'[4] Both Achebe and Nwapa here refer to the need to maintain the highest levels of transparency and integrity in addressing the extremely sensitive, seemingly intractable issue of payment of royalties to African writers. It is important to understand the enormity of the task Nwapa assumed. In publishing writers other than herself she not only tied up her own resources in the production (that is in the editing, printing, marketing, distribution, etc.), but was also obligated to pay the writers their royalties on sales realised. This was in spite of the very low levels of these sales and the fact that the receipts from the sales did not even begin to approach the cost of production. In effect, Nwapa's publishing house would have had to be subsidising virtually every published title! Additionally, the cost of illustrators also proved to be quite considerable[5] and this impacted on the quality of a number of her books. It was undoubtedly Nwapa's commitment to produce culturally-relevant, visually attractive and entertaining material for children that led to the production of her picture books and the liberal use of colours in children's stories. However, in this area Nwapa was unable to find the right balance between talented illustrators/artists and the appropriate technology at an affordable price. The quality of the finished product was thus quite unprofessional looking and would not have been competitive, especially in the children's genre. Virginia Dike aptly captures this difficulty: '[I]n several books the physical quality seems to be compromised by financial constraints: the paper is opaque, the printing is too heavy and bold for easy reading and the illustration lacks finish.'[6] This weakness in no way detracts from the vision, energy and commitment of Nwapa in assuming this pioneering role as the first African female publisher/writer. The publishing business was and remains extremely difficult especially in the socio-political and economic circumstances of the then and present-day Nigeria for both women and men. The challenges and

---

[3]Ibid.
[4]Quoted in ibid., p. 190.
[5]James Gibbs, ed., *Handbook for Africa Writers* (Oxford: Hans Zell Publishers, 1986), p. 23.
[6]Quoted in Ezenwa-Ohaeto, 'Breaking Through: The Publishing Enterprise of Flora Nwapa', p. 196.

opportunities she encountered through her publishing business were a de facto reality given the prevailing political and economic realities and *not*, as Ezenwa-Ohaeto has suggested, even remotely related to 'her gender.'[7] His statements such as '[Nwapa] demonstrated to other female writers and entrepreneurs that it is possible for women to make such achievements in spite of the restrictions on her gender'[8] or '[f]or a woman and a writer who set out to create a small publishing concern, the success of her enterprise exceeded expectation'[9] are gratuitously patronising and merely serve to perpetuate the very stereotypes of African womanhood which Nwapa, through her books, consistently resisted. *Nwapa's achievements and failures transcend gender.* Her achievements should not be classified as such because she was a woman. Her achievements are noteworthy because in the face of considerable odds Nwapa distinguished herself by her vision and actualisation of what was possible in post-conquest Nigeria and by clearly identifiable contributions to the literary field. Her achievements would be no less worthy or spectacular if Nwapa had been a man, or indeed of a racial background other than African. Chukwuemeka Ike elaborates: 'There is no doubt that Flora Nwapa wrote primarily about women. She did not, however, write exclusively for women, neither did she live in a world exclusive to women. It would, therefore, be a disservice to her memory for female or male scholars and readers to see continuing interest in her works as an affair for women only.'[10] In all, Tana Press/Flora Nwapa and Co. publications published 25 titles written by both women and men. These include Nwapa's own titles: *Mammywater* (1980), *My Tana Colouring Book* (1979), *My Animal Colouring Book* (1979), *The Adventures of Deke* (1980) *Journey to Space* (1980), *The Miracle Kittens* (1980), *One Is Enough* (1981), *My Tana Alphabet Book* (1981), *My Animal Number Book* (1981), *Women Are Different* (1986), *Cassava Song and Rice Song* (1986), *Wives at War and Other Stories* (1986), *The First Lady* (1993) *Two Women in Conversations* (1993) and *The Sycophants* (1993). There remain a number of unpublished manuscripts written by Nwapa herself including *The Lake Goddess* which is currently being prepared for a posthumous publication.[11]

---

[7]Ibid., p. 197.
[8]Ibid.
[9]Ibid., p. 198.
[10]Chukwuemeka Ike, 'Foreward,' in Umeh, ed., *Emerging Perspectives on Flora Nwapa*, p. xxiv.
[11]Marie Umeh, 'Introduction: Historicizing Flora Nwapa,' in Umeh, ed., *Emerging Perspectives on Flora Nwapa*, p. 10.

Flora Nwapa died in 1993 at the age of 62. One of her outstanding contributions to the goal of African renaissance is the promotion of the philosophy of an autonomous political-economic space for women and the strengthening of the African family, in keeping with African traditional norms and values. She also advocates the promotion of an African intellectual quest which emphasises the indigenisation and local control of all aspects of literary and other educational work in Africa, including the writing, publication, criticism, distribution and use in Africa's centres of learning. Before her death, she had in fact earmarked the establishment of the Flora Nwapa Foundation to contribute to the pursuit of this goal. Nwapa's greatest achievement however remains her forthright challenge to the distortion and ahistoricity of the racist anthropological writings on the position and role of women as well as the nature of the relationship between men and women in Igboland/Africa prior to the European conquest.[12] In challenging the long-established 'tenets' of this scholarship, Nwapa consistently demonstrates in her literary work the elevated position that women had in her society ('I did not see women as second-class citizens,' she often told interviewers[13]) and the complementary nature of the relationship between men and women during this epoch of history. These crucial facets of Igbo society rested on the powerful institution of motherhood, itself embodied in the overarching spirituality of the earth goddess – *ani, idemili* or, as in the case of Ugwuta, *uhamiri*. For Nwapa, the European conquest of Africa radically altered this state of affairs with devastating consequences for women and by extension the society as a whole. Consequently, the future for

---

[12]While it is true that Africans cannot be viewed as homogenous, there are significant social/cultural similarities which African peoples share, especially as regards the *status* and *role* of motherhood. Indeed, if there exists any definitive ideology binding on most African societies, despite differences that may have occurred due to geography or in some cases, history, it is motherhood. Furthermore, the half-a-millennium long European encirclement, conquest and occupation of Africa has created *interlocking layers of shared experience* for all African peoples – in Africa and the diasporan spaces in the Americas, Europe and elsewhere that have emerged in the aftermath of the invasion. See for instance, J.A. Sofola, *African Culture and African Personality* (Ibadan: African Resources, 1973), Cheikh Anta Diop, *Cultural Unity of Black Africa* (London: Karnak House, 1989), Joseph Holloway, ed., *Africanisms in American Culture* (Bloomington and Indianapolis: Indiana University, 1991), Margaret Busby, ed., *Daughters of Africa* (London: Jonathan Cape, 1992), Oba T'Shaka, *Return to the Afrikan Mother Principle of Male and Female Equality: Vol I* (Oakland: Pan African, 1995).
[13]Quoted in Umeh, 'Introduction: Historicizing Flora Nwapa,' p. 10.

Africa, she always contended, lay in the re-incorporation of these time-honoured values in societal gender relations. While this study examines Nwapa's literary contributions, it focuses overwhelmingly on the sociological and political impact of her writings and her objective, indeed commitment, to tell the African woman's story of this epoch. As we shall establish, it is to the credit of Flora Nwapa's foresightedness that she was the first person to raise and articulate these ideas in writing long before any other comparable literary, historical or sociological investigation of the subject by African women *on* themselves.

2

The historical and contemporary context of gender definitions

Gender roles

The characterisation of being female in Africa, particularly in West Africa and most specifically among the Igbo, is examined in this chapter. We shall be focusing on the social and cultural context of gender definition primarily in Igboland prior to its conquest by Britain at the beginning of the 20th Century, as well as the impact of this conquest on gender relations subsequently. In the first instance the attempt is to understand the values, the political, the economic, and cultural institutions that were created by, and supported the very existence of women in Igbo society, defining the totality of their activities including relationships with spouse, children, the extended family, and the greater community at large. This, in effect, would constitute an 'auto' or self-definition. In later chapters we will examine 'other' definitions of women's status and roles in society and contrast the two (*internal* and *external*) perspectives on women and analyse why an external definition of them has in fact shaped and perpetuated a 'global' definition of African women, and the agenda behind these definitions.

In her book on gender and sex in Igbo society, Ifi Amadiume, perhaps for the first time in African sociological discourse, draws the important distinction between the notions of gender and *biological* sex. She states: 'the flexibility of Igbo gender construction meant that gender was separate from biological sex. Daughters could become sons and consequently male. Daughters and women in general could become husbands to wives and consequently males in relation to their wives...'[1] In other words, the political power wielded by these women,

---

[1] Ifi Amadiume, *Male Daughters, Female Husbands: Gender and Sex in an African Society* (London: Zed books, 1987), p. 15.

their ambition and aspiration for authority, privilege and power - all seemingly male attributes - could be and were readily assumed by women (i.e. people of the female *biological* sex) in which case they were then defined as 'males', their 'femaleness' or 'femininity' notwithstanding. The implications of these 'dual-sex' roles are far-reaching and crucial to an accurate understanding of how these African women defined themselves. Indeed, the main objective of this study is to ascertain how the novelist Flora Nwapa understood and interpreted the response(s) of the women of her society to issues of concern to these women. In so doing it is essential to locate this analysis within the context of an historical and sociological setting, from which one could then interrogate the literary/sociological contributions which Nwapa makes to Igbo Women's Studies. What exactly were the key roles necessary for society's members to play in order to ensure the continuity of the community? To what extent did women assume roles/engage in these activities? Were these roles played out in a manner different from the men in society? The process of creating a particular world-view, indeed a world order, by this society, relevant in its entirety to, and addressing solely the needs of their members, defined the various activities that the nation's constituent members subsequently engaged in. It appears, therefore, that societal chores/tasks were carried out by both men and women except where limiting biological factors existed. The ascription of the 'male' role to women occurred only to the degree that attributes characteristically and ostensibly associated with men were acquired by women. In ordering society there appears to have been an awareness of the need for both sexes to exist in harmony with nature.[2] Thus gender roles were not *a priori* rigidly codified by an all-embracing state superstructure. Rather, roles were defined by limiting biological factors, limitations which were subsequently *rationalised* by society. For example the role of a man as defender of the nation would appear to stem from the physical superiority he exercised over his female counterpart. It was 'natural' for him to play this role! 'Defender of the nation' became a male role, and females assuming this attribute were defined as 'male'. The crucial point here of course is that females could, in spite of the 'maleness' of the role, assume this attribute. This point is further explained by the Igbo who insist that a good male cook is tantamount to *nwoke naesi nni ka nwanyi*, that is 'a man who cooks like a woman.' The role of cooking is closely associated with that of mothering and nurturing, a necessary prerequisite of which is the ability to

---

[2]Diop, *Cultural Unity of Black Africa,* especially pp. 177 - 180; Molefi Kete Asante, *Kemet, Afrocentricity and Knowledge* (Trenton: Africa World, 1990), pp. 83 - 100.

provide for, and support dependents - food being one crucial element. This 'natural' tendency for woman/nurturer also to be preparer of food is then rationalised by society as a female 'role'. Males assuming this cook/nurturer role are therefore seen, in this respect, as assuming a female role. *The institutionalisation of these sex roles did not however occur to such an extent as to render the roles non- interchangeable.* In other words tasks normally associated with one sex could quite easily be assumed by the other sex.

The Igbo were and remain a republican people where participatory democracy (involving all of society - men and women) was actively practised and taken very seriously. In effect, republicanism was real to the Igbo and was not merely an ideal to which society aspired. In all communal discussions, whether in times of conflict or in addressing the direction of societal advancement at any particular time, *all* the individuals had the right to be heard and responded to.[3] Society was certainly not idyllic and the attempt here is not to romanticise the operation of these value systems. There remain, nonetheless, practical spheres within the constituent Igbo principalities and states and the Igbo nation as a whole where these values as described were expressed. There were of course exceptions, as invariably there must be when common, overarching characteristics of any society are being defined. First, there are those sectors of society such as the *osu* (those dedicated to the gods, outcasts) which were defined as culturally excluded. However, even here parallel patterns of operation were observed within the *osu* community, who apart from the issue of marriage maintained normal relations with other (non-*osu*) members of society. Secondly, in the monarchical states of the Igbo such as Onitsha, Ugwuta, Aboh and Osommari where institutionalised hierarchical structures and class stratification were present, it is conceivable that these societal standards may not have operated in as unfettered a manner as they did elsewhere in Igboland. Nevertheless, it is important to reiterate that there were minimal restrictions placed on either sex on the aspiration for the attainment of those spheres of societal activity expressed through the pursuit and achievement of human enterprise and opportunities. In Igboland women were involved in five key socio-cultural roles: spiritual, economic, political, educational, and in their role as mothers. In examining the manner in which women performed each of these roles, our focus will be purely from the independent, pre-conquest African experience.

---

[3] Cf. Chinua Achebe, *Hopes and Impediments* (Oxford: Heinemann International, 1988), pp. 113 - 114.

Independent, pre-conquest definitions of gender roles

It is important to stress yet again Ifi Amadiume's argument - that the roles an individual could play in pre-conquest Igboland were by no means sex-specific. In other words, performing the variety of tasks existent in society and specifically tasks linked to the acquisition of societal resources - power, authority, wealth, land, etc. - was not dependent on the biological sex of the individual. Thus, this African society could not be described as 'patriarchal' in the conventional sense of the word, say in a European World, where the state apparatus of society was often exclusively the preserve of the male. In contrast what one had in Igboland was a level of *complementarity of activity* between the sexes aimed at achieving the smooth functioning of society.[4] However, if and when a particular goal/means of survival or continuity of society, or a component of that society (family or lineage) became threatened, or indeed when an individual within that society decided on a path different from that usually associated with their sex, then the cultural flexibility of the polity *ensured* that this societal complementarity was sustained, within the context of alternately defined roles. A woman could then take on a 'male' role to ensure that the 'greater communal good' was preserved, that the said goal was achieved, and that the coherence of society, family, lineage, etc, was fully ensured. As Amadiume states, 'Roles, rights and interests were maintained and safeguarded by men and women in culturally constructed categories which sometimes meant that sex did not correspond to gender.'[5] And yet, great flexibility notwithstanding (a feature of Africa's gender system rendering the use of the concept 'patrilineal' meaningless), it could be argued that there remained some evidence of 'advantage of circumstance' intrinsically male; the roles associated with the male sex and gender more often than not *coincided -* one following naturally from another. This did not occur in the case of the female sex, although her gender could undergo a 'redefinition' to create for her, if required in a particular circumstance, access to the activities of a male gender. Hence an 'equality' or equal access by both sexes to all of society's resources

---

[4] U.D. Anyanwu, 'Gender Question in Igbo Politics,' in U.D. Anyanwu and J.U. Aguwa, ed., *The Igbo and the Traditions of Politics* (Enugu: Fourth Dimensions, 1993), pp. 119 - 120. For a discussion on the importance of 'complementarity' in other African cultural references, see Marimba Ani, *Yurugu: An African-Centred Critique of European Cultural Thought and Behavior* (Trenton: Africa World, 1994) p. 174; pp. 242 - 244.
[5] Amadiume, *Male Daughters, Female Husbands*, p. 21.

(i.e. completely unfettered, unimpeded access to all of society's resources regardless of one's natural state of being) did not occur in the strict sense of the word. It is true that permutations of gender roles could and did occur to accommodate any circumstance clearly indicating a lack of rigidity in the definition of sex roles; nonetheless sex roles did exist. Thus and to this extent, 'principles of social inequality [class and sex] were therefore present in [African] indigenous society... [H]owever there was nothing approaching the rigid traditional Western feudal system or later class system.'[6] The point we must not lose sight of, however, is that women were, and are seen as *different* from men, but the Igbo never problematised this 'duality' of social existence: 'where something stands, something else will stand beside it.'[7] Women's roles, crucial to the very survival of society itself, represented the embodiment of all the essential components of an African World-view. The importance of their role and the reverence it embodied in the eyes of society's members as a whole (male and female) were self-evident and accepted by society. There was, therefore, not the need to demonstrate, as for instance is often the case in the tradition of Western World feminism, the existence (or lack of it) of some notion of parity between the two sexes.[8] It could therefore be argued that the current persistent need of African scholars (Amadiume most notably) to demonstrate to the world at large the complementarity of African male and female roles, but more specifically the flexibility of these female roles and gender attributes that have been intrinsic in the cosmological sensibilities of the African World for ages, amount to a repudiation of the stifling effects of patriarchy (in all its manifestations) as African societies increasingly began to be subjected (through conquest) to an 'alternative' world-view of male/female relations. However, this brand of scholarship appears to define the value of women in society in terms of their ability to acquire and assume Western stereotypical 'male roles'. In this context, it is a scholarship that is sadly caught up in the web of the very value system it is attempting to critique. Two errors are committed here. First, gender is ascribed to attributes (such as, for instance, power and authority) where Africans do not define the 'masculinity' or 'femininity' of such attributes. The Igbo language itself is an excellent example

---

[6]Ibid., p. 31.
[7]See Chinua Achebe, 'Words of Anxious Love,' *The Guardian* (London), 7 May 1992.
[8]Interestingly though, Melanie Phillips's conclusions in her study on the subject, *The Sex Change Society: Feminised Britain and the Neutered Male*, are more oriented to the African position just stated. See Phillips, 'Women behaving disgracefully,' *The Sunday Times* (London),12 October 1999, p. 6.

of this phenomenon. It could be argued that it is the value placed by the Igbo on their attained level of republicanism - specifically, the recognition of individual rights to equal participation in societal affairs - that has contributed to the evolution of the Igbo language as it exists today. The Igbo language actively attempts to avoid the pitfalls of explicit sex-identification, one example of this being the fact that the language does not actually ascribe any gender to pronouns. For example, the pronouns 'he' or 'she' and related categories (e.g. him/her) do not exist in Igbo language. Very importantly, the use of the 'male' as collectively representing humanity (e.g. as in 'mankind') does not occur in Igbo. Thus, the Igbo literal translation of the concept 'mankind' which is *umu-nwoke* is not synonymous with the *genderless* pronoun *madu* which means 'people', in the way that 'mankind' is interchangeably used with people/humanity/humankind in English language. Neither *umu-nwoke* nor indeed *umu-nwanyi* (women) could therefore ever be considered or used as a substitute for the collective reference to a people/humanity.

Secondly, the other error committed in this scholarship is that male roles are then used as the yardstick against which women's liberation or the degree to which they have a voice in the ordering of their society is assessed. This study, in contrast, will demonstrate that women were intrinsically important, *in their own right*, with little need to undergo gender transpositions to increase their access to societal resources. In effect her role deriving from being a woman (i.e. a biological female) already and originally *embodied* all these. The concern here therefore, is not so much with 'male daughters' who in any case constitute a minority at any point in time, but with *daughters* - women, mothers. Adiele Afigbo aptly captures this error when he asserts: '[T]his ... approach and stance is wrong because it arises from a false cosmology ... which *sees man as the ultimate measure of things*' (emphasis added).[9] The Igbo world-view was that of a society where self was *defined* in terms of the other/greater human community; where the fulfilment of self was predicated very clearly on the merger between self and other. In effect, seeming dichotomies in society had to be reconcilable - between men and women, between individuals and communities, between the physical and spiritual.[10]

---

[9]A.E. Afigbo, 'Women as a Factor in Development,' in Martin Ijere, *Women in Nigerian Economy* (Enugu: Acena Publishers, 1991) pp. 46 - 51.
[10]Cf. Asante, *Kemet, Afrocentricity and Knowledge*, p. 83.

Socio-cultural roles

In considering the interrelationship of social and cultural factors (that is the behaviour patterns, traditions, value systems, as well as the expectations of the individual vis- à-vis society and vice versa) that characterise Igbo and the wider African society, it is important to understand exactly what these roles entailed.

Spiritual

Events which pertained to the transcendental nature or the 'soul', the sacred or non-temporal nature of society, were and remain very important in Africa as a whole. Marimba Ani has shown in *Yurugu: An African-Centered Critique of European Cultural Thought and Behavior*: 'In the ancient religious traditions of Africa...we find again and again the pre-dominance of the mother goddess; the valorisation of the female principle; the earth symbol.'[11] Ani's study highlights the linkages between 'Mother Earth' - loving, gentle, fertile, productive, supportive, juxtaposed with an inherent power to produce effect, energy, force - and general female attributes. In other words, those female sex roles/functions which are traditionally attributed to women were crucial to the continuity, indeed the very existence of society. Women, therefore, seen solely as females, played a critical role in society (especially in the economy and subsistence) - a role which could never be undertaken by males. Hence, Ani's assertion that '[t]he female principle is the foundation of the [African] cosmological conception'[12] is essentially correct. Amadiume aptly illustrates the efficacy of this conception with the Igbo. She discusses the myths surrounding the origins of the Igbo. In one version the goddess *idemili* is seen as central to, and very prominent in the establishment of society. As Amadiume states 'the female gender had the more prominent place in myth and indigenous religious and cultural concepts - the supernatural, a goddess, is female. The stream, Iyi Idemili, is the source of divinity... Thus [society] inherits industriousness from females; the most highly praised person in Nnobi is a hard-working woman.[13] The very strong spiritual role of women is in fact replicated throughout Igboland. Ikenna Nzimiro states that in Onitsha, the *omu* (the queen of women) like her male counterpart, had the right to perform ceremonials: 'The *Omu* appointed the female titled officials, each of whom had duties corresponding to

---

[11]Ani, *Yurugu*, p. 171.
[12]Ibid., p. 172.
[13]Amadiume, *Male Daughters, Female Husbands*, p. 29.

the equivalent male *Ndiche Ume* ... and they acted as the *Omu*'s advisory and executive council.'[14] The point is that in this society there existed a parity between females and males, that is through its gods and goddesses, in defining the people's spiritual base. Consequently, those individuals selected/nominated to administer these spiritual requirements were equally respected and revered by all members of society. This point is well illustrated among the Yoruba. In his discussion of women of power and influence among various West African nations, Afigbo sites the example of *iya Mode*, the priestess designated to oversee the 'veneration of the spirits of departed kings.'[15] He states: '[T]he king looked upon her [*iya Mode*] as a "father" and addressed her as such. So important was her job that the monarch [would] salute her kneeling - the only mortal to whom he gave such honour.'[16] In the duality of roles assumed by the priestess (woman and priestess/emissary of the gods or goddesses), the female 'receded' in the face of the spiritual ... In other words, the power vested in this particular role of priestess was not and could not be ignored or disrespected regardless of what other roles may have been ascribed to her. As Christopher Ejizu has argued: '[r]itual experts who happen to be women such as diviners ... doctors ... and the category of married women known as the *Umu-Ada/Umu-Okpu*... possess small-sized *ofo* twigs which they used for ... events such as in meetings and settling disputes among their ranks. Ritual experts among them use theirs very much like their male counterparts to communicate with their spirit patrons.'[17] The role of women in the divination/spiritual life of society is particularly evident in the literary works of many African writers.[18] The complementarity of female and male represented as the embodiment of a particular principle or quality and controlling a particular element or

---

[14]Ikenna Nzimiro, *Studies in Ibo Political Systems* (London: Frank Cass, 1972) p. 55. *Omu* is the Onitsha title for queen. The *omu* society refers to the society for Onitsha titled women who collectively would have directed considerable affairs, most notably the economic, within society.
[15]A.E. Afigbo, 'Women in Nigerian History,' in Ijere, ed., *Women in Nigerian Economy*, p. 26.
[16]Ibid.
[17]Christopher Ejizu, *Ofo: Igbo Ritual Symbol* (Enugu: Fourth Dimension, 1986), p. 52. The *ofo* is a symbol of authority held by the titled or those in positions of power/authority. Ejizu has shown that the power vested in women 'ritual experts' (via the acquisition of the *ofo* twig) is no different from that of their male counterparts. Similarly, the *umu-ada/umu-okpu* are patrilineage daughters. They wield considerable influence within the family, again similar to the male members of the family.
[18]Achebe, Soyinka, Nwapa.

phenomenon of nature clearly emerges. Similarly, the earthly representatives of these spiritual embodiments are to be found equally distributed across both sexes.

Economic

Leonard Barnes concluded his study of African economic life by noting that 'African women must be the most industrious human beings who ever lived; and even African men, who admittedly cannot hold a candle to their sisters and their wives, work as well as any, and better than many...'[19] Women's economic independence was a feature of traditional Africa. Despite the grim dislocation of contemporary Africa's social existence (on which we shall be elaborating later on in this and other chapters), women's economic independence remains a much cherished and crucial component of female heritage, contributing to, and participating in the day-to-day management of family and community life. From all evidence available, African women (with reference in particular to the Igbo and Yoruba) largely controlled their own economic activity as well as the proceeds/profits from this. They were not expected to render account of these resources to any other members of the family or community - *including* spouses. In discussing the process of marketing and women's economic activities, Amadiume states, and it is important to quote her at length:

> Except for palm wine and yam which were sold by men, most marketing was done by women, so that most of the cash passed through female hands from the sale of either their own or their husband's goods. Following the principle of sexual division of labour and gender division of crops, women kept their own profit and what was considered theirs; nothing considered as female and nothing belonging to women was sold by men. *But women marketed most of what was considered to be male and belonging to men, and kept some of the profit.* The control of cash and goods by women was as a result of their monopoly of the market place.[20] (emphasis added)

To this Nina Mba adds: 'Up to 1900 ... the riverine Igbo areas [states located on and around the River Niger delta], women controlled the markets, constituted the local and long-distance traders, were in a position to amass more

---

[19]Leonard Barnes, *African Renaissance* (London: Victor Gollancz, 1969), p. 69.
[20]Amadiume, *Male Daughters, Female Husbands*, p. 39.

wealth than men, and participated fully in decision making.'[21] Mba argues that the control of markets in Onitsha was entirely in the hands of the *omu* society. Not even the *obi* of Onitsha was sufficiently privileged to control or directly participate in this industry in his own society. Mba's study of the Yoruba corroborates this position. That Yoruba women largely controlled not only their own economic activities, but also the management and the marketing of such activities is clearly illustrated. Through the craftswomen's guilds which were run by the women themselves, women were able to plan, organise, produce, market, sell and retain the profits generated from the sale of their commodities. Mba notes that in the markets all the women selling a particular commodity were organised in a managerial association which was headed by the *iya egbe* (mother of the association). All profits from trading or from the crafts sold belonged completely to the women themselves to utilise as they wished. Yoruba women undoubtedly possessed a high degree of autonomy in their economic life. They participated actively in key areas of the economy, often gaining as much wealth as men and largely controlling and managing the entire sphere of economic activity in their country.[22] In his own study of both the Igbo and Yoruba, Afigbo argues, like Mba, that all main areas of economic activity - i.e., agriculture, trade and manufacture - were controlled predominantly by women.[23] On the agricultural front, they provided the labour not only to cultivate the crops but also process the harvested food products. Local and retail trading was monopolised by these women. Among certain Igbo states, particularly those on or bordering on the Niger delta, long distance trade (and therefore wholesale trade) was also exclusively controlled by women. Additionally, as a result of intermarriage, women were able to create and promote vital trade links and contacts, thereby facilitating their control of the industry. Women were also in control of manufacturing, particularly with regard to the production of cloth, pots and other household items.[24]

It is thus clear to see the critical role played by African women in pre-conquest times in the economic progress and development of their various nations. What emerges is a societal world-view which demonstrates an evolution of roles which is not based on a predominant male world-view aimed at securing and ensuring the continuity of the latter's own power base, definition

---

[21]Nina Mba, *Nigerian Women Mobilized* (Berkeley: University of California, 1982), p. 32.
[22]Ibid., pp. 7 - 15.
[23]Afigbo, 'Women in Nigerian History,' pp. 28 - 29.
[24]Ibid., pp. 28 - 30.

and control of society. Rather, what predominates is a world-view that is highly *gender-complementary*. Its evolution, particularly pertaining to economic development, seems to have been influenced by factors such as the ecology of the area (i.e. the quality of land/soil, dictating the types of crops that could be grown), gender ideas (whether grounded in myth, the supernatural or reality), and the relationship between these ideas and levels of specialisation and productivity - that is sex divisions of economic labour.[25] The woman's control of the use of the proceeds of her economic activity is also indicative of the fact that the philosophy underlining the development of this particular organisational arrangement of society would have been heavily influenced and impacted by a female perspective as much as the *male's*, within of course the general and overarching context of society's communal good and progress.[26] In other words interests were clearly defined by sex. Men and women negotiated and subsequently developed and institutionalised structures that adequately safeguarded these interests.

Political

So what role did women of these societies play in the administration and management of public affairs? Women played a prominent role in public affairs in pre-conquest Africa. Besides the few monarchical Igbo states of the Niger delta, the 'village group' constituted the basic political unit. This consisted of a conglomerate of dispersed villages which in turn were comprised of lineage groupings able to trace their descent back to one common ancestry - male, female or both. Afigbo, Amadiume and Mba have shown that women had access to, and utilised structural or formal political power. As Amadiume states, '[P]olitical administration was embedded in the religious structure [where] we find both patriarchal and matriarchal ideologies juxtaposed in the indigenous political structure.'[27] Lineages in turn comprised of extended families (sub-lineages in effect), made up of patrilineage members of both sons and daughters. Serious matters transcending a particular unit or sublineage were dealt with by the council of lineages which included the heads of all sublineages. At all council meetings *both men and women were present and could express their views* - a point which further emphasises the uniqueness of

---

[25]Cf. Amadiume, *Male Daugters, Female Husbands*, pp. 29 - 30, p. 39. See also Oba T'Shaka, *Return to the Afrikan Mother Principle of Male and Female Equality*.
[26]T'Shaka, Ibid., p. 190.
[27]Amadiume, *Male Daughters, Female Husband*, p. 52.

complementarity and negotiation as hallmark of historical Igbo society. The Igbo were therefore not preoccupied with attempting to demonstrate levels of equality between men and women. Differences between men and women (particularly those originating from the biological/anatomical) were of course readily acknowledged. However, these differences did not constitute a barrier to either sex in the pursuit of human achievement/advancement in the political, economic or social spheres of existence. In most Igbo societies there were, and remain presently (although their roles have been drastically altered) women's councils, women-led, and women-managed organisations. All issues and affairs pertaining to women were seen to through these various organisations. It is clear that in settling all matters of dispute, or even in the day to day management or planning for society's needs, great degrees of negotiation took place to accommodate varying positions before mutually agreed goals were embarked upon. It is also pertinent to recall that within these organisations at any one time, there were categories of women who took care of male interests and women who took care of women's interests. In this way the affairs of society were democratically negotiated with minimal imposition of conflicting interests. At any point in time, women in Igbo society would be called upon to play one of the roles described above. For example, in settling disputes within the family, the *umu-ada* who, in effect, were no longer directly within the family (as a result of marriage out of the family), would be particularly attentive to ensuring the preservation of the interests of their patrilineage family and would have the responsibility of representing those interests. The wives on the other hand would be committed to addressing those issues which directly pertain to the preservation of the welfare of the women who have married into the family and were now directly part of the family. Thus, there is constantly a 'duality' of roles for Igbo women: at certain times they would play the role of a *wife* directly addressing the collective interests of women (wives) in the family, while at other times they would focus on their responsibility as a *daughter* in their patrilineal family from whence they have come!

It is interesting to note that one of the effects on Igbo women of the rapidly encroaching European conquest of their nation was the emergence of mass political action, which transcended the autonomous Igbo village unit.[28] This form of political mobilisation culminated in the 1929 Women's War against the British. The war took the form of highly organised, clearly articulated protests

---

[28]See A.E.Afigbo, 'Revolution and Reaction in Eastern Nigeria: 1900 - 1920,' *Journal of the Historical Society of Nigeria*, Vol. 111, No. 3, pp. 539 - 557.

and attacks against the new British-created institutions especially those of the courts, taxation, local government infrastructure and the individuals appointed to oversee these.[29] The new officials were generally seen as renegades and collaborators of the conquest regime.[30] Also under attack were the imposed imperial currency (pound sterling) and the taxation of women. The immediate implication of the use of the new currency was that the value of local labour and the costs of goods and services were now determined in this medium (i.e by the British), creating an obvious loss of economic power/ independence, especially for women. Another site of contention was the imperial regime's taxation on women. The women felt that such taxation was ethically reprehensible. A leading organiser during the period had declared: 'What have we women done to warrant our being taxed. We women are like trees which bear fruit. You should tell us the reason why women who bear seeds should be counted [and taxed].'[31]

With the obvious erosion of traditional means of dealing with disputes, and perhaps more pertinent, with the imposition of a conquest regime on their people, such mass action became inevitable. Historically, Igbo women had managed to evolve and develop a system for imposing individual and/or collective sanctions on the power structures of society if they felt that certain policies/ decisions/actions were inimical to their wellbeing. It was evident from the outset that the root of the women's revolt against the British was not so much the issue of taxation, but rather a deeply felt political, moral, psychological, and, in particular, a *cultural rejection* of the imposition of alien policies and forms of authority which, in the women's eyes, lacked any form of legitimacy. As Adiele Afigbo succinctly describes it, '[the Women's War] was an instance of cultural nationalism.'[32] The result was the development of a well-orchestrated, extremely efficient, and effectively managed movement with far-reaching implications and consequences for Igboland. No doubt the legacy inherent in this history of women's political struggle, initiative and leadership constitutes an important lesson for contemporary African societies in re-defining and implementing an alternative culture-specific plan for re-development and reconstruction. Following the Igbo women revolt, there also emerged elsewhere in Nigeria and further afield in the West African region,

---

[29] Afigbo, 'Women in Nigerian History,' p. 37; Mba, *Nigerian Women Mobilized*, especially ch. III.
[30] Mba, *Nigerian Women Mobilized*, pp. 91 - 93.
[31] Quoted in Ibid, p. 76.
[32] Afigbo, 'Women in Nigerian History,' p. 37.

highly developed *non-literate* women, translating political consciousness into action - working sometimes in unison with men, and at other times independently.[33]

There was the institution of the *omu* or queen among certain communities in Igboland (mainly the Niger delta states). The appointed *omu* acted more like a spokesperson for the women in her community, representing them at the *Obi* (king) Council, but also exercised great political influence over the rest of society.[34] Accession of the *omu* to the throne did not differ significantly from that of the *obi*, with the ritual and insignia of the latter paralleled by that of the *omu*. Whilst the *omu* was installed by the *obi* the latter could not however depose her. The importance of the office of the *omu* was dramatically demonstrated in 1884 when the reigning *omu* (Nwagboka) had to be one of the signatories to the treaty signed that year between Queen Victoria of England and the Onitsha state.[35] U.D. Anyanwu has discussed various ways in which institutional arrangements created avenues for women's involvement in Igbo politics. As groups as well as individually, women exercised enormous influence on the decisions taken on various subjects by men at all levels of the sociopolitical structure primarily because 'Igbo perceptions of leadership or headship did not approve of authoritarian principles.'[36] Tradition demanded that the man, as head of the family, must seek and obtain the consensus of all members before embarking on a particular course of action. Women served on Council of Elders and their views 'were listened to with respect and taken seriously into account when decisions were being reached.'[37] There was also direct involvement in the routine or formal politics of most Igbo communities. For example in Nnobi, cited earlier in Amadiume's study, patriarchal and matriarchal ideologies juxtaposed in the indigenous political structure such that women served as ritual elites and became title holders. Anyanwu has shown how Nnobi is by no means unique in its political structure and organisation from many other Igbo village states and principalities notably Obowo, Ohuhu, Uboma, Nsu, Ihitte and Mbaise where women took part directly (through their *umuada* and *umuopku* associations) in the political management of their

---

[33]Ibid., pp. 30 - 37. See also Mba, *Nigerian Women Mobilized,* pp. 290 - 304.
[34]F.E. Ekejibua, 'Omu Okwei: The Merchant Queen of Ossomari,' *Nigerian Magazine,* No. 90, 1996, pp. 213 - 220.
[35]Mba, *Nigerian Women Mobilized,* p. 25.
[36]Anyanwu, 'Gender Question in Igbo Politics,' p. 116.
[37]Afigbo, 'Women in Nigerian History,' p. 27.

societies.[38] Yet, women's participation in the running and development of their community was not limited to these forums. Women's political organisations, described by Judith Van Allen as the 'base of women's political power,'[39] served to make sociopolitical decisions ostensibly about women, but in reality and of wider significance, about the overall interest and welfare of society as a whole. Thus, as Anyanwu puts it, 'women were structurally *visible* in the Igbo political system' (emphasis in the original).[40] The complementarity, indeed the closeness of male and female roles in society, is here made clearly evident. 'Collaboration rather than rivalry was the main feature in male-female relations in Igbo politics.[41] The definition of society as well as the administration of it were without doubt a *shared responsibility* between the sexes in Igboland.

Motherhood

To the vast majority of African women, womanhood is inextricably bound with marriage and child bearing, perhaps almost as strong a phenomenon now as in pre-conquest times. 'The traditional power of African women,' Amadiume has argued, 'had an economic and ideological basis which derived from the importance accorded motherhood.'[42] Motherhood therefore remains essentially the ultimate fulfilment/manifestation of being female in Africa. Motherhood however includes not solely a woman's capacity to conceive and have a child, but an overall philosophical thrust that clearly incorporates a familial and communal responsibility. Motherhood, for Africans, remains the embodiment of love, nurturing, wisdom or temperance (constantly acting as a mediating voice of reason in the home and community) and strength. An erosion of this philosophical base in the functioning of contemporary society is evident, although elements and the framework of an earlier (now latent) value system remain intact. This essence of mothering embodies the collective responsibility of women (including those who have not borne children) to steer society's growth through its youth in a particular direction and according to prescribed

---

[38]Ayanwu, 'Gender Questions in Igbo Politics,' pp. 116 - 120.
[39]Judith Van Allen, '"Sitting on a Man": Colonialism and the Lost Political Institutions of Igbo Women,' in Sharon Tiffany, ed., *Women and Society* (Montreal: Eden, 1979), p. 27.
[40]Anyanwu, 'Gender Question in Igbo Politics,' p. 117.
[41]Ibid., p. 120.
[42]Ifi Amadiume, *Re-inventing Africa* (London & New York: Zed Books, 1998) p. 112.

norms and values as defined by the overall society. Mothering incorporates an intuitive appreciation for, and responsibility to infuse in society's children, a spiritual base that honours and reaffirms the sanctity of life in all its dimensions, and consequently the social responsibility society's members have for one another. This, then, is the basis upon which the monumental task of motherhood operated and currently operates in much of Africa, although increasingly to a lesser extent. The social institutions through which this occurred will be examined shortly. The fulcrum of femaleness in Africa has always been, and remains intrinsically linked with motherhood and the family. Family in the African sense of the word literally consists of a group of persons connected by blood or marriage, including aunts, uncles, cousins, grandparents, and in-laws. As J.A. Sofola asserts, '[t]he family institution has the characteristics of solidifying the relationship between two different families or lineages, rather than between individuals only...Marriage in Africa is a union of the lineages for purposes of procreation, companionship, assistance, etc. and the continuity of the relationship.[43] Within this institution of marriage and family, the woman essentially constitutes the stabilising/harmonising force both within the individual family as well as the greater society.[44] Stability and balance within society derived from an adherence to societal norms and values handed down through the ages. It was believed that the transgression of these laws had immediate repercussions, most notably harvest failures and premature deaths. The impact of these transgressions were deemed to be felt more acutely by women, given their role as mothers. Afigbo discusses how, for these reasons, 'women were inclined to insist on rigorous observance of any rules and regulations whose observance society saw as *sine qua non* for a peaceful, ordered and prosperous existence. In this sense women were a very important source of social stability.'[45] It is interesting to note the different means employed by these women to promote societal harmony and stability. While women's roles as 'keepers of rules and regulations' could be defined as bordering on the conservative, we have, however shown how these women simultaneously acted as a powerful instrument of social change and progress, individually and collectively. Innovation and an exploration of the new, combined with tradition and value for the old to create a society that recognised the intrinsic uniqueness and contribution of each sex, were clearly the norm of the African social scene.

---

[43]Sofola, *African Culture and the African Personality*, pp. 5 - 6.
[44]Afigbo, 'Women in Nigerian History,' p. 31.
[45]Ibid.

It is important to note that the African system of marriage involves the bestowing of gifts upon the family of the bride by the family of the bridegroom - the so-called bride wealth. Thus marriage ceremonies in Africa, no doubt differing in specificity from nation to nation, principality to principality, were characterised by a sharing of gifts between the two 'uniting' lineages, signalling a commitment on both parts to play their very crucial role of working towards ensuring a continuity and harmony in the relationship.[46] Three distinctive components of the African family unit - the underpinning institution of society are noted. These are Motherhood, Fatherhood, and the Extended Family.[47] We shall hence discuss the roles/tasks inherent in motherhood while also establishing that there was no dichotomy, no rupture, between what appeared to be the highly politicised life of a woman and the 'benignly' perceived role of the woman as wife and mother - the ultimate fulfilment of being female in Igboland and most of Africa. Five pertinent functions of the role of motherhood will now be examined.

1. Nurturing

The act of promoting development, physical and psychological, is at the core of motherhood. The physical closeness between child and mother for the 9-month gestation period is continued by the African mother after birth, exemplified most clearly in the carrying of her baby on her back. In this way physical contact is maintained continuously and a feeling of reassurance and security is constantly given to the child regarding his/her well-being. It is as if every groove, every hump, indeed every distinct characteristic of the mother's back is imprinted on the subconscious of the child - conveying warmth, love, security. Breast feeding also promotes and enhances the bonding process between mother and child, providing not only physical sustenance and nourishment, but also psychological well-being. Normally it is the mother who, for the first several months of the child's contact with other human beings, is at the centre of his or her very existence. It is the mother who touches, holds, embraces, carries, kisses, etc., and, very importantly *sleeps with the child.* In Africa, sleeping arrangements between mother and child were and continue to be characterised by close physical contact. When sleeping, new borns are

---

[46]T'Shaka, *Return to the Afrikan Mother Principle of Male and Female Equality,* especially ch. 8.
[47]Ibid., p. 259 and Sofola, *African Culture and the African Personality,* pp. 5 - 6; pp. 66 - 123.

separated from their mothers only in exceptional circumstances such as during acute ill-health; by sleeping next to the mother, the newborn is ensconced not only in her physical presence, but, some would argue, her spiritual essence also.[48] The premise upon which this high degree of physical contact was predicated lay in an ethos which recognised that for an individual to develop into a well-adjusted, useful, and contributing member of society, there must be cultivated in the child certain pre-disposing elements - *self assurance, self-confidence and self-love.*[49] The method adopted by Africans to cultivate a culture of sharing and support for the other, which was critical for living in a communitarian society, was by fostering, through this physical and psychological support for the mother, a sense and an appreciation of human warmth, acceptance/approval, and security.[50] This uniquely female role is described by Afigbo as an 'up-building role.'[51] According to him this role 'involves encouraging the right kind of growth and development through the imparting of abiding moral and spiritual values. And the imparting of these values in turn involves the show of love...It is indeed a role that has always been needed in public life where there is often so much coarseness and ugliness, so much tension and violence, so much corruption and insincerity, so much materialism and time-serving.'[52] Marcella Gerber's study on the psycho-motor development of African children in their first year of life, and the influence of maternal behaviour on a sample of children from Kampala, Johannesburg, and Dakar, reveals a striking level of precocity in the African child raised along these African traditional lines discussed by Afigbo.[53] Gerber concludes that the closeness of the relationship between mother and child seems to result in advanced mental and physical development in early childhood - a characteristic seemingly lost in African babies not raised in this manner.[54]

Interestingly, the functions defined above are not the exclusive preserve of

---

[48]T'Shaka, *Return to the Afrikan Mother Principle of Male and Female Equality*, pp. 273 - 74. See also Paul Reisman, *Freedom in Fulani Social Life* (Chicago: University of Chicago, 1977), p. 122.
[49]Felix Boateng, 'African Traditional Education: A Tool for Intergenerational Communication,' In Molefi Kete Asante and Kariamu Welsh Asante, eds., *African Culture* (Trenton: African World, 1990), pp. 110 - 111.
[50]Cf. Afigbo, 'Women as a Factor in Development,' pp. 49 - 52.
[51]Ibid., p. 50.
[52]Ibid.
[53]Marcella Gerber, 'Psycho-Motor Development of African Children,' *Journal of Social Psychology*, Vol. 47, 1958, pp. 185 - 195.
[54]Ibid.

the biological mother in most African communities. Rather, there are a host of women (related by blood or not) who take on this role of nurturing. In a manner similar to that carried out by the biological mother, these women, singly or collectively, take on an implicit responsibility to see to the total physical and psychological well-being of the child. They will, in the absence of, or jointly with the mother, see that the baby is held, cuddled/embraced, carried, fed, bathed, etc. Later for the child, this same community of women continue their role as nurturers, seeing to the emotional and physical needs of their children - as means and knowledge permit. It is as if, in the true spirit of the communal nature of African society, an implicit communal responsibility is acknowledged by these women for the collective well-being of their progeny, and specifically their role as nurturers of the community's off-spring.

2. Child bearing

Women of Africa saw (still see) their position in society as crucially linked with such institutions as marriage and kinship; they are essentially responsible for the propagation and the survivability of the nation, the people, the race. Traditionally, marriages in Africa constituted more of a union between two lineages or families than between the individuals involved. It therefore became the duty of the two families to ensure the success and survival of the union. Among the Bambara (Senegal, Mali, Guinea), the phrase *a toro mousso kele la* is used to describe the loss of life of a woman at childbirth. It means, 'she fell on the battlefield in the line of duty.'[55] It is important though to emphasise that the fate of women in preconquest Africa was not *subordinated* to the realisation of the requirements for the continuation of the lineage, as it is at times mistakenly suggested.[56] Instead, the fate of women was the *central consideration* of the realisation of the requirements for the continuation of the

---

[55]Alpha Boubacar Diallo, 'Maternal Mortality in Senegal - Implications for Africa,' *African Peoples Review,* Vol. VI, No. 2, May-August 1997, p. 10.
[56]See for instance, UNAIDS, *Gender and HIV/AIDS: Taking stock of research and programmes* (Geneva, March 1999); K. Carovano, 'More than Mothers and Whores: Redefining the AIDS Prevention Needs of Women,' *International Journal of Health Services,* Vol. 21, 1992, pp. 131 - 142; C. Rwabukwali et al., 'Culture, Sexual Behavior, and Attitudes Towards Condom Use Among Baganda Women,' in D.A. Feldman, ed., *Global AIDS Policy* (Connecticut: Bergin & Garvey, 1994), pp. 70 - 89.

lineage.[57] African women in pre-conquest times were not 'sitting ducks' on whose behalf decisions regarding the most intimate and sacred of functions - child bearing and child upbringing - were made. The psychological preparation for the enormous task of motherhood, specifically child bearing, was of course undertaken by tutors at the appropriate age group (most often pre-marriage) for members of the same age group. Here, young women were given the information available to the tutors and passed on both from past generations and contemporary experience. The information provided covered issues such as puberty, sexuality, pregnancy, childbirth, breast-feeding, diet/weaning, child-upbringing, maternal health, etc. Additionally, there was provision or potential provision for continuous support not only from the mother/mother-in-law, but from relatives, friends and indeed the entire community. In Igboland, the role of women as the key to the continuation of the lineage in particular and society as a whole is a responsibility which the vast majority of women welcome and cherish.[58] Society depends on her and encourages her in this task, and she responds by providing society with a new generation of valuable resource on which the continuity of society so heavily depends. As Afigbo puts it, '[motherhood] is the ultimate source of the physical [hu]manpower which we need for development.[59] The often individualistic approach to child rearing often seen in some parts of the world remains largely alien to African sensibilities, which are firmly in line, philosophically, with a culture that is committed to honouring its past by ensuring the viability of its future through the individual as a member of a communitarian society. All evidence suggests that the African community, *as opposed to the institutions of the nation state*, continue to depend on and encourage women through the indigenous supportive structures of the extended family and women's support groups in this undertaking of child bearing. The fact that the nation-state remains aloof and indifferent in its support to women, via the poor provision of basic antenatal services, drugs, postnatal services and general support to mother and child, must not be confused with the supportive network within the community, however materially deficient this network may in actuality be. African women did not and do not feel resentful of a role they perceive as 'naturally' theirs - a role in which women are central to the provision of the most valuable resource to society, and thus its continuity.

---

[57]T'Shaka, *Return to the Afrikan Mother Priniciple of Male and Female Equality*, pp. 199 - 200.
[58]Amadiume, *Male Daughters, Female Husbands*, especially ch. 4.
[59]Afigbo, 'Women as a Factor in Development,' p. 49.

3. Companionship

For the African woman, companionship has essentially constituted being the anchor, the bedrock, on which the entire marital relationship revolves. It is the woman who consistently exhibited responsibility as confidante, helper, friend, and lover. In normal times (characterised by crisis-free periods), the planning for the needs, survival, and the progress of the family was conducted jointly by husband and wife. Although available data and other evidence suggests leisure-time activity often being undertaken separately with one's age and gender group,[60] husband and wife both participated in obligatory family social occasions/ceremonial activities. In other words, complementary and independent activities of both individuals co-existed with little resulting trauma. Pointedly, companionship entailed a 'supportive sacrifice', a sustaining, calming, reassuring and comforting support or anchor to her family during times of difficulty, as well as non-stressful times. In reality, the concept of the African woman as companion is essentially the manifestation, or the embodiment of this most African of concepts, namely, to be *one's brother's/sister's keeper*. The African woman, as companion, was fundamentally a help-mate whose main concern throughout her existence was with ensuring that her family (her husband, herself and children) reached their greatest potential, and that all relatives (from both husband and herself) were supported and helped as much as possible in the pursuit of their goals. African orature, literature, folklore and history are full of examples of women acting out this role. The visit to the deity or sage (with or without her spouse) to consult or confer on a particular troublesome problem; the planning with her spouse regarding the way forward for the children, whether with regard to their education, career, or any other pressing problems; the generation of additional resources needed to address a financial difficulty or to help out a relative in distress; the commitment to the maintenance of harmony in the home; accommodating differences of temperament and personality in her spouse, and finally moral support, all embodied and demonstrated the function of companionship for the African woman.[61] Indeed a one-to-one relationship in which the woman acted as companion only to her spouse and/or vice versa, was rare in the African value system. The harmony of the relationship between husband and wife therefore lay with the couple's *adeptness at handling situations involving divergent*

---

[60]Amadiume, *Male Daughters, Female Husbands*, especially ch. 3.
[61]T'Shaka, *Return to the Afrikan Mother Prinicple of Male and Female Equality*, pp. 161 - 232; Sofola, *African Culture and African Personality*, pp. 66 - 123.

interests of kinsfolk and their own marriage.[62] In its most advanced form, a relationship marked by a lack of conflict between kinsfolk and the 'specific marriage' relationship, constitutes a strong social support unit, sustained by love, respect and sensitivity for all members involved. Equally important, it serves as a restraining or cautioning influence for those members who exhibit unacceptable, disruptive behaviour towards other members or those likely to bring the family unit as a whole into disrepute. The attainment of higher levels of commitment needed to bring about this degree of harmony in the family - constructing and maintaining a strong and cohesive unit - remains the fundamental basis of the development of African community spirit over the ages.[63]

4. Provider

We have already discussed the economic role women play in African society. To reiterate briefly, agriculture, trading and craft-making/manufacturing formed, in the main, the basis for economic activity for African women. The dual roles of motherhood and income generator did not prove in any way conflictual. 'There is not therefore the house wife/home/unproductive/apolitical separation from public/ production/ politics'[64] characterisation of social existence involving African women. Economic independence was a fundamental 'right', a way of life for women and no other requirement of, or duty to society, attempted to interfere with this most important of activities. Invariably, women used up the proceeds from their economic endeavour to provide generously to their family and the community at large. Historically, African society fully recognised, and valorised their women's economic independence. We earlier indicated how in the aftermath of the conquest of African society, there occurred a loss of power and status for women. Furthermore, within the principal institutions of the African nation-state, women's access to the means of economic independence has remained minimal. We have sought to establish the historical and traditional roles of women as co-provider and at the epicentre of economic stability within the African family in this study. This role needs to be re-integrated as a matter of priority in the African sociocultural ethos. Re-integrating this economic role in Africa has the potential for impacting upon the manner in which women and families respond

---

[62]Sofola, *African Culture and African Personality*, pp. 136 - 142.
[63]Ibid.
[64]Amadiume, *Reinventing Africa*, p. 195.

to the economic pressures and realities of contemporary society. As Leonard Barnes reminds us in his study of African society, '[these] women must be among the most industrious human beings who ever lived...'[65] This industriousness has always been pursued primarily for the following purposes: motherhood and economic independence.

Whether as nurturer, child bearer or provider, African women have always prided themselves as having a communal/social responsibility to the needs of their society, either through the mobilisation of collective action as we have seen, or in the provision of individual support. Historically, women exhibited the highest standards of public conduct and possessed both a social conscience and a sense of social responsibility in addressing the needs of their society.[66] This philosophy and the social institutions through which these were expressed continue to operate in contemporary society, albeit at a much reduced capacity.

5. *Educator/manager*

The family in Africa, and most especially the mother in the early years, plays a crucial role in socialising and educating the child - from birth till adulthood.[67] The nature and dynamics of this process of acculturation differs from nation to nation and from region to region. Yet, there are some general trends that characterise each major period in the child's development which are of interest. The first three to five years of the child's life constitute a phase largely featured by a high degree of indulgence, but with some degree of discipline regarding acceptable and non-acceptable behaviour. This process of socialisation takes place primarily in the family. During this period the use of toilet facilities and the process of eating independently of the mother are mastered; in other words, the mastery of basic psychomotor skills and learning the medium of communication take place.[68] Also during this period, the child is socialised, quite subconsciously, into appreciating a communal way of life - not only is s/he loved, caressed, played with by *both* mother and father, but the child is also allowed to interact freely with numerous relations including brothers, sisters, grandparents, aunts, uncles, cousins, etc. This is the process during which the child's feeling of belonging to the family group is imbibed and solidified. Sanctions and rewards for quality of behaviour are also readily applied in order

---

[65]Barnes, *African Renaissance*, p. 69.
[66]Cf. Afigbo, 'Women as a Factor in Development,' p. 50.
[67]Sofola, *African Culture and African Personality*, pp. 66 - 123.
[68]See Gerber, 'Psycho-Motor Development of African Children'.

to ensure that the foundations of acceptable behaviour are firmly laid.

During the next phase of life (usually from about age 5 - 10), the presence of the extended family members assumes a more significant and high profile role in the child's life. The child's participation in carrying out family chores and/or his/her involvement in helping in the family's income generating activities begins to be defined. The child now accompanies his/her mother to the farm/market and begins to assist with less arduous tasks. It is here that an appreciation of the integration of activities of family members for the attainment of family objectives is begun.[69] His/her circle of interaction is now enlarged and strengthened through an initiation into age-bands which henceforth (that is from around age 10 onwards) serves as the child's most important medium of education and socialisation, including training for the assumption of adult roles and the concomitant responsibilities of marriage, mother/fatherhood, etc. Consequently up until the child becomes a part of an age-band, or comes under the tutelage of the father (particularly in the case of sons), it is the mother who is *primarily responsible* for the education and socialisation process, ensuring that the child's foundation for development into a balanced, disciplined, and responsible youth is well grounded and remains so throughout the period of childhood and into adulthood.

Finally, if we define a manager as one who organises/directs the affairs of an enterprise, business or institution, then African women would be aptly named as such for they manage the affairs of the household, coordinating the roles of numerous family members and ensuring that the family functions as a balanced, cohesive and productive unit.[70] The welding together of the multiplicity of duties outlined in the preceding pages provides us with some insight into the nature and diversity of the individual skills which women have to possess, skills which in today's terms, would include knowledge of such areas as finance (money management), management of the entire domestic affairs while possessing a keen sense of awareness of political as well as social issues in their community.

Fatherhood

Motherhood co-existed with fatherhood and family life subsequently thrived because of the emotional, spiritual and financial support provided by the man

---

[69]Boateng, 'African Traditional Education,' pp. 110 -111.
[70]Cf. Amadiume, *Reinventing Africa,* pp. 115 - 117.

of the house. Just as in the case of motherhood, fatherhood was defined by certain distinct roles and responsibilities binding on fathers. There were serious sanctions when these responsibilities were violated. The father embodied the symbol of responsibility and discipline in Africa.[71]

1. Provider

For the vast majority of the people of Africa, the synonymity between father and provider is an established cultural ethos. Similarly, that a man's destiny, quite literally, lies solely in his own hands, making him the arbiter over his life, is a concept which the majority of the peoples would clearly identify with. This ethos is captured in every genre of artistic creativity in Africa. In Chinua Achebe's classic novel, *Things Fall Apart*, the following extract could not have been more expressive:

If ever a man deserved success, that man was Okonkwo. At an early age he had achieved fame as the greatest wrestler in all the land. That was not luck. At the most one could say that his *chi* or personal god was good. But the I[g]bo people have a proverb that when a man says yes his *chi* says yes also. Okonkwo said yes very strongly; so his *chi* agreed. And not only his *chi* but his [people] too, because it judged a man by the work of his hands.[72]

Whether through a businessperson, a farmer, craftperson, spiritualist, philosopher, scientist or physician, the African male had societal and familial/personal obligations clearly defined. The mechanism for achieving these tasks were firmly inculcated in the individual throughout the transitional period from childhood to adulthood. The goal was to ensure, to paraphrase an old Yoruba adage, that 'shame does not befall the family,' a fate that invariably occurred when individuals fell short of set objectives. It was not that Africans were intolerant of failure. On the contrary, a man who tried and failed was respected for his effort and assistance was given to support him - in the form of advice, morale building or finance. What was clear was that laziness, lack of effort, lack of commitment to succeed, were attributes that were generally frowned upon within African populations. These often attracted major repercussions if evinced in an individual. For marriage to occur, the young man had to convince his family that he was able to create and maintain and provide

---

[71]See for instance, Meyers Fortes, *Oedipus and Job in West African Religion* (Cambridge: Cambridge University, 1959).
[72]Chinua Achebe, *African Trilogy* (London: Pan Books/William Heinneman: 1988), pp. 34 - 35.

for his own household, working consistently and steadily (building his house, maintaining his farm, etc), as well as contributing to the well-being of the extended family.

2. Leadership & companionship

Male companionship to their women operated much in the same way as did the female to their males.[73] It was mutual anchorage, providing in the main psychological support in reference to the family's needs and overall well-being. With his wife/wives, individually and/or together, and including other members of the family, the 'man of the compound' was assured of an elaborate emotional support system to deal with life's quest both at the 'closest' lineage (head of family/lineage, head of family/ influential member of lineage) level and the wider community. He was seen as the head of his own family - ensuring that all the latter's needs were catered for, and that the smooth functioning of the integral parts enabled the whole to work efficiently. He, of course, achieved this *in collaboration with his wife/wives* whose roles were crucial to a successful outcome as we have already shown. Africans had unambiguously assigned their males and females with varying, clearly articulated roles, each considered as being of equal value and indispensable as the other.[74] As indeed Anyanwu has shown, 'collaboration rather than rivalry was the main feature in male-female relations...'[75]

3. Educator: setting standards

Educator was a role that the father strongly assumed as the child moved into adolescence and beyond, especially for male children. Tutorship with regard to the assumption of the family occupation, from farming to business to craftspersonship, etc, became the father's main preoccupation. But more importantly, *the father set standards* - standards of achievement, standards of success, and standards by which the child's definition of self could coherently emerge.[76] The child listened to, absorbed, respected and followed these standards. The father's standing in society was very important, but his

---

[73]T'Shaka, *Return to the Afrikan Mother Principle of Male and Female Equality*, especially ch. 6.
[74]*Ibid.*
[75]Anyanwu, 'Gender Question in Igbo Politics,' p. 120.
[76]Cf. Amadiume, *Male Daughters, Female Husbands*, p. 93.

aspirations for his children were even more pronounced. Regardless of his achievement, the fundamental, underlining, and distinctive spirit and philosophy of African peoples were embodied in a prayer (still strongly adhered to in contemporary times) that the next generation (the child's) achieve, produce, excel, survive, and in general, live, and enjoy life in ways the preceding generation (the father's) had never been privileged.[77] There was, however another recognised crucial ingredient necessary for this prayer to materialise. This was the element of hard work.

4. Disciplinarian

To shield the household from danger, injury, or attack was obviously a major role of the father and head of the household.[78] By virtue of the physical advantage he had over the womenfolk in the household, the father had to ensure that the household enjoyed good security. It was a fundamental requirement of his male role, and a man unable to control and ensure the smooth functioning of the household was harshly judged by his peers in society. The nature of the rules governing the household was, broadly speaking, defined by society at large. However, the mode of implementation and the individual adaptation or interpretation of these rules were of course personal to the individual household. The father set the tone, in effect of governance. However, since women were nearly always the real power in the household, managing in totality and implementing the integral essentials of this complex government, they could effectively ensure that the rules were either adhered to or subverted. The necessary partnership between the father and mother/mothers in conducting what ostensibly appeared to be a male function was therefore clear to see. It was a subtle partnership, but a highly necessary one, spelling the difference between the success and the failure of the efficient management of a household.[79]

---

[77] In Igbo language, as well as in many other African languages, these sentiments for generational advancement are commonly expressed in day to day family reflections, meditations, and prayers.
[78] Fortes, *Oedipus and Job in West African Religion*.
[79] T'shaka, *Return to the Afrikan Mother Principle of Male and Female Equality*, pp. 184 - 188.

Extended familyhood

The Yoruba have a saying which roughly translated as follows into English: 'what a child refuses to learn at home, society (life) will invariably teach it'. It is important to recall that the extended family in Africa does not only involve individuals related by blood or marriage, but a community of individuals which assumes responsibility and concern for its members. It was this willingness and capacity to, for example, praise a neighbour's son or daughter who succeeded in accomplishing some feat, or similarly challenge a friend's son or daughter whose public behaviour was less than ideal, or speak out publicly in support of, or against a position of importance to the well-being of that society, that in reality defined an African extended family. It is on this definition that the following analysis of the functions of this role are predicated. Two primary functions can be discerned from the African extended family: social support and education.

1. Social support

The primary and most important role of the African extended family system lies in its function as provider of social support. The maintenance of order and harmony in the larger society through a strengthening and organisation of the basic family unit was the philosophy on which this system was built. First, the extended family was designed to actively foster a cooperative spirit between kith and kin (those related by blood and marriage).[80] This meant that an active interest was taken in the well-being of the affairs of members of the families by their own constituent members - culminating in a rallying round in times of need. The commitment to support members was characterised by a sense of obligation and in effect acted as a form of social security (both psychological in being part of a family/group, as well as financial) for all members. Secondly, the extended family sought to curtail levels of negativity (envy, offensive action, etc.) within the family, not only by one member to another, but also by a member to a non-member of the household.[81] Here the eldest members of the family had, in particular, an important role to play. Grievances that could not be dealt with directly by the individuals concerned were inevitably referred to the elders within the family who would subsequently convene a family meeting

---

[80]Cf. Sofola, *African Culture and African Personality*, pp. 66 - 123 and T'shaka, *Return to the Afrikan Mother Principle of Male and Female Equality*, p. 259.
[81]Ibid.

with the distinct intention of resolving the outstanding contention. Finally, the individual's absorption into the larger group of family always acted as a means of 'check and balance' in ensuring that the limits of conventional/appropriate behaviour (as defined by those societies) were not transgressed. Hence, the ever present restraining hand of the family circle embodying its own contributory community responsibility ensured that serious offences of the type so commonplace in contemporary society were virtually negligible. No one could hide under the anonymity of individualism![82]

2. Educator

The process of socialising an individual in accordance with society's norms and values was a continuous process. It began at childhood with the parents, as we have indicated, and culminated in the greater society at adulthood. The role of the extended family - in effect an intermediary educating role - was a key function of this system of family organisation. Ensuring the maintenance of a pattern of behaviour appropriate to the role one occupied was its remit. As the child grew into adulthood and assumed a variety of roles (many external to the immediate family), it was this group of 'extended' individuals who guided, suggested, cautioned, experimented, explored, and discussed a variety of issues of mutual interest with the child.[83] Within the 'extended' family, the sanctions available to enforce and reinforce desired behaviour were often less rigid that within the immediate family structure - especially where the father or mother was involved. In this social circle therefore, the motivation by participants was to learn and explore and/or question the existing norms. It was usually in this enhanced gathering which could take place in the informal setting of a story-telling group, or in the more formal structure of an age-group that the rationale, the morals, the legitimacy, indeed the ethos of the people/nation was communicated, discussed, explored, accepted or rejected and manifested in later life. Whilst this socialisation process was in fact didactic, it was nonetheless flexible enough to accommodate differing opinions among participants, ensuring a productive exchange and fertilisation of ideas.[84] It is now evident that in historical Africa, the definition of gender roles were undertaken by *women as well as men*. Just as men in their prescribed tasks, women of this era were the

---

[82]Cf. Victor Uchendu, *The Igbo of Southest Nigeria* (New York: Holt, 1965), p. 50.
[83]*Ibid*. See also Sofola, *African Culture and African Personality*, pp. 66 - 123.
[84]Gay Wilentz, *Binding Cultures* (Bloomington & Indianapolis: Indiana University, 1992), pp. 12 - 14.

subjects of their own world and they *themselves* defined the nature of their politics, their economic activity, their familial relationships and responsibilities vis-à-vis their menfolk. The nature of their interaction with the larger community of which they were an integral, contributing, valued and respected component was negotiatory and accommodating but always with a clear sense of pursuing their own self-interest - i.e. the welfare of women in that community. That the contemporary image of African women, in addition to their roles and their relationship with the rest of society are largely construed and quite often constructed as subordinate and marginalised, is clearly indicative of the tragedy of subjugation of a people that has characterised the history and heritage of Africa.

Collapsing economies

There is little doubt from the historical, sociological and anthropological literature available, a number of which we have reviewed and referred to above, that the European invasion of Africa resulted in serious dislocations in African society. It created a disequilibrium within the balance of power relations which traditionally existed between individuals and communities, between the physical and the spiritual, and, perhaps most importantly, between men and women. Unfortunately, during the past 40 years of the restoration of African independence, there has been no attempt by Africans themselves to correct this disequilibrium. Rather, this has become more entrenched with time. The overall socioeconomic situation in Africa has so seriously deteriorated in the past 20 years, creating even more strains and tensions in the corporate life of African community existence. There is clearly an inability of the state to satisfy society's basic needs, hence the resultant marginal success of African development progress in the midst of immense human and natural wealth. Indeed what characterises the contemporary African nation-state, 40 years after decolonisation, is the limited nature of structural change to the 'inherited' infrastructure. African economies, with hardly any exception, continue to produce agricultural or mineralogical products at a primary level, as was the case during the period of conquest. It is therefore highly ironical that Vincent Ballore, the chief executive of the Ballore Group, a leading French exporter who has operated in the west African region for 150 years, recently issued the following statement about his vision for Africa's economic prospects for the new millennium: '[Africa] will be the essential supplier of raw materials in the future including palm oil, latex, coffee, cocoa and timber...'[85] Alas, this African economic profile of primary producer of minerals and agricultural products which currently accounts for a paltry 2 per cent of world trade, hardly deviates from the role that Africa has been playing in global economic activity since its days of conquest by Europeans. It would appear that African leaders who 'inherited' the African state after colonialism accepted the proposition and were quite content to operate within its context, that their economies would continue to play the role of 'mono-commodity' or 'dual-commodity' economies. This is in spite of the ever-changing international economic relations which have witnessed the spectacular transformation of economies such as Malaysia, Thailand and South Korea, which only a few years back were in the same league as these African primary-commodity producer countries. African leaderships have woefully failed to transform their economies to serve their population's needs. There was no attempt to incorporate the underlying African cultural and work ethos (extensively reviewed above) into the workings of the newly independent state. Scarcely any sustained investment in, or mobilisation of society's human resources occurred in the new Africa as society was still perceived and valued, internally and externally, in terms of its ready availability for the exploitation of its vast natural resources. What is also significant in this unstructured African economy is that Africa has now emerged as a net exporter of capital to the West - a fact that challenges a cardinal tenet of development economics.[86] The depressing statistics of the past decade provides sufficient evidence of the extent of dispossessiveness which Africa is forced to carry as a result of this crisis. In 1981, Africa recorded a net capital export of US$5.3 billion to the West. In 1985 this figure jumped to US$21.5 billion. This is the same year that the world witnessed the devastating tragedy of the Ethiopian famine on their television screens. Three years later the crisis of Africa's levels of transfer deteriorated. Africa's net capital export to the West in 1988 was US$36 billion. In other words for each day in 1988, Africa's net capital export to the West was US$100 million. By 1992, this figure became US$50 billion. In 1997, it rose to US$70 billion. Given the average annual increases since this financial haemorrhage began in 1981, Africa's net capital

---

[85]See 'Eight countries, one destiny,' *Newsweek* (New York), 15 November 1999, Special Advertising Section - p. 7.
[86]See Herbert Ekwe-Ekwe, *Africa 2001: The State, Human Rights and the People* (Reading: International Institute for African Research, 1993) for an excellent discussion of the African political economy of this period from where the statistics quoted here are derived.

transfer to the West in the year 2000 is estimated to be at least US$100 billion. None of these figures includes the national accounting of the Arab states of north Africa nor those of South Africa and Namibia. According to international financial institutions such as the IMF and World Bank, Africa's current debt to West is about US$300 billion. This figure is about 100 per cent of continent's gross national product.[87] Turning specifically to Nigeria which has been under military rule for most of the past 40 years, we observe a socio-economic situation comparable to or perhaps even worse than the overall continental statistics. Nigeria currently owes the West US$30 billion and will spend about US$2 billion on debt-servicing alone this year.[88] This amount represents one-third of the US$6.7 billion it has in its foreign reserves.[89] Such is the crisis in the Nigerian economy that the new civilian government that came to power in May 1999 has now realised that it cannot pay the minimum monthly wage of US$ 75 to workers, which it had earlier promised. Presently, 65 per cent of Nigeria's population of 120 million lives 'below the poverty line' and about 40 per cent or a total of 50 million 'wallow in abject poverty.'[90]

Alienation and wars

Structural alienation from the political process typifies the overall disposition of people in the contemporary African state. The overwhelming majority of the people are not involved in the process of their own governance and of course one obvious and serious consequence of this is the ease with which political differences and disagreements often deteriorate into major conflicts and wars. This is dictated largely by the unresolved nature and character of the state vis à-vis the constituent nations and nationalities. It would appear that the underlying structural basis of independence, or, more correctly, the restoration of independence in Africa, has never really been clearly defined. There does not appear to have been an agreement on the fundamental working character and role of the nation-state by the constituent nations and nationalities that make up the state. Not surprisingly, the nature of the state that emerged after the European conquest had, and still has no organically-shared essences for national

---

[87]The Report of the South Commission, *The Challenge to the South* (Oxford: Oxford University 1992), p. 229.
[88]*The Guardian* (Lagos), 28 July 2000.
[89]Ibid.
[90]Ibid.

cohesion and set goals. Most African conflicts have therefore centred on whether or not nation/nationality A or B wishes to remain in the existing state (European-created) in which it finds itself, or whether it wishes to join another state, or alternatively, declare itself independent! It is precisely because of this unresolved historical factor of conquest that Africa remains a tinderbox, exploding uncontrollably from time to time with the devastating consequences that the world has come to expect in the last 30 years. Until there is a far-reaching restructuring of political and economic relations within the state to ensure inclusive participation by all nations and peoples, conflicts in Africa will remain endemic.

Since the end of the Second World War in 1945, more than 100 wars have been fought in Africa, the Middle East, Latin America/ Caribbean and Asia, resulting in the deaths of 36 million people.[91] This figure represents about 70 per cent of the total number of people killed during the Second World War. Significantly, out of those 36 million casualties in the world's contemporary wars, 12 million or one-third or these are Africans. These Africans have died in civil wars fought since the 1960s in Congo, Nigeria, Ethiopia, Sudan, Rwanda, Burundi, Liberia, Uganda and Sierra Leone, as well as in countries where Africans fought against direct European conquest regimes such as South Africa, Namibia, Zimbabwe, Mozambique, Kenya, Angola and Algeria. Countries like Congo Democratic Republic, Republic of Congo, Sierra Leone, Liberia, Ethiopia, Eritrea, Somalia, Rwanda, and Burundi are still ravaged by simmering conflict or the aftermath of one, and the spill-over consequences on contiguous states and regions have been devastating. Africa currently has the world's largest numbers of refugees displaced from wars. As can be imagined, the effect of these wars on the African family has been profoundly tragic - bereavement, separation, disorganisation, displacement. Life in a refugee camp in a foreign land with a missing father or mother or daughter or son has taken a heavy toll on Africa's legendary family cohesiveness. The effect on children is particularly grave. As casualties in the war theatre mount inexorably, the recruitment of children from the refugee camps and elsewhere into the military intensifies. According to a study by *The Economist*, Africa presently has 81,000 child-soldiers (boys and girls) fighting in its major wars in east, central and western regions.[92] Proportionately, this figure represents one of the highest recruitment of child-soldiers in the world. These wars have in turn attracted a

---

[91]See Herbert Ekwe-Ekwe, *Conflict and Intervention in Africa* (London and Basingstoke: Macmillan, 1990).
[92]See 'Children Under Arms,' *The Economist* (London), 10 July 1999, p. 22.

preponderant range of interventionism, especially in the military sphere, by both continental and noncontinental powers. Inevitably, Africa must resolve the contentious issues that fuel the current conflictual existence of most of its peoples before achieving urgently needed socioeconomic transformation. If people are not actively involved in the affairs of their society, issues of human and civil rights as well as civic responsibilities will be subverted, creating societies which are clearly not at peace with themselves.

Indigenous institutions: real Africa

Besides prevalent and incessant conflicts, the other area of phenomenal failure of the African state since the restoration of independence focuses on the lack of harmonisation or synthesisation between the institutions of the state and the rich resource of the indigenous African systems of government, economy, gender, and other inter-personal relationships which we discussed earlier on. Just as in the period of the European occupation of Africa, the African successor-state has shut off the *real* Africa, that sector of social existence that impacts directly on the overwhelming majority of people, from the centres and dynamics of power of the so-called nation-state. Precisely as a consequence of this glaring exclusion, the vast majority of Africans, just as it was the case during the European occupation, are not involved in issues of societal development, societal change, and societal reconstruction. To underscore the extent of this exclusion in the way that it relates to the economy of a typical African country, for instance, it should be noted that at any given time frame only 1 to 10 per cent of the population are employed in the state/quasi-state sector. The rest of the population, an average of 90 per cent, are employed in the private sector. This sector ranges from the farming enterprise where majority of Africans work, producing the food that feeds society, to the famed market stalls (that women often control) and shop keepers which, in the contemporary African state of general economic collapse, are just about the only noticeable sites of societal economic vibrancy. With the absence of the ubiquitous transnational companies that dominated the African wholesale/ retail trade in the past, the current African market place and shopkeepers in many an African town or city now sell virtually everything - ranging from building construction materials to motor cars! Yet, the contributions to the country's Gross Domestic Product of this highly productive and critical 90 per cent work force, the hub of African socioeconomic mainstay, are neither recognised nor incorporated into national accounting figures.[93]

Apart from not tapping into the reservoir of autonomous indigenous economic activity for overall national economic planning, the African successor-state also ignores the sociological and cultural realm of societal inheritance at its own cost. One critical area where this has occurred is gender relations which in the past was the fulcrum on which the complementarity of shared expectations and goals between men and women in society was hinged. The long stretch of instability that has plagued the state sector in the past 30 years, leading now to its virtual collapse, has pointedly had a devastating impact on especially men who mostly worked there. Thousands of men dismissed from their posts in the past decade in the wake of massive shut downs of state and quasi-state enterprises, quite often under the rubric of International Monetary Fund-directed 'structural adjustment programmes,' now increasingly find themselves unable to fulfil their provider roles as fathers and sons in their families. Ironically, women, who were generally excluded from the principal institutions of the state during the period and ran their own businesses in the markets and elsewhere, are increasingly emerging as major breadwinners in their families. Women do not however equate this new sociological role with some elevated power position either in their relationship with spouses or with the rest of society. After all, they plough the profits of their businesses into the up-keep of the family! Men, on the other hand, have felt a growing discomfiture with what is now appearing as a redefinition of roles in a key sphere of responsibility at home.[94] Surely, this is a development that has not helped gender relations in Africa. Indeed, the relationship between African men and women has never been more strained, more misunderstood, less enduring, and seemingly in perpetual friction than ever before. Perhaps the single greatest contributing factor is that in Africa's historical past, unlike now, women were highly valued in society purely and entirely for being women. As Adu Boahen has argued, '[a] highly regrettable social impact of colonialism [and its aftermath] is the deterioration that it [has] caused in the status of women in Africa...'[95] Hitherto, African society immensely valued the role of its women for

---

[93]See, for instance, United Nations Regional Project on HIV & Development for Sub-Saharn Africa, *Annual Report*, 1999, Dakar, September 1999, especially ch. 7.

[94]Femi Nzegwu, *Gender & HIV: A Position Paper*, United Nations Development Programme/Regional Project on HIV & Development, Dakar, June 1999

[95]Adu Boahen, 'Colonialism in Africa: its impact and significance' in Boahen, ed., *General History of Africa: Vol VII* (London/California/Paris: Heinemann and the University of California and UNESCO, 1985), p. 802.

three reasons. First, it was very conscious of the fact that the success of its gender relationship based on complementarity would only work if women (and men) had the freedom to fulfil their expectations in the community. Second, it clearly understood and appreciated the fact that the family was the direct beneficiary of an independent and prosperous womanhood. Third, it recognised the fact that while defining general social norms and duties for each sex - male and female, there was a need to ensure that individuals were not restricted in the degree to which they could pursue their highest aspirations within these expected norms, or indeed venture outside these norms should they so choose. This state of affairs no doubt contributed to a more cohesive and more accommodating society as we showed earlier on. Furthermore, it accounted for greater stability in the nature and quality of male-female relationships. From this intrinsic value for womanhood, it appears that certain discernible features within male-female relationships followed. First and perhaps most important was a willingness by both parties (but especially husbands) to accommodate the needs of one another (most especially wives) to express individual aspirations/creativity, most notably demonstrated in the co-existence of a life quite independent of home and spouse. The role of women in innumerable market guilds across Africa, trading both locally and further afield from home, underscores this point. Second, there was the existence and articulation of clear expectations of women and men towards one another, as well as the extended family within their marriages. In other words, it was clear to all parties concerned what it meant in their society (of that era) to be a good wife or husband. And finally, life was dedicated, on balance, to the well-being of, and the advancement of the family unit rather than the individual member. All decisions and activities related to the success of the family followed from this most primary of premises. It is important to stress that a central concern for the family did not imply that the unique needs of the individual were ignored. Indeed, the advancement of the family meant that a delicate balance had to be struck between the overall needs and interests of the family and that of the individual members. It is inconceivable that a stable and happy family unit could exist in the absence of accommodating the needs and aspirations of the constituent members as realistically as possible.

Essentially, the European conquest and occupation of Africa has meant that the scales have turned against the complementary gender relations which ensured the well-being of the African family in the past. The society that valued and highly encouraged a woman's independence has regrettably given way to one in which a man is 'less than a man' if he has an independent and prosperous wife![96] The openness of society and its willingness to accommodate the needs and aspirations of all its members have long dissipated, making way for a society which emphasises male domination and a bogus, arrogant, and self-delusory need for the male to assume the entire responsibility for the care of large family networks. Expectations of wives towards husbands and vice versa also appear to have become less clearly defined when viewed across time. A mutuality and balance in relationships earlier witnessed is now decidedly absent. With the shift in the power relationship between men and women in the former's favour, men have sometimes failed to bring to their relationships with women the crucial levels of respect, consideration, trust and candour (in other words, a necessary mutuality) that have in effect undermined the family. In responding to this power shift in society which has clearly placed women at a disadvantage, women have justifiably acted to ensure their survival by making adjustments to the family structure that have ensured the continuity of the lineage and society as a whole, but increasingly at the expense of the 'sanctity' and cohesiveness of the immediate family/marriage structure.[97] So, motherhood, ever intrinsically a dominant feature in the consciousness of the African woman remains intact. However, because of women's current levels of insecurity within marriage vis-à-vis their spouses, there is a greatly diminished taboo about opting out of this previously most sacred of African institutions. Not all women are, however, in a position to opt out, or indeed seriously question their unequal, perhaps even abusive treatment which have continued to put women and their families as a whole at risk. The vast majority of women will cite as the reasons for this level of vulnerability, the lack of independent means, or the need to ensure the benefits of having a father in the family (especially with respect to sons) are not lost. The cost to Africa of this current state of gender relations is undoubtedly incalculable. It has damaged the cohesiveness of the African family at a crucial time of major challenges to it caused by the ravages of conflicts and wars, the cataclysmic upheaval in the economy of the nation-state, and the scourge of the AIDS/HIV epidemic. It is inconceivable to contemplate any concerted effort towards an African societal reconstructionary endeavour which does not tackle as a matter of priority the full reactivation of the continent's historic complementarity of gender relations.

Across Africa though, despite the overarching burden of the state 'inherited'

---

[96]Flora Nwapa, *One is Enough* (Enugu: Tana, 1981), p. 17.
[97]Theodora Akachi Ezeigbo, 'Myth, History, Culture, and Igbo Womanhood in Flora Nwapa's Novels,' in Umeh, ed., *Emerging Perspectives on Flora Nwapa*, p. 63 and p. 72.

from the European occupation and the punishing strains this places on African corporate life, there are extant, empirically classifiable pre-conquest African sociological structures and value systems which not only summarise the essence of the African social existence discussed above but do continue to largely shape the lives of the overwhelming majority of the people. That the African state since the restoration of independence is yet to incorporate this sociological heritage into building a new Africa is one of the inexplicable tragedies of the continent. Generally, we can isolate seven broad areas of this indigenous African sociological heritage:[98]

1. The family, broadly defined to incorporate its 'extended' range of grandparents, uncles, aunts, cousins, etc., is the epicentre of African social existence. The family gives each individual their identity and reference.

2. The concept of being one's brother's/sister's keeper is a demonstration of the African support system which ensures that the individual is not an isolated migratory being in society, but is a ready recipient of love, care, responsibility and justice from the rest of his/her family and the community at large, and he/she is expected to reciprocate accordingly.

3. Shared ownership/easy access to critical means of livelihood such as land or water resources. The African land tenure and ownership system has ensured that for stretches of millennia, except in the wake of foreign invasions and the resultant disfigurement and distortions of local values in some cases, every one in African society has access to land. Land is inalienable, as it is inextricably linked to the spiritual and economic wellbeing of society.

4. The communitarian ethic characterises the linchpin of African societal organisations. Right from birth, the human being has a stake in their community with a critical balance struck between the objective rights of the individual to pursue life's challenges and goals and their contributions to the totality of community development. This attribute in fact ensures the society's biological, spiritual and socioeconomic survivability and transformation.

5. Respect for the old and the elderly. Even where not explicit such as in the

---

[98]Adapted from the broad categorisation of Sofola, *African Culture and African Personality*, especially ch. 4.

monarchical states of Africa that would depend on royal lineages for the accession to the throne by a prince or princess, a gerontocracy of one form or the other was a common feature of African government.

6. Generosity and hospitality. African generosity and hospitality to the stranger or foreigner is an established fact. Indeed, some critics have argued that this African attribute has tended to work against overall African interests in recent historical experience.[99]

7. Optimism. African peoples, by and large, have a charitable and optimistic disposition to life and life's mission.

The African nation-state, essentially that structure of socioeconomic relations that emerged after centuries of European occupation of Africa has for all intents and purposes collapsed. Whilst several factors account for this collapse, as we have shown, one reason appears primarily responsible: the lack of shared consensus for the fundamental character of the state by the constituent nations and nationalities and the attendant widely prevalent abuse of power and leadership privileges, whether it is a Nigeria or Sierra Leone, a Congo or Rwanda nation-state. The colonial or conquest state that was the originator of the contemporary African nation-state *neither underwent any structural transformation to serve African needs and aspirations, nor did the new states draw upon crucial African cultural values of state and societal management.* Thus, the philosophy of life espoused by the vast majority of Africans remains diametrically in contrast to that of the nation-state in which they are situated. Indeed, the post-colonial African nation-state has continued to incorporate the conflictive, chauvinistic, hierarchical and exploitative character of the epoch of conquest and occupation.

Renaissance

While it is not historically feasible in any circumstance for Africa to return wholly to its pre-conquest political and sociological order, it is however imperative that Africa incorporates critical attributes of its cultural heritage in any new emerging state system, as has happened in all other nations world-wide.

---

[99]See, for instance, Cheikh Anta Diop in Carlos Moore, 'Conversations with Cheikh Anta Diop,' *Presence Africaine*, Nos. 3/4, 1993, p. 380.

Top on the agenda for this restoration is of course the complementarity of gender relations, the time-proven anchor of societal stability. 'African women [must once again] carry into the arena of public life the up-building qualities and duties which, over the centuries, made them the nurturers and stabilisers of society.'[100] The new African state system should look at the re-construction of contemporary political systems, drawing on Africa's rich cultural heritage to build institutions of government that are much more accountable to the people; a system which restores to women their lost social, political, and economic status and to both women and men their historical mutuality in relationships; a system in which the process of decision making is decentralised and universally more inclusive, drawing on, and incorporating opinions from all sectors of society. Such constituted bodies would be obliged to seek and respond to consultation from all sectors of society, drawing on historically and, where relevant, existing systems of mobilisation, education, conflict resolution, and management to address issues pertaining to the progress of African society and the guarantee of human and civil rights. In the new arrangement the following structures would particularly be reorganised: (1) the post-colonial political, social and economic marginalisation of women (2) the family, children and societal values (3) the low priority given to human capacity development (4) the hierarchisation of nations and nationalities (5) the lopsided and disarticulated nature of the African economy that currently serves export needs (6) the content and structure of education (7) the delivery of health care. As we indicated earlier on, the ideational and cultural value systems encompassing the attributes necessary for this required African *renaissance* are in place in any given African nation-state, but tragically not incorporated into ongoing 'developmental' perspectives and programmes. In effect the new African state must be built firmly on those attributes emanating from its internal human resource. Surely in Africa, as elsewhere in the world, the resource that is responsible for the development and transformation of society must be the human beings who live there.

---

[100]Afigbo, 'Women as a Factor in Development,' p. 51.

3

Colonial definitions and interpretations of gender in Africa: the adherents

Despite 40 years of the restoration of African independence, the European colonial definitions of gender in Africa predominate and still constitute the basis upon which policies affecting African society are conceived, planned and implemented, both by foreign as well as the vast majority of African governmental/institutional structures. There is yet no serious or sustained attempt in Western academia (and media) to confront the ravages and the aftermath of the Western conquest and occupation of Africa, an event that has been one of the key features in the shaping of contemporary history as we know it. The West has not offered any apologies or reparations to Africans for the heinous crimes perpetrated in Africa in the course of the last 500 years. These have included slavery involving the forced exportation of millions of Africans to the Americas and the Caribbean and also to other parts of Africa (especially eastern and southern Africa), widespread genocide involving millions of Africans during the period, the direct occupation of lands and the exploitation of African human and natural resources, and the resultant creation on the African scene of what Claude Ake has succinctly described as a 'disarticulated economy'[1] – the bane of current African social existence. Chimalum Nwankwo has argued that the West's standard approach to avoid confronting its responsibility of 'owning up' to what it has done in Africa is to 'explain away' this history by continuously finding ways of implicating Africans themselves in the catalogue of tragedies of the epoch.[2] The minimalist intention for this exercise, Nwankwo contends, is for the rationalisation of Western action however grave the latter may have been, whilst the maximalist or ultimate

---

[1] See Claude Ake, *A Political Economy of Africa* (Harlow: Longman, 1981), especially chs. 3 and 5.
[2] Chimalum Nwankwo, 'The Lake Goddess: The Roots of Nwapa's Word,' in Umeh, ed., *Emerging Perspectives on Flora Nwapa*, p. 335.

strategic goal is that of total evasion.[3] In the specific realm of colonial writing and criticism, the impact of this approach has been the 'conflagration of African value systems lit by all forms of invidious and deracinating stances. Action without fear of consequence is privileged over action with circumspection.'[4] This chapter explores how these definitions have come to be perpetuated. In reviewing the sociological and anthropological literature on African women as a whole and Igbo women in particular, one is therefore not shocked as would otherwise have been the case, by the degree to which these 'scholarly works' are steeped in racist, africophobist, unhistorical and at times ahistorical analyses and conclusions. Often, the African reader of these works has little difficulty in confirming Abena Busia's stark observations made some years ago that the '"Africa" being discussed here has very little to do with any Africa Africans themselves, from whatever part of the continent, might recognize as "home".'[5] The standard epithets used in describing African women (and men) in the literature range from 'primitive' to 'tribal', 'backward' to 'savage'. It is important to note that such modes of representation have hardly changed significantly in contemporary times - here and there essentially synonymous terms or euphemisms may be used but the racist and eurocentric underpinnings remain. An inevitable disturbing outcome of this scholarship is of course that it provides contemporary society (particularly in the Western World) with the 'knowledge base' to define and interact with the African humanity. The discipline of anthropology has been the main culprit in this regard, recognised among many Western scholars as 'the one social science which is capable of growing into a unified body of social theory [being] preoccupied with [studying] ... tribal man.'[6] Hermeneutic derivatives from anthropology have since broadly formed the foundation for the development of subjects, courses and indeed discourses on virtually every sphere of African humanity in the Western academia and media. In contemporary Western or Western-influenced academic institutions, 'primitive' may have given way to the prefix 'ethno' or 'ethnic' but the meaning conveyed remains unchanged: in studying perspectives of African existence or quite often any other non-Europeans deemed culturally

---

[3]Ibid., pp. 337-339.
[4]Ibid., p. 336.
[5]Abena Busia, 'Manipulating Africa: The buccaneer as "liberator" in contemporary fiction,' in David Dabydeen, ed., *The black presence in English literature* (Manchester: Manchester University, 1985), p. 168
[6]Kenneth S. Carlston, *Social Theory and African Tribal Organizations* (Urbana: University of Illinois, 1968), p.ix.

dissimilar, one is not just studying peoples but 'ethnic' peoples or 'tribes'; one is not a musicologist studying African music but an 'ethnomusicologist' studying 'ethnic' music; one is not a linguist but an 'ethnolinguist' because the site of study is 'ethnic' languages or 'vernaculars'; one is studying 'ethnic relations' when describing the relations amongst African peoples, not intra-national or, perhaps, inter-national relations, etc, etc. Western scholarship on Africa sediments in this way and forms the basis for all interaction between the West and African peoples. Several of the works critically examined in this chapter abound in a catalogue that ranges from an astonishing partial reading or mis-reading of the African historical and sociological heritage to a blatant distortion of this reality. What this practice attests to is either a glaring lack of understanding of the range of African societies and cultures the authors in question claim to be studying or writing about, or just a case of rationalising or explaining away the crimes and consequences of the Western conquest and occupation of Africa as we have highlighted above. Indeed Western colonial or conquest scholarship is characterised by a profound lack of the very 'objectivity' which, ironically, Western academia takes great pride in propagating. In the main, European colonial views on the status of women in Igbo/African society do not differ radically in their overall conclusions as much as in the detailed observations of these various peoples and nations. Differences in studies are superficial and do not inform the critical reader of the values and norms that give rise to varying historical experiences and world-views.

The 'subordinated woman' trope: reflections and interrogation

In effect, the European colonial typecast of the status of the African woman in her society is encoded within a retrograde spectrum - ranging from male dominance to total and complete female subordination! The anthropological works that best encapsulate this spectrum are undoubtedly those of Sylvia Leith-Ross and Phoebe Ottenberg. The extent of Leith-Ross's study of Igbo women carried out in the 1930s is no doubt more comprehensive in scope than Ottenberg's which took place 20 years later. Whilst Ottenberg concentrated on the the Igbo principality of Afikpo, Leith-Ross studied the principalities of Nneato, Nguru and Owerri, in addition to Igbo women domiciled in the seaport commercial town of Port Harcourt. On the key subject of women and gender relations in Igbo society, Leith-Ross's conclusions are more contradictory. In one breadth, she describes Igbo women as 'ambitious, go-ahead, courageous, self-reliant, hard-working, independent,'[7] and in yet another breadth, she thinks that the 'woman is the working partner to a greater degree than the man.'[8] Still on the same subject, Leith-Ross notes that Igbo men respect their women 'in a way again so original and so modern that Europeans have only just begun to think of it.'[9] Ottenberg's position on Igbo gender relations is unequivocal: '[B]efore the establishment of the British government [in Igboland] in 1902, an [Igbo] woman was literally in a position of physical and economic dependence on her husband.'[10] She adds: '[R]elations between men and women are characterised by strong male domination ... innate superiority of men over women ... backed by men's control over land and the supernatural and by sanctions of the village men's society, one of whose admitted purposes is to "keep women down."'[11] Whilst E. E. Evans-Pritchard did not specifically study Igbo women, his conclusions on his study of African women in east and central Africa, whom he collectively describes as 'primitive women' (significantly, the same nomenclature that both Leith-Ross and Ottenberg use in their categorisation of Igbo women), reflect the 'subordinated African woman' trope that preoccupies colonial scholarship on gender: 'a woman passes at marriage from under the authority of her father to that of her husband.'[12] Kathleen Frank, a latter day literary critic of African women's literature employs this genre with vengeance in her discussion of Nwapa's *One is Enough* (as well as Ama Ata Aidoo's *Our Sister Killjoy*, Mariama Bâ's *So Long a Letter* and Buchi Emecheta's *Double Yoke*) to conclude that 'these novels embrace the solution of a world without men: man is the enemy, the exploiter and oppressor. Given the historically established and culturally sanctioned sexism of African society, there is no possibility of a compromise, or even truce with the enemy.'[13] Yet, Frank's assertion that the 'culturally sanctioned sexism of African society' is

---

[7] Sylvia Leith-Ross, *African Women: A Study of the Ibo* (London: Routledge and Kegan Paul, 1939), p. 230.

[8] Ibid.

[9] Ibid.

[10] Phoebe Ottenberg, 'The Position of Women among the Afikpo Ibo,' in William Bascom & Melville Herskovitz, ed., *Creativity and Change in African Cultures* (Chicago & London: University of Chicago, 1959), p. 214.

[11] Ibid., pp. 207-208.

[12] E. E. Evans-Pritchard, *The Position of Women in Primitive Societies and Other Essays* (London: Faber and Faber, 1965), p. 51.

[13] Kathleen Frank, 'Women Without Men: The Feminist Novel in Africa,' *African Literature Today*, No. 15, 1987, p. 15.

'historically established' is no where demonstrated in her essay. On the contrary, she in fact states, in the same study, that the subject 'remains a vexed issue, and clearly all the sociological and literary votes on this question of the source, nature, and extent of the oppression of women in Africa *are not yet in*' (added emphasis).[14] Until the latter occurs, it appears that the reader or the observer at large would need to assume that Frank's claims of the 'culturally sanctioned sexism of African society' should be taken for granted! The same assumption also has to be made with respect to Marie Umeh's position on the subject. In her review of Buchi Emecheta's *Double Yoke*, Umeh contends that the choices available to the possibilities of African women's liberation are fraught with immense difficulties: 'In order to be liberated and fulfilled as a woman she must renounce her African identity because of the inherent sexism of many traditional African societies. Or, if she wishes to cherish and affirm her "Africanness" she must renounce her claims to feminine independence and self-determination.'[15]

As a result, Umeh is very pessimistic about the future for African woman: 'Either way [the African woman] stands to lose; either way she finds herself diminished, impoverished.'[16] Right from the outset, Umeh glibly characterises Igbo society as 'patriarchal' without any attempts to rigorously demonstrate what this exactly means in Igboland historically. In effect, she relies on the theoretical insights of Kate Millet, Simone de Beauvoir and Germaine Greer to arrive at the predictable destination of her project: 'Igbo women are enslaved to Igbo traditions which subjugate them.'[17] Interestingly though, Umeh has since shifted her position on Igbo women as presented above. An incredible *volte-face* occurs in her contribution to the subject in a recently published collection of essays by several scholars on the memory of Flora Nwapa, a collection which she in fact edited.[18] Surprisingly, Umeh now rejects '[t]he popular Eurocentric view ... that the position of African women is one of subordination to husbands,

---

[14]Ibid., p. 16.
[15]Marie Umeh, 'Reintegration With The Lost Self: A Study of Buchi Emecheta's *Double Yoke*,' in Carole Boyce Davies and Anne Adams Graves, eds., *Ngambika: Studies of Women in African Literature* (Trenton: Africa World, 1986), p. 175.
[16]Ibid.
[17]Ibid., p. 174.
[18]See Umeh, ed., *Emerging Perspectives on Flora Nwapa*.

and the repression of talents outside the domestic realm.'[19] Surely, this is a far cry from Umeh's claims in her earlier study when she inferred that 'traditional Igbo ... society frustrate[s] the gifted women from the realization of herself as an entity.'[20] Now, she realises that Nwapa's 'honest portrayal of Ugwuta women insists on the complementary nature of the society, beginning with the mixed-gender age grade system, a mystical Lake Goddess, who guarantees women, as well as men, power, prominence and peace.'[21] Pointedly, in an interview which Umeh had carried out with Nwapa in 1993 (about a year before the death of the novelist) and the text of which was published in the same volume of essays, she had asked the novelist: 'What do you think of Leopold Sedar Senghor and Ali Mazrui's statements that "African women have always been liberated"? In other words, is there any truth in the statement?'[22] Nwapa's emphatic reply: 'For me, yes!'[23] In turn, Umeh's response cannot cease to amaze: '*Ugwuta traditional society certainly nurtured you into being an independent thinker.* It appears that you don't even wince before you perform a task' (added emphasis).[24] Finally, Umeh asked the novelist whether she was a 'radical feminist,' to which Nwapa said: 'I don't think I'm a radical feminist. I don't even accept that I'm a feminist. I accept that I'm an ordinary woman who is writing about what she knows. I try to project the image of women positively.'[25] There are important features of Nwapa's 'disclaimer' that no doubt impinge on the reading and criticism of her work and we shall be returning to an examination of these as this study progresses. While it is true that the novelist later modifies her non-identification with the label of 'feminism' with the concept 'womanist,'[26] it is highly presumptuous of Molara Ogundipe-Leslie to argue that Nwapa's non-acceptance of the former concept is due 'to the successful intimidation of African women by men ... Male ridicule, aggression and backlash have resulted in making women apologetic and have given the term "feminist" a bad name.'[27]

---

[19]Marie Umeh, 'The Poetics of Economic Independence for Female Empowerment: An Interview with Flora Nwapa,' in Umeh, ed., *Emerging Perspectives on Flora Nwapa*, p. 662.
[20]Umeh, 'Reintegration With The Lost Self,' p. 171.
[21]Umeh, 'The Poetics of Economic Independence for Female Empowerment,' p. 664.
[22]Ibid., p. 668.
[23]Ibid.
[24]Ibid.
[25]Ibid.
[26]Ibid., p. 671.
[27]Quoted in Frank, 'Women Without Men,' p. 33.

On the contrary, Nwapa is unequivocal about her mission as a writer (in the interview with Marie Umeh) and her views hardly suggest that of somebody being 'successfully intimidat[ed]' by someone else:

> I try to project the image of women positively. I attempt to correct our men folks when they started writing, when they wrote little or less about women, where their female characters are prostitutes and never-do-wells. I started writing to tell them that this is not so. When I do write about women ... I try to paint a positive picture ... because there are many women who are very, very positive in their thinking, who are very, very independent, and very, very industrious.[28]

Susan Andrade's concern to construct a dichotomised 'tradition'/'modernity' architecture from her reading of Flora Nwapa's works is a variation on the theme of the 'subordinated African woman' trope in African literary criticism that we have been considering so far. She makes her contribution to the genre through a more circuitous path though, alleging that Nwapa's *Efuru* has a 'blind adherence to Igbo tradition.'[29] This tradition, according to Andrade, is 'patriarchal' and she accuses Nwapa of eliding this assumed feature of pre-conquest Igboland in order to ensure the novelist's 'privileging of the discourse of tradition over that of modernity.'[30] As a consequence of this, Andrade concludes, 'Efuru's desire to be traditional threatens to subvert the text's manifest assertion of female independence.'[31] What is undoubtedly astonishing in this brand of criticism is its ingrained pretentiousness. Here, the critic is making an extraordinary demand on the novelist. Critic Susan Andrade literally wants novelist Flora Nwapa to *re-write* the story of her historical heritage to conform to the critic's chosen framework of discourse which posits the 'subordination of African women' in Africa before the European invasion of the continent. This demand is made despite the fact that Nwapa has shown consistently throughout her writings (and speeches and interviews) that Igboland, prior to conquest by Britain in the late 19th century/early 20th century, does not conform to the sociological typologisation

---

[28]Umeh,'The Poetics of Economic Independence for Female Empowerment,' pp. 668-669.
[29]Susan Andrade, 'Rewriting history, motherhood, and rebellion: naming an African women's literary tradition,' *Research in African Literatures*, 1990, 21,1, p. 104.
[30]Ibid., p. 97.
[31]Ibid., p. 105.

called 'patriarchy'. It is also on this assumed ubiquitous 'African patriarchy' that Florence Stratton employs as the launching pad for her study on African literature and gender.[32] She conflates three important eras of African history – the pre-conquest period of African independence, the conquest phase of European occupation, and the contemporary post-conquest period of the restoration of independence. As we shall show shortly, the importance of this tactic for Stratton is that it creates for her the opportunity to quote some key sociological texts out of epochal contexts in an effort to maintain her claim of an inexorable 'African patriarchy' throughout history. Stratton argues that whilst the 'canonical' texts of a number of Africa's leading writers including Chinua Achebe, Wole Soyinka, Ngugi Wa Thiong'o and Leopold Sedar Senghor may be concerned with critiquing European imperialism in Africa and the consequence of this history on Africa's lost independence and cultural heritage, the literature produced has nonetheless valorised the 'patriarchal order' of pre-conquest Africa which 'oppressed African women.'[33] She notes that a common feature that is discernible in the writings of the four writers quoted above is the exclusion of African women as active agents in history. This 'inactive silence'[34] of African women in the writings of these African authors, Stratton charges, is comparable to the 'silence' and 'exclusion' of the African subject which African writers (men and women) over the years have attributed to colonial literature such as Joseph Conrad's *Heart of Darkness*, Joyce Carey's *Mister Johnson* and William Shakespeare's *The Tempest*. To underscore her point, Stratton turns the title of Achebe's *Things Fall Apart* into a parody captioned 'How Could Things Fall Apart For Whom They Were Not Together?'[35] which she then uses as the heading of one the chapters of her study. But even more outrageous to African sensibility, *women's as well as that of men*, is Stratton's comparison of *Things Fall Apart* with *Heart of Darkness*,[36] one of the most notorious pieces of africophobist literature ever written. Chinua Achebe may not have developed all the female characters in *Things Fall Apart* as sufficiently 'complex individuals'[37] comparable to such male characters as Okonkwo, Ezeudu, Nwoye and Uchendu but this is precisely an authorial

---

[32]See Florence Stratton, *Contemporary African Literature and the Politics of Gender* (London and New York: Routledge, 1994).
[33]Ibid., pp. 1 - 55.
[34]Ibid., p. 35.
[35]Ibid., ch. 1.
[36]Ibid., p. 171.
[37]See C. L. Innes, *Chinua Achebe* (Cambridge: Cambridge University, 1990), p. 22.

artistic device which crucially reinforces the central thrust of the novel, namely that the democratic and egalitarian 'dual-sex' gender principle that characterises the relationship between men and women in Igbo society is undermined if there is any weakening of either of the constituent units of the dyad.[38] In this case, what is undermined in the construct is the 'female principle' that incorporates the 'moral system which (sic) generates the concepts of love, harmony, peace and cooperation, and forbids human bloodshed and imposes a check on excessive and destructive masculinism.'[39] Okonkwo's career as a respected wealthy farmer (who comes originally from a family of very poor financial circumstances), a war hero, and indeed an influential member of Umuofia's political leadership, begins to plunge into crisis after crisis soon after he violates the 'female principle' of Umuofia after he murders the son of a kinsman.[40] Okonkwo is exiled by his community for seven years as a result and he never recovers his eminent status in Umuofia before his eventual suicide (which occurs soon after he kills an agent of the expanding British colonial regime). Contrary to Stratton's obvious misreading of *Things Fall Apart*, the novel in fact demonstrates quite clearly that the disequilibrium evident in the working of the 'dual-sex' gender principle in Umuofia does lay the grounds for the ultimate British conquest of the country – or, things eventually falling apart in the society!

We still have further observations to make on the subject of the partial development/total non-development of the character of the African subject of history or the silence imposed on this personage by colonial literature. This subject is only a concern to African writers (and critics) because it is organically linked to the colonial writer's consciously expressed efforts to achieve two crucial goals in his/her project at hand: (a) to deny the European strategic objective of the African conquest and (b) to demonise the African, *female and male alike*, in order to rationalise the conquest. Even if Stratton were correct that women characters in *Things Fall Apart* or in any other novels by Chinua Achebe were partially-developed, that, in itself, does not make the latter's novel(s) sexist or a 'patriarchal project'. African women are neither demonised nor is their humanity questioned in any way in any of Achebe's writings. No one would suggest that because critic Charles Larson claims that the characters in

---

[38]Cf. Carole Boyce Davies, 'Motherhood in the Works of Male and Female Igbo Writers: Achebe, Emecheta, Nwapa and Nzekwu,' in Davies and Graves, ed., *Ngambika*, p. 246.
[39]Amadiume, *Reinventing Africa*, p. 122.
[40]Achebe, *The African Trilogy*, p. 105.

Things Fall Apart (men, as well as women) 'are not fully developed,'[41] then this amounts to Achebe's demonisation or dehumanisation of the African men and African women in the novel. Not even Larson himself would lay such a charge! For Florence Stratton therefore, it is clear that by exaggerating the import of the female character development in *Things Fall Apart*, she ends up offering a superficial reading of the position of women in the novel. Indeed, as we have just indicated, a careful examination of the central tenet of *Things Fall Apart* shows clearly that the background to the fall of Okonkwo (the hero) and the ultimate tragedy that wreaks Umuofia's independence is in fact the hero's *violation* of the 'female principle' in society. This occurs when Okonkwo murders, albeit inadvertently, the son of the respected Ezeudu during the course of the latter's funeral. Fused with the 'male principle' in the dyadic relationship of Igbo dual-sex complementarity, the 'female principle' emanates from the goddess *ani*, the most revered in the Igbo pantheon. The Igbo describe any violation of the requirements of *ani* as *nso ani*, taboo-to-earth, or a crime against the goddess. Punishment for such a violation can be severe indeed, ranging from a reprimand to exile similar to that which Okonkwo receives in his own case. Rather than being absent or silent, women and women's vital interests are very much interwoven in the meticulous heuristic heritage of Umuofia chronicled in *Things Fall Apart*. The test of this is essentially the fact that Okonkwo's attempt to ignore or override the female component of this male-female duality of an inheritance triggers his fall and the ultimate collapse of society. For the people of Umuofia, both female and male, *things indeed do fall apart* as a result. As we shall demonstrate in this study, the ultimate safeguard for women's political, economic, juridical and spiritual rights in Igboland was the control that women, *themselves*, historically exercised over their own autonomous organisations which in turn reinforced the operationalisation of society's 'dual-sex' gender system. Such is the profound legacy of African women's historic role in the progress and development of their society that Annie Lebeuf arrives at the following conclusions in her study on African women:

By the habit of thought deeply rooted in the Western mind, women are relegated to the sphere of domestic tasks and private life, and men alone considered equal to the task of shouldering the burden of public office.

---

[41]Charles Larson, *The Emergence of African Fiction* (London and Basingstoke: Macmillan, 1978), especially ch. 2 and 6.

The anti-feminist attitude, which has prevented political equality between the sexes from being established in our country until quite recently ... should not allow us to prejudge the manner in which activities are shared between men and women in other cultures, more particularly, so far as we are concerned, in those of Africa.[42]

Another problem with Florence Stratton's contribution to the 'subordinated African woman' trope of literary criticism is that she either resorts to carefully selected quotations from key sociological texts which, right from the outset, reject the fundamental premise of her argument (of pre-conquest 'subordinated African woman'), or she maintains a silence over areas of such texts altogether without any attempts to offer a critique of dissension. The way that Stratton uses Amadiume's *Male Daughters, Female Husbands* in her discussion typifies our observation. First, Stratton makes the following claims: 'While all contemporary societies can be classified as patriarchal, in that each operates a social system characterized by male dominance, they are differently patriarchal, for each constructs gender differently.'[43] Then, she states:

There is also evidence to indicate that some societies are more flexible than others in their construction of gender. This is what Amadiume and others have argued was the case in a number of African societies until the beginning of this century when, under colonialism, rigid European gender definitions were imposed, which altered male-female power relations to the detriment of women.[44]

It is not clear what time frame Stratton is referring to as 'contemporary' in the first quote above. Does she mean in the 1990s? If so, since when, prior to the 1990s decade, would be incorporated in the 'contemporary'? It appears many years, indeed centuries prior to this decade and we can assert that this is the case because of Stratton's reference to Amadiume in the follow-up quote: 'This is what Amadiume and others have argued was the case in a number of African societies ...' But the problem with this reference is that there is nowhere in *Male Daughters, Female Husbands* that Amadiume describes Igbo society,

---

[42]Annie Lebeuf, 'The role of women in the political organizations of African societies,' in Denise Paulme, ed., *Women of Tropical Africa* (Berkeley: University of California, 1963), p. 93.
[43]Stratton, *Contemporary African Literature and the Politics of Gender*, p. 14.
[44]Ibid.

prior to the European conquest, as a patriarchal society or a variant of one for that matter. On the contrary, she is emphatic that Igbo society was not patriarchal prior to British conquest:

> In the indigenous society, the dual-sex principle behind social organization was mediated by the flexible gender system of the traditional culture and language. The fact that biological sex did not always correspond to ideological gender meant that women could play roles usually monopolized by men, or be classified as 'males' in terms of power and authority over others. As such roles were not rigidly masculinized or feminized, no stigma was attached to breaking gender rules. Furthermore, the presence of an all-embracing goddess-focused religion favoured the acceptance of women in statuses and roles of authority and power.[45]

In sharp contrast to the society governed by the 'dual-sex principle' described above, this is how Amadiume describes the sociology of gender power relations in Igboland after the latter's conquest by Britain in late 19th century/early 20th century:

> Western culture and the Christian religion, brought by colonialism, carried rigid ideologies which aided and supported the exclusion of women from the power hierarchy, whether in government or the church in the modern society. This rigid gender system meant that roles are strictly masculinized or feminized; breaking gender rules therefore carries a stigma.[46]

The two quotes above from *Male Daughters, Female Husbands* definitely do not refer to the same historical epochs. The first refers to pre-conquest Igboland whilst the latter refers to Igboland since the conquest, incorporating the present or contemporary as Amadiume is quick to reiterate: 'As a result of Western influence... men now manipulate a rigid gender ideology in contemporary sexual politics and thereby succeed in marginalizing women's political position, or in excluding them from power altogether.'[47] For Amadiume, in effect,

---

[45]Amadiume, *Male Daughters, Female Husbands*, p. 185.
[46]Ibid.
[47]Ibid.

'contemporary' Africa clearly refers to the two latter epochs of African history presented above, namely the European-conquered and post-conquest societies. As for Stratton, 'contemporary' Africa refers to Africa 'of all time'. Stratton is aware of this sharp disagreement with Amadiume and it is astonishing to state the least that she does not criticise the latter's obviously conflicting position on a subject on which the entire basis of her charge of an inexorable 'African patriarchy' is constructed. Instead, she conflates Amadiume's epochal frames employing *Male Daughters, Female Husbands* in selective citations often directed at the latter two historical epochs of African history where the two agree on a 'patriarchal' characterisation of power and authority (example: 'Amadiume tells of a northern Nigerian state [in the 1970s] "which outlawed rented accommodation for single women, considering them all to be prostitutes against whom punitive action should be taken"'[48]). Finding *Male Daughters, Female Husbands*'s position on pre-conquest African women not all together comfortable especially as its author at the end calls for the reestablishment of the 'dual-sex' gender system of the past as a solution to the present marginalisation of women in Nigeria politics, Stratton invokes Molara Ogundipe-Leslie's dogmatic marxist reading of African women in history as the sociological background of her discourse.[49] Obviously, this is a more appropriate reference for Stratton's project. According to Ogundipe-Leslie, the six-tier 'mountain of burden' that African women are 'subjected to' has gone on throughout time: from pre-conquest Africa to the present. The sixth tier of this 'mountain' is particularly oppressive:

> Women are shackled by their own negative self-image, by centuries of the interiorization of the ideologies of patriarchy and gender hierarchy. Her own reactions to objective problems therefore are often self-defeating and self-crippling. She reacts with fear dependency complexes and attitudes to please and cajole where more self-assertive actions are needed.[50]

---

[48]Stratton, *Contemporary African Literature and the Politics of Gender*, p. 16.
[49]Omolara Ogundipe-Leslie, 'African Women, Culture and Another Development,' *Journal of African Marxists*, February 1984. For a similar marxist and quite often reductionist reading of African history as the background for literary criticism, see the otherwise informative Chidi Amuta, *The Theory of African Literature* (London and New Jersey: Zed Books and Institute for African Alternatives, 1989).
[50]Ogundipe-Leslie 'African Women, Culture and Another Development,' pp. 35 - 36.

Whilst uncritically 'relying in this undertaking on Omolara Ogundipe-Leslie's analysis'[51] ensures that Stratton maintains her ideological position of a 'generic' and pervasive 'African patriarchy' throughout her study, it is perplexing how someone who subscribes to this view of 'weighed down' African women could appreciate or understand the independence, the drive, the enterprise, and the spirituality of women encapsulated in the 'dual-sex' gender organisation of Igbo society that Flora Nwapa so comprehensively demonstrates in *Efuru* and *Idu*. Stratton indeed devotes one chapter of her book to examine Nwapa's writings but even the access to the latter's work hardly changes her position. It is therefore not surprising that despite reading Nwapa, Stratton would contemptuously dismiss the African liberation struggle from European conquest in the following manner at the end of her study: 'patriarchal nature of both European imperialism and African nationalism, a coincidence of interests and complicity between two groups of men who share a will to power.'[52] In contrast, despite her dedicated service to the British imperialist mission in Igboland 70 years ago, Sylvia Leith-Ross displayed a greater respect for the sovereignty of the Igbo people:

> True democrats, no one was better than themselves but yet they were somehow better than anyone else. This self-assurance was sometimes a little frightening. The Ibo men and women are so continually in the right and so busy proving that every one else is in the wrong... They tolerate us because they need us. They do not look upon us resentfully as conquerors but complacently as stepping-stones. What will happen when they can, or think they can, mount alone and have no further use of the stepping-stones, no one can tell.[53]

Indeed, Leith-Ross's research in Igboland in 1934 remains one of the best known colonialist studies on Igbo women. Unlike her latter day adherents who are often content to adhere to preconceived and usually stereotypical sociological/historical assumptions about African women without making further or continuing efforts towards interrogation, Leith-Ross was more rigorous, more circumspect and more honest with the motives or goals of her research. Leith-Ross was unequivocal in stating that her studies were aimed at

---

[51]Stratton, pp. 14-15.
[52]Ibid., p. 172.
[53]Leith-Ross, *African Women*, p. 357.

the service of the British occupation regime in Igboland, especially coming in the wake of the Igbo Women's War of 1929.[54] To underline her credentials for this task, Leith-Ross referred to the fact that her husband was a colonial administrator in northern Nigeria, her brother was also in the colonial service and her father had been on the British naval squadron that stormed and captured Lagos some decades earlier.[55] In contrast, contemporary colonial writers and/or critics, especially those belonging to the category that we recently examined, operate within the ethos of the presumed objectivity of Western academia but are often anything but objective in their enterprise. Florence Stratton acknowledges some affinity with Leith-Ross (who 70 years earlier had been the recipient of a generous scholarship from a British research foundation to study Igbo women) when she describes herself as a privileged 'First World' researcher who studied African literature with research grants - 'an opportunity afforded much more frequently' to people who share a similar background to herself than those she describes as 'Third World' researchers.[56] But there is another affinity that the Strattons of contemporary colonialist writing on African women share with Leith-Ross and this has to do with the objective of their tasks. As we have already stated, Leith-Ross's was aimed at the consolidation of British imperialism in this part of west Africa. As for the Strattons, theirs is geographically and intellectually broader and more ambitious: they constitute a perspective in Western feminist discourse which wants to perpetuate the notion that the West, as Chandra Mohanty has observed, is the 'primary referent in theory and praxis.'[57] They try to achieve this by recycling stereotypical, essentially racist assumptions about African women/African humanity whose origins are often from anthropology or its more contemporary variant, 'development studies', both of whose main theorists and proponents have been Western males. This is precisely why this intellectual practice typifies what Gayatri Chakrovorty Spivak refers to as a 'fall back on a colonialist theory'[58] that advances Western global hegemony. For instance, instead of the racist binaries such as civilised/uncivilised or civilised/primitive or civilised/savage

---

[54]Ibid., pp. 39 - 44.
[55]Ibid., p. 41.
[56]Stratton, '"The Empire, Far Flung": Flora Nwapa's Critique of Colonialism,' in Umeh, ed., *Emerging Perspectives on Flora Nwapa*, p. 128.
[57]See Chandra Mohanty, 'Under Western Eyes: Feminist Scholarship and Colonial Discourses,' *Feminist Review*, No. 30, 1988, pp. 61 - 62.
[58]Gayatri Chakravorty Spivak, *In Other Worlds: Essays in Cultural Politics* (New York: Methuen, 1987), p. 179.

which were the standard references in Leith-Ross's focus on the European and the African, Stratton *et al* employ the not-too-dissimilar racist dualisms of developed/underdeveloped, developed/developing, first world/third world whilst discussing the same subject of the European and the African. Surprisingly, or so it appears, there is indeed some awareness of the political implications of this form of intellectual project. In an unguarded moment of candour, rather than a disclaimer, Stratton, for instance, admits that 'many traces of colonial contamination remain in my essay' on Leith-Ross and Nwapa. It is not without significance that she follows this admission by quoting from Robert Young's *Colonial Desire: Hybridity in Theory, Culture and Race*: 'The nightmare of the ideologies and categories of racism continue to repeat upon the living.'[59] The racism and cultural arrogance that often pervade the literature of the contemporary adherents of colonialist writing on Africa is astonishingly virulent, making the racism in Leith-Ross's book and those of her other colleagues nearly a century ago appear less anachronistic.[60]

So, despite its own racist commentaries and references where African women are routinely described as 'uncivilised', 'untutored savages' and 'primitive', Leith-Ross's scholarship on the Igbo was quite often more painstaking an endeavour than the present day variety. It records invaluable insights into the social organisation of both women and the 'dual sex' gendered heritage of Igbo society that are indeed compelling references for serious scholarship in the current era for those who so desire. As Elizabeth Isichie has argued, '[These were] eyewitness descriptions from missionaries, soldiers and administrators. But these were of course, themselves, agents of [the colonial occupation]. Nevertheless their descriptions, supplemented by studies of Ibo society...do show us the lineaments of Ibo society before it was subjected to the ... experience of alien conquest and rule.'[61] What is at stake here is not so much the objectivity of the findings of the research engagement itself, given the unambiguously stated political aim of the project made by the researcher(s) in question (as we indicated earlier in the case of Leith-Ross). Rather, it is that a

---

[59]Robert Young, *Colonial Desire: Hybridity in Theory, Culture and Race* (London: Routledge, 1995), p. 28.
[60]Cf. Amadiume, 'Cycles of Western imperialism: feminism, race, gender, class and power,' in Amadiume, *Reinventing Africa*, pp. 183-198 and Amadiume, 'In the company of women: love, struggle and our feminisms,' in Amadiume, *Reinventing Africa*, pp. 199-207.
[61]Elizabeth Isichie, *The Ibo People and the Europeans* (London: Faber and Faber, 1973), p. 71.

picture which should help clarify some of the contemporary intellectual debates that are a concern in our present study is indeed discernible from these exercises of the past, despite the charged conflictive and contradictive circumstances of the times. We shouldn't forget that the power relationship between researchers such as Leith-Ross and the African subject *being researched upon* was clearly *uneven*, with the researcher coming from a European conquest state or from elsewhere in the European/Western World,[62] studying peoples under European political and cultural subjugation. The researchers could not, in the majority of cases, speak the local African language, and so could not understand the underlying complexities of the social phenomenon they witnessed. Their reliance on interpreters who, more often than not, would have come from nations or nationalities *already* occupied by Europeans, further added strain on the quality of the outcome of the research. Furthermore, given the staggering disparity between the researcher's educational profile and that of the interpreter, the latter was in no intellectual position to relate or participate as an equal in the hermeneutic interplay or process demanded by the research in question. That these Western researchers approached the study of African societies with preconceived ideas about them was inevitable. The methodology employed was fatally flawed. Trite, superficial questions were asked about attitudes and behaviour steeped in a complex history of social norms and behaviour. To the research questions posed these researchers obtained answers which could not have been but tinged with a desire to please or at least not antagonise the researcher (either directly from the subject being interviewed, or from the interpreter, or indeed from both!), unmistakably seen by the Africans as part of the European collective which held such power over their lives. Even when observations were made, the validity of the conclusion reached and the accuracy of the interpretations thereof would have to be impaired given the disadvantaged point from which the researcher was operating - very little or no understanding of the language, very little or no understanding of the culture, very little or no understanding of the context within which these observations were being made, and minimal identification with the subjects being studied, even if only on a 'human' basis. The yardstick of analysis was invariably wrong. European culture was the ultimate measure of 'civilisation' and that which could not be understood within this context was perverse! This was the background

---

[62]Cf. Karen Blixen who was Danish but lived in British-occupied Kenya where she acquired a luxurious farm and wrote about Africans, usually contemptuously.

behind Western intellectual work on Africa and little has changed since then.[63] Evans-Pritchard's strident racist discourse on this subject reveals that, in spite of itself, there was a definite awareness of data distortion and misinterpretation even on the part of these researchers and writers. Yet, they persisted in presenting to the world their perverse readings as fact as Evans-Pritchard himself recalls in a controversial valedictory lecture at the end of a long academic career during which he published innumerable books on Africa whose titles hardly failed to incorporate the epithet, 'primitive'. Here, Evans-Pritchard's reflections which should be quoted in full have an arresting ring of irony for the contemporary colonial-writing practitioner who is more likely to be a woman:

We have to bear in mind, therefore, that the accounts of the social life of savage peoples on which the early anthropologists based their conclusions were usually written by men, and men from middle class homes and often, especially when from this country, with an evangelical background. The measure by which they judged the status of savage women was ... [by] their own mothers and sisters. Their observations were then strung together by anthropologists from, broadly speaking, the same class, who furthermore saw themselves as progressive thinkers in the forefront of the assault on the last strongholds of superstition and privilege, tending in consequence to write about savage customs and beliefs with an eye to the changes they wished to bring about in their own institutions. The evidences were for the most part so incomplete and so conflicting that by selection, presentation and emphasis a writer about primitive peoples could do much to discredit what he was opposed to ... It is difficult, if not impossible to evaluate objectively woman's position in any particular primitive society or in primitive societies in general. In the end any judgement is based on our own opinions and practices ... and is likely to be superficial, a judgement based on appearances strange to us rather than on the social realities behind them.[64]

Evans-Pritchard concludes: 'On the whole the findings of modern

---

[63]For an excellent discussion of the implications of this brand of scholarship, see Chinua Achebe, 'Impediments to dialogue between North and South,' in Achebe, *Hopes and Impediments*, pp. 14 - 19.
[64]Evans-Pritchard, *The Position of Women in Primitive Society and Other Essays*, pp. 38 - 40.

anthropologists are in agreement that women's status among primitive peoples has been misunderstood and underestimated.'[65]

Economic independence

According to Phoebe Ottenberg, Igbo women were 'literally in a position of physical and economic dependence' on their husband prior to the British conquest of Igboland. The picture painted by Ottenberg's portrait in defining the Afikpo Igbo is in direct contradiction to the large body of meticulous research that has been conducted by nationals and foreigners alike during this epoch of Igbo history. Ottenberg's portrait depicts an Igbo society where women's trading was regulated and controlled by men, including the profits generated from the trade which a husband could keep, 'feeding and clothing her in return.'[66] As we showed earlier on in the previous chapter, Igbo women's economic independence was a crucial feature of national social existence. Ottenberg must surely have been studying women from elsewhere! In contrast, Leith-Ross notes: 'The woman... has crops of her own which she sometimes plants apart ... All the ... crops, perhaps not in theory but in practice are the women's own property ... [A]nything left over from the household wants can be sold in the market. The money thus earned is kept by the woman who can spend it as she pleases...'[67]

A major source of economic advancement for women is linked to the introduction of cassava as a food crop. Ottenberg alleges that cassava is seen as a 'woman's crop' and therefore 'beneath the dignity of men.'[68] To Ottenberg, this is further evidence of the sexual subordination of women. There is in fact a historical and public health background to the presence of cassava in Igboland which Ottenberg either is unaware of or chooses to ignore. While cassava had been available in the coastal parts of Igboland as early as the 17th century,[69] it

---

[65]Ibid., p. 42.
[66]Ottenberg, 'The Position of Women among the Afikpo Ibo,' p. 214.
[67]Leith-Ross, *African Women*, pp. 91 - 92.
[68]Ottenberg, 'The Position of Women among the Afikpo Ibo,' p. 214.
[69]The introduction of cassava to Igboland is thought to have occurred either via international trade between Africans and indigenous American populations (for an excellent historical treatise on this subject, see Ivan Van Sertima, 'Evidence for an African Presence in Pre-Columbian America,' in Van Sertima, ed., *African Presence in Early America* [New Brunswick and London: Transaction Publishers, 1992], pp. 33-35)

only became a prominent food crop in the 20th century (after the 1914/1918 World War) following the widespread influenza epidemic.[70] The most devastating impact of this epidemic on the population was the extremely high rate of male mortality which caused a 'mass withdrawal of male labour from the rural economy.'[71] This, naturally, affected the production of yam, the prominent agricultural crop of the Igbo people, which is mostly cultivated by the male. In effect it became increasingly difficult for most households to depend on yam, hence the increasing importance of cassava in the diet. This example of yam and cassava - 'male' and 'female' crops - presents an excellent metaphor for understanding the important distinctions between gender and sex, and it highlights the misinterpretations of language and social systems that can occur in the event of the transposition of a researcher's value system onto their subjects, especially when the latter is from a different cultural/racial background. Yam, the 'male' or 'king' of crops, is so called because the perception that the Igbo have of this crop in its functions is a representation of 'maleness'. In the previous chapter we defined some attributes of maleness that *were intrinsically* male as being strength/power, protector/guardian of the nation. The role of the yam crop in the household diet was major. Various forms of preparation of yam constituted the main component of the household meal. In this respect, yam was in every sense a 'male' crop. Cassava, along with all the other 'female' crops, on the other hand, exhibited female traits – without them the household collapsed! It is to the historical background of its emergence as an important crop in Igboland, the ecological flexibility and adaptability of its cultivation, and the *feminised household signification* of the crop that Flora Nwapa invokes in an incantatory poem entitled, *Cassava Song:*

> We thank the almighty God,
> For giving us cassava
> We hail thee cassava

---

or via Portuguese traders on the west African coast during the 17th century - see Don Ohadike, *Anioma* (Athens: Ohio University, 1994), p. 202.

[70]The influenza pandemic of 1918-1919 which spread to Africa from Europe claimed two million lives in Africa (excluding North Africa) and one-half of a million in Nigeria alone whose population was only 18 million at the time. Mortality was highest among the age group 20-45. For a detailed discussion of this topic, see Ohadike, *Anioma,* p. 202.

[71]Ibid., p. 201.

The great cassava.
You grow in poor soils
You grow in rich soils
You grow in gardens,
You grow in farms.

You are easy to grow
Children can plant you
Women can plant you
Everybody can plant you.

We must sing for you
Great cassava, we must sing
We must not forget
Thee, the great one.[72]

Thus, cassava, as well as other 'female crops', provided a dietary balance for the family - the additional, necessary, supplement needed for the health and growth of the household. 'Female crops' complemented, supplemented, and when necessary, substituted for 'male crops'. Two distinct roles provided through two distinct crops - each playing a unique and vital complementary role in support of the household, and each genderised in the tradition of the Igbo for whom the use of language was an art! The idea, therefore, that the same Igbo man who routinely enjoys his cassava crop with his family would turn around and view this crop as 'beneath his dignity' smacks of irrationality; essentially, what is evident here is a researcher's lack of understanding of the significance of a cultural practice that is not her own. It is therefore not surprising that Ottenberg believes that the division of labour in Igboland is 'characterised by strong male domination.' As a result, she concludes that Igbo society exists on the basis of an 'innate superiority of men over women... backed by men's control over land and the supernatural and by sanctions of the village men's society, one of whose admitted purposes is to "keep women down."'[73] Once again, Leith-Ross's reflections of her own study of Igboland directly contradict Ottenberg's. Leith-Ross distinctly refers to the *fluidity* in sex-roles and the division of labour between the sexes. She observed that tasks considered men's

---

[72]Flora Nwapa, *Cassava Song and Rice Song* (Enugu: Tana, 1986) p. 1.
[73]Ottenberg, 'The Position of Women among the Afikpo Ibo,' pp. 207 - 208.

or women's work were interchangeably performed by members of the opposite sex. A case in point: 'The man does all the building work... Yet this work is not actually taboo for a woman... Similarly, I have seen a boy making a mat, which is purely women's work, for his sick mother. In agriculture, division of labour is strictly in theory, variable in practice... In practice, one will see women firing the undergrowth, men weeding, men planting both "men's" and "women's" yams [cassava or cocoyam] and vice versa.'[74]

The market is the central focus of the economy of Igboland and a quote from an account published in the Church Missionary Record in July 1866 is illustrative of the vitality of this social and cultural institution in the country: 'Their market consists of ... produce of every sort. Provisions in abundance. It abounds in corn, palm-wine, rum, fish, deer's flesh ... fowls, tobacco, yam, eggs, spices, pine-apple, palm-oil, bananas, and plantains, cassava, cloths, guns, powder, pipes...'[75] Elizabeth Isichie has argued that if one compares Igboland with other parts of Africa, the activity of the country's economic life and the vast number of its markets are strikingly noticeable.[76] Here it is important to stress once again that these institutions were primarily controlled and managed by women. It is about these same centres of economic activity that Leith-Ross comments: 'One would think [that the] practice of visiting different markets two or three times a week with all its attendant bustle and fatigue would be gladly dispensed with [as most of these activities could be done] without stirring from the women's respective villages.'[77] Although Leith-Ross concedes that these markets were much more than trading sites for the members of the community, she could not even begin to appreciate the significance of the markets especially that they were in fact *sites for the propagation of vast and sophisticated support net-works*, functioning as enabling mechanisms for women to carry out what were extremely demanding roles.

Unlike their earlier counterparts, the present-day adherents of the 'subordinated African woman' trope maintain a silence over the role of women in the ever changing dynamics of the socioeconomic conditions of contemporary Africa. Such an inquiry would have opened up new sites for subjecting their working assumptions on African women to further scrutiny. As we indicated in the previous chapter, the long stretch of instability that has

---

[74]Leith-Ross, *African Women*, pp. 89 - 90.
[75]Quoted in Isichie, *The Ibo people and the Europeans*, p. 75.
[76]Ibid., p. 76.
[77]Leith-Ross, *African Women*, p. 87.

wracked the African nation-state in the past 30 years has had incalculable consequences on the continent's social life. The International Monetary Fund-directed so-called 'structural adjustment programme' that has been institutionalised in most African economies in the last 20 years has had a devastating impact on Africa. During the period, Africa has uninterruptedly been a net-exporter of capital to the West - a fact that dramatically repudiates one of the fundamental tenets of 'development studies' and the relationship between North and South. Indeed, since 1985, Africa's net capital transfer to the coffers of Western governments and Western-led financial institutions has averaged US$20 billion per annum,[78] a startling feature of Africa's crisis that has forced Michel Camdessus, the former managing director of the IMF, to publicly and dramatically acknowledge his organisation's contribution to Africa's current plight.[79] As we have already shown in the previous chapter, major economic/societal disruptions have occurred in the wake of arbitrarily implemented 'structural adjustment' and 'privatisation' programmes aimed at meeting IMF specified targets for reducing government spending and cutting down deficits across most of Africa. Most of those made unemployed have been men who now increasingly find themselves unable to support their families, creating dangerous strains in social/family cohesion. Elsewhere in the economy, thousands of African farmers, again mostly men, have abandoned the cultivation of a range of such 'cash crops' as cotton, groundnut and sisal because of the virtual collapse of the prices of these products in the Western commodity markets especially in the past 20 years.[80] Women, who in the past were not employed in the state sector are now assuming the overwhelming role of day-to-day family support. As for men, there is a growing sense of a lack of fulfilment in the obvious sociological tasks of a father or a son in the family as the economic crisis persists. It is conceivable that the long-term impact on gender relations if the crisis is not soon resolved will create even greater fissures in the African family.

---

[78]Ekwe-Ekwe, *Africa 2001*, pp. 75 - 76.
[79]See 'IMF Says sorry to Africa,' *West Africa* (London: 31 January - 6 February 2000).
[80]For an insight into the range and depth of the virtual collapse of the prices of Africa's key agricultural products exported to the West during the period, see The Report of the South Commission, *The Challenge to the South*, pp. 59 - 60.

Political

As should be expected, the colonialist school of the 'subordinated African woman' extends its focus to politics. Despite the history of the influential role played, not by some socially-grounded elite, but ordinary women in ordering the Igbo nation, the persistent thrust of the dominant Western scholarship's views about *these same women's* so-called 'subjugation' exist to such a degree that one wonders whether this misrepresentation remains a question of just a lack of understanding, or, more likely, a deliberate effort to pervert the sociocultural integrity of an African society that presents us with an alternative and 'surprisingly' advanced world-view. Ottenberg's view that Igbo women were 'totally subordinate to men' in society and wielded no real political influence is best summed up in the phrase, 'to keep a woman down,' itself the prevalent theme that acquires a broad African continental transmutation in Rosaldo and Lamphere's edited *Women, Culture and Society*.[81] Evans-Pritchard dramatises the essence of this thinking when he notes: 'the adult primitive woman is above all a wife, whose life is centred in her home and family.'[82] He adds: '... a woman passes at marriage from under the authority of her father to that of her husband...'[83] Similarly, Ernestine Friedl links dominance of males to control over the production and distribution of resources/wealth and sees this as crucial in assessing the degree to which women can acquire political power.[84] It is indeed difficult to conceive of how such conclusions could have been drawn from a study of Igbo women given, in particular, the history of the 1929 Women's War. The sophisticated levels of political organisation witnessed have been attested to by virtually all critical observers.[85] The speed with which information on the war was communicated across most of Igboland and to a wide area of neighbouring Ibibio country, the organisation of mass meetings, and protest rallies were indeed impressive. It was this degree of disciplined and organised action that led Leith-Ross to comment, albeit with some incredulity,

---

[81] M. Z. Rosaldo and L. Lamphere, ed., *Women, Culture and Society* (Stanford: Stanford University, 1974).
[82] Evans-Pritchard, *The Position of Women in Primitive Societies and Other Essays*, p. 46.
[83] Ibid., p. 51.
[84] Ernestine Friedl, *Women and Men: An Anthropologist's View* (Stanford: Holt, Rinehart & Winston, 1975), p. 61.
[85] See, for instance, Mba, *Nigerian Women Mobilized* and Afigbo, 'Women in Nigerian History'.

that '[r]emembering the Aba riots of 1929, the extraordinary rapidity with which these thousands of women had mobilized, their organisation and discipline, one could not help wandering whether there was not some vast network of secret societies binding the women together and to some central authority.'[86] Annie Lebeuf has no such incredulity in her discussion of the Igbo women's councils which played a crucial role in mobilising their members during the war: 'These councils are responsible for everything concerning agriculture and the interests of women in general ... If anyone, man or woman, contravenes any of their decisions, they can take sanctions against them and they have great authority in judicial matters.'[87] Leith-Ross agrees that the men support the independence of these councils, but she does not quite see these structures as constituting another arena of the Igbo 'dual-sex' gender construction of their society: '[I]ndeed the majority of men approve of [the women's councils] and wish them to keep their power. This may be partly due to the fact that they trust the integrity of the women ... more than their own. They also know that women wish to preserve the peace of the town as it enables them to carry on their trading, and they seem also to think that the women have a greater sense of abstract justice.'[88] Besides their more inclusive work for women's interests, the councils also have advisory roles in other political institutions in society especially those that cater for men's interests and those that safeguard the overall development and survivability of the community. '[W]hen one has listened to one of their meetings, seen the order, the good sense ... one cannot help feeling what a pity it is that not more use can be made of these women and this surprising organisation.'[89]

Spiritual/philosophical

The Igbo never had a religion defined as a particular institutionalised system of beliefs, outlining their relationship with a deity or deities. The spiritual life of the Igbo, like most Africans, was closely interwoven with their very existence. Christopher Ezekwugo defines it as '[a] system of life accommodation in

---

[86]Leith-Ross, *African Women*, p. 105.
[87]Lebeuf, 'The role of women in the political organizations of African societies,' p. 113.
[88]Leith-Ross, *African Women*, p. 107.
[89]Ibid., p. 107.

relation to an overall norm.'[90] Spirituality was individualised to the extent that one's *chi* (personal god) provided direction and guidance to the individual. As he states, 'the Igbo [person] believes firmly in and gives proportionate worship to the true God, who for him [or her] is not a god-out-there in the distance and too difficult to reach. [S/he] sees God very near to [her/his] as [her/his] protective deity and family member. This makes [her/his] personal relation to God something natural and spontaneous,'[91] illustrated by 'natural and unfeigned devotion.'[92] He adds of the Igbo religious perspective: '[R]eligion is the soul of [humanity's] individual and social life. It embraces every aspect of [humanity's] life.'[93] Ezekwugo believes that the heart of Igbo religion is contained in the concept of *chi* which has been '...completely neglected and overlooked or woefully misrepresented...'[94] Chinua Achebe points out that '[E]very person has an individual *chi* who created [them] ... [The Igbo] postulate the concept of every [person] as both a unique creature and the work of a unique creator.'[95] But the most controversial interpretation of the importance of the concept of *chi* in Igbo philosophical thought and religion belongs to Donatus Nwoga, who for many years was a leading scholar on Igbo culture and literature at the University of Nigeria at Nsukka. Nwoga is convinced that it is someone's *chi*, not the concept of the 'Supreme God' (which he considers as 'stranger' in Igbo philosophy/religion), that is central to the Igbo 'consciousness of transcendental power.'[96] These references offer a fascinating insight into the endeavour of African scholars to reconstruct the corpus of the African philosophical heritage that has often been the focus of deliberate distortions or outright demonisation in European colonialist writing. Ezekwugo maintains that an area of monumental failure in colonialist scholarship on the Igbo and other Africans has been its inability to study, understand, and report on the complexity of the religions and cultures of the people. Quite simply, this was as a result of the 'unwillingness of the early Europeans ... to recognise Africans as human

---

[90]Christopher Ezekwugo, *Chi: The True God in Igbo Religion* (Alwaye: Pontifical Institute of Philosophy and Theology, 1987), p. 6.
[91]Ibid., p. xiv.
[92]Ibid.
[93]Ibid., p. 4.
[94]Ibid., p. xiii
[95]Chinua Achebe, 'Chi in Igbo Cosmology,' in Achebe, *Morning yet on Creation Day* (London: Heinemann Education Books, 1975), p. 98.
[96]Donatus Nwoga, *The Supreme God As Stranger in Igbo Religious Thought* (Ekwereazu: Hawk, 1984), p. 33.

beings...'[97] Ezekwugo is right to emphasise that in a people's religion is embodied the '"soul" of human life'[98] through which all acts are animated. 'In the light of this [fact] it makes no sense to speak of a people ... without a religion.'[99]

With these reflections in mind, we once again return to Leith-Ross who warns against 'the danger of over-estimating the present powers of the Ibo women to understand and inwardly digest religious or ethical teaching.'[100] She sees the world of the Igbo as being ridden with superstition, a spirit-filled environment in which sickness and death occur not by natural causes but as a result of displeased spirits in need of 'constant propitiation.'[101] She goes on to comment, once again in direct contradiction to her initial observations: 'I cannot feel, as one is so often told, that their lives are obsessed with fear...If you listen in the twilight you hear the comfortable sounds of a sleepy village; if you watch the faces in the morning, they are smooth, unstrained. Surely terror-ridden people do not walk so freely, talk so loud, are not so bright of eye and sleek of body ... Were one to put a group of black men and women and a group of white, one would destroy the illusion that it is they who are the slaves and we who are the free.'[102] Finally, perhaps the greatest recognition of womanhood and the importance ascribed to that role is exemplified in the femaleness of *ani*, the earth goddess of fertility, and the most revered deity in the Igbo pantheon who Michael Echeruo has described as the most likely candidate to be designated the 'supreme god' of the Igbo.[103] Thus, the Igbo worship of *ani* which Leith-Ross herself acknowledges as consisting of the 'essentials of Ibo religion,'[104] is surprisingly not seen by her at the same time as evidence of the singularly important role of women in Igboland.

In conclusion, the Igbo attitude to compassion and charity work, or the lack of these, constitutes another interesting site of reference in Leith-Ross's studies. She recalls an encounter she had with a leper during the course of her research. She had given a blanket to the leper to use as a cover during the rainy season.

---

[97]Ezekwugo, *Chi*, p. xiii.
[98]Ibid., p. 6.
[99]Ibid.
[100]Leith-Ross, *African Women*, p. 116.
[101]Ibid., p. 121.
[102]Ibid., pp. 120 - 121.
[103]Quoted in Elaine Savory Fido, 'Okigbo's *Layrinths* and the Context of Igbo Attitudes to the Female Principle,' in Davies and Graves, eds, *Ngambika*, p. 223.
[104]Leith-Ross, *African Women*, p. 117.

Leith-Ross claims that a great shout of laughter erupted from a crowd watching which, in her opinion, 'did not begrudge it him,' but who, lacking in this capacity for largesse, found it inconceivable and comical that the blanket had been given to the leper 'towards whom [she] was under no obligation.'[105] Igbo tradition is steeped in a deep reverence for individual achievement and effort. A person's capacity to utilise his/her own talents to achieve great success is looked upon with great respect and admiration in their community, as Okonkwo's sterling example in *Things Fall Apart* demonstrates.[106] Leith-Ross's gesture, seen by her to highlight her sense of pity and magnanimity, was undoubtedly perceived differently by the on-looking villagers. This was clearly a case of differing cultural interpretation on how best to support someone in need. It is highly likely in this example that the villagers may have felt that Leith-Ross's gift to the beggar falls into that category of charity work which the Igbo are very contemptuous of, and so decry in the popular saying, 'giving a man a fish rather than teaching him to fish'. The burst of laughter from the villagers would be consistent with that act of derision! According to Igbo philosophy on this score, if indeed the villagers' stated reaction was motivated by the assessment that we have proffered, a truly magnanimous gesture on Leith-Ross's part would have been judged to have occurred if she had enabled the leper to alter his destitute condition *permanently* – creating the opportunity for the leper to discontinue the life of dependency and poverty and embark on a more independent existence. Igbo philosophy lays particular emphasis on the concept of helping others to help themselves, and not helping others only to the extent that they remain dependent on someone else for future help.[107]

Motherhood

Filomina Chioma Steady has discussed the importance that African women and society as a whole attach to motherhood. She argues that this attribute and the whole subject of child upbringing arguably account for the 'most fundamental

---

[105]Ibid., p. 128.
[106]See Achebe, *The African Trilogy*, especially pp. 34 - 40.
[107]See, for instance, Ejizu, *Ofo*, pp. 118 - 119 and Ogbu Kalu, 'Ethical Values In Igbo Tradition of Politics,' in Anyanwu and Aguwa, eds., *The Igbo and the Tradition of Politics*, pp. 16 - 17 .

difference between the African woman and her Western counterpart.'[108] We should now explore how colonialist writers and critics have examined this subject in their work. Leith-Ross's study of Igbo women extends to family bonds, specifically the emotional bond between parents and children. Families shared meals and children's needs were given priority since 'being the weakest they must be fed first.'[109] The closeness, even after the children had become adults, married, and left home, was noted. 'One of the most attractive features of Ibo family life is this affection, shown not only by the proud father lifting an ecstatic baby onto his shoulder but by younger children patiently hushing a tiny form to sleep, motionless and cramped, a tiny head in the crook of their own tiny arms.'[110] In spite of these observations, Leith-Ross maintained that Igbo women lacked an understanding of love: 'I should say her emotional lags behind her intellectual development.'[111] Writing even more broadly on African women as a whole, Evans-Pritchard concurs: 'The primitive girl ... would find it difficult to understand either sentimental love, or what it has to do with marriage...'[112] Furthermore, Evans-Pritchard returns to the crucial subject of the independence of African women in marriage for what appears as an opportunity for re-evaluation, having earlier dismissed it outright - 'a woman passes from under the authority of her father to her husband.' The outcome of the re-evaluation throws his position on the subject into even greater confusion and contradiction as the following three quotes demonstrate:

A married couple have their family *life together* with their children in their home ... A husband goes about his affairs, not only in public affairs but in his social life also, without having to take his wife with him; and a wife leads her own social life without his constantly being present.[113] (emphasis added)

[T]he *sense of companionship* between men and women, particularly

---

[108]Filomina Chioma Steady, *The Black Women Crossculturally* (Cambridge: Schenkman, 1981), p. 29.
[109]Leith-Ross, *African Women*, p. 84.
[110]Ibid., p. 104.
[111]Ibid., p. 114.
[112]Evans-Pritchard, *The Position of Women in Primitive Societies and Other Essays*, p. 47.
[113]Ibid., p. 49.

between husbands and wives, *is not so strong* as in our own society.[114] (emphasis added)

...[T]here is *less merging of personalities*, less loss of that distinct quality of the sexes.[115] (emphasis added)

How the African woman who supposedly at marriage 'passes from under the authority of her father to her husband' is able to maintain the independence of responsibility and action obviously implied in each of the latter three quotes above is nowhere answered nor resolved by Evans-Pritchard. Furthermore, Evans-Pritchard comments on the wide circle of family and sense of community available in African societies: 'There are any number of persons a child calls and to some extent acts towards and thinks of as "father", "mother", "brother", "sister"... Consequently there is a large spread of the intra-family sentiments and interests over a very wide range of [relations].'[116] This vast network of social support, Evans-Pritchard implies, is however negative because it, in some way, dilutes the bonding/emotional ties between parent and child. This is illustrated, according to him, on the death of a parent: 'The primitive son or daughter may suffer the loss acutely but it is not the disaster it is to us.'[117] More stale and distasteful examples follow, further dehumanising African people, and reducing them to some sort of weird species of existence. At the end, what is clear here is a deliberate effort by a leading European World academic of his age to disregard, distort, and indeed demonise what is often or evidently 'value' and 'difference' between the African cultural heritage and that of the European, driven largely by the ideological quest to rationalise the British/European conquest and occupation of Africa. The more contemporary colonialist writers equally operate within the overarching imperatives of this rationalising enterprise as we have already shown. Just as the earlier writers on this subject of African motherhood, they share very similar views that the African woman is very much subordinated to her husband. But much more than the former, the contemporary colonialist writer is concerned with what could be termed the 'too-mothering' role of the African woman, a reference to the central and enduring theme of motherhood in the writing of leading African female writers including Flora Nwapa, Buchi Emecheta, Ama Ata Aidoo, Grace Ogot, Bessie

---

[114]Ibid.
[115]Ibid .
[116]Ibid.
[117]Ibid.

Head and Mariama Bâ, as well as the importance also attached to the subject by influential male writers such as Chinua Achebe, Leopold Seder Senghor, Wole Soyinka, Ngugi Wa Thiong'o, Christopher Okigbo and Ayi Kwei Armah. Marie Umeh is very critical of the mothering and associated roles of women 'inherent... [in] many traditional [African] societies.'[118] She feels that the effects of these roles on the current and future wellbeing of African women is 'devastating.'[119] The African woman, Umeh claims, as earlier cited, is 'caught in a bind. In order to be liberated and fulfilled as a woman she must renounce her African identity ... Or, if she wishes to cherish and affirm her "Africanness" she must renounce her claims to feminine independence and self-determination.'[120] Umeh's claims are untenable. This is because there is no sociological or historical study of any group of African women that indicates that African women, *themselves*, find their mothering roles in society and their consciousness of possessing an independent space of responsibility and action dichotomised or indeed contradictory in any way. On the contrary, our study so far has shown that women in Africa view mothering as well as other societal tasks that they are involved in as totally inclusive, or as Felicia Ekejiuba of UNICEF has argued,

> For the African woman, mothering is supreme. Women are asking for economic empowerment so as to be able to take care of their children and they are also calling for equitable distribution of resources and opportunities and the removal of all constraints that obstruct women's development and progress.[121]

Maryse Condé completely misses the underlying exhilarating humour and irony evident in the exquisite composite portrait of women's lives and chores that Nwapa paints in her novel, *Efuru*. Condé's response to this picture incorporates the predictable demonising and pretentious preoccupation of colonialist criticism on the African humanity. She writes that Nwapa creates a 'disturbing picture of narrow-mindedness, superstition, malevolence, and greed and fear in

---

[118]Umeh, 'Reintegration With The Lost Self,' p. 175.
[119]Ibid.
[120]Ibid.
[121]Quoted in Ezeigbo, 'Myth, History, Culture and Igbo Womanhood in Flora Nwapa's Novels,' p. 73.

traditional Africa and might go contrary to what she has thought to defend.'[122] No such thing! There are no features of a range of behaviour that Nwapa creates in the novel that could not occur in similarly close-knit communities elsewhere where women enjoy some autonomy in their daily lives. These include the women looking after a relation's or neighbour's child as the parent goes to the farm or market, or undertaking some other task for someone in the village, or the occurrence of the occasional discussion over some captivating story or the envy that some success could attract. This is a story in which the novelist gives some insight into the space that women inhabit and organise independently of men in their society that helps the reader to appreciate the working of the Igbo 'dual-sex' gender complementary system. 'The mothers of Africa, Nwapa shows, also have voices, anger, rival aspirations, their own lives. Most of all, they are as much the subjects of communal history as their ... sons.'[123] Essentially, what Nwapa does here is to challenge the usual dogmatic portrayal of Igbo society as 'patriarchal' which critics such as Condé who subscribe to colonialist interpretations of African history and literature tend to make. It is therefore not surprising that at the end Condé fails to grasp the defining lesson of Efuru's triumph in *Efuru* (we shall be elaborating on this in the next chapter) when she concludes her study by noting: 'No happiness can be achieved for a woman unless in childbearing... Efuru for all her qualities and gifts, considers her life as valueless since she fails to have a child.'[124] Similarly, Katherine Frank, another critic of the colonialist school, arrives at the same faulty conclusion on the subject when she alleges: 'In [Africa] for a woman to lack reproductive power is to lack all power, indeed to be deprived of her very identity and raison d'etre in life.'[125] On the contrary. Even though Efuru is childless at the end of the novel, we are told unambiguously that she 'slept soundly that night.'[126] She is a wealthy business woman, beautiful and a privileged worshipper of *uhamiri*, the lake goddess, the most revered deity in her community. The fact that Efuru has a similar personality profile as *uhamiri*,

---

[122]Maryse Condé, 'Three Female writers in Modern Africa: Flora Nwapa, Ama Ata Aidoo and Grace Ogot,' *Presence Africaine*, 82, 2, 1972, p. 136.
[123]Elleke Boehmer, 'Stories of Women and Mothers: Gender and Nationalism in the Early Fiction of Flora Nwapa,' in Susheila Nasta, ed., *Motherlands* (London: Women's Press, 1991), p. 19.
[124]Condé, 'Three Female Writers in Modern Africa,' pp. 134-136.
[125]Frank, 'Women Without Men,' p. 20.
[126]Flora Nwapa, *Efuru* (London: Heinemann Education Books, 1966), p. 221.

including the goddess's state of childlessness,[127] means that even on the crucial subject of motherhood the Igbo have an in-built flexibility within their 'dual-sex' gender system which ensures that a woman who fails to become a mother can be successful and respected in society by embarking on other goals. As Elleke Boehmer succinctly puts it 'fecundity [is] important, not entire.'[128] Condé is equally critical of the feminist credentials of another African writer, Grace Ogot. Here, she is particularly incensed by Ogot's political and literary reading preferences: 'One feels tempted to advise her to join some Women's Lib. Movement to see how European females question the code of values and behaviour imposed upon them, and to replace her Bible by Germaine Greer's book.'[129]

Boehmer has shown how Africa's leading male writers have found the theme of motherhood critical in some of their writings. 'Africa, the continent ... is both the beloved land and mother.'[130] The action of a group of Nigerian officials who wrote a new national anthem invoking the 'father-image,' unlike the previous anthem that referred to Nigeria as 'our sovereign motherland,'[131] would amount to a glaring example that goes against the grain of this continent-wide reverence for the institution of motherhood. The presence across Africa of innumerable female deities in the people's pantheon of gods and goddesses, several of which are among the most revered and worshipped by male and female alike in the population, has undoubtedly ensured that 'motherhood' is treated with spiritual sensitivity that goes beyond the issue of fecundity. In Igboland, the people usually refer to the female deities as 'mother' with all the reverence that this connotes.[132] We should recall that motherhood is a crucial derivative from the 'female principle' which is that constituent feature of the 'dual-sex' gender system which not only foregrounds the possibilities of fecundity, but is the fountain of society's moral authority which oversees the conceptualisation and the working of attributes of love, peace, harmony and goodwill. Both male and female members of society (as well as children) therefore have an immanent

---

[127]Ibid.
[128]Boehmer, 'Stories of Women and Mothers,' p. 18.
[129]Condé, 'Three Female Writers in Modern Africa,' p. 142.
[130]Boehmer, 'Stories of Women and Mothers,' p. 3.
[131]See C. L. Innes, 'Virgin Territories and Motherlands: Colonial and Nationalist Representations of Africa and Ireland,' *Feminist Review*, No.47, Summer 1991, pp. 10-11.
[132]Ezeigbo, 'Myth, History, Culture and Igbo Womanhood in Flora Nwapa's novels,' p. 71.

stake in their identification with this heritage. It is this that leads Wendy James to argue that for Africa, 'there is a deeper and historically more enduring level at which the nature and capacity of women are given primacy in the definition of the human condition itself.'[133] Novelist Mariama Bâ apparently expresses some concern over the 'nostalgic praise to the African mother whom, in his anxiety, man confuses with Mother Africa.'[134]

This concern does not in anyway challenge the validity of the entrenched African spiritual reverence to motherhood by both female and male. Given its abiding ethos across Africa, it is a reverence whose practice could hardly be exaggerated nor misunderstood. Therefore, individual or collective African male (or indeed female) expertise or success in writing, politics, business or any other profession for that matter, need not be dependent on an evaluation of how effectively or otherwise they show reverence to the motherhood principle. 'Women [are] regarded as the very embodiment of African society and custodians of African culture. They therefore command ... the highest respect.'[135] Given this background, it hardly makes any sense to accuse any African of idealising or romanticising the position of motherhood in their society as some colonialist writers and critics have tended to typecast the contributions of especially African male authors on the subject. These critics have claimed that African male authors have generally 'appropriated' the womanhood/motherhood trope as symbol for idealistic or romantic projects, or, as Elaine Fido describes this orientation, the writers employ 'myth to create fantasies which deny the reality' of African historical experience.[136] In Stratton's contribution to this discourse, she employs very distasteful language in her review of a number of African male authors, including Leopold Sedar Senghor, Chinua Achebe and Wole Soyinka. Her use of language in this regard borders on africophobist writing not too dissimilar to earlier colonialist writings discussed in this study.[137] According to Stratton, the 'crime' that leading African male authors have committed in their canonical works on African literature is

---

[133]Wendy James, 'Matrifocus on African women,' in Shirley Ardner, ed., *Defining Females: The Nature of Women in Society* (London: Croom Helm, 1978), p. 160.
[134]Quoted in Mineke Schipper, 'Mother Africa on a pedestal: the male heritage in African literature and criticism,' *African Literature Today*, 15, 1987, p. 47.
[135]Amadiume, *Reinventing Africa*, p. 104.
[136]Fido, 'Okigbo's *Labyrinths* and the Context of Igbo Attitudes to the Female Principle,' p. 224.
[137]See Stratton, *Contemporary African Literature and the Politics of Gender*, especially Part I.

that on this subject of African motherhood, they have dared to 'romanticise' the theme as part of their respective projects to safeguard 'African patriarchy'![138] Despite Stratton's position which reveals her lack of understanding of the background history and sociology of the 'motherhood' heritage we sketched above, Senghor, Soyinka, Achebe, Ngugi, Okigbo, Armah and any other African male authors for that matter, as well as their female counterparts, are *justifiably entitled* to celebrate the motherhood corpus of their inheritance as evocatively as they wish. It is hard to imagine any other known facet on the African sociological scene that has enhanced male-female relationships and the spirituality of social existence as much as the institution of motherhood. This is the legacy that has captivated the interest of African women and men of letters in the past and there is no reason to suggest that it will cease to be the case in the foreseeable future.

Western education: the key to women's liberation?

Colonialist administrators, writers and critics have for many decades argued that Western education serves as the liberating force for women of Africa. This section will demonstrate that contrary to this deeply entrenched belief about African women, Western education for both men and women has served strategically to establish and then perpetuate European World social constructs of subordination in Africa. The crisis in Africa presently is one of a seeming inability of a people to plan, formulate and implement policies designed to advance the interests and wellbeing of their people. This problem lies squarely at the door of Africa's *mal-education*. Within this construct, European value systems ranging from gender relations as we have shown so far in this study, to the overarching socioeconomic order that defines day-to-day life are promoted and highly coveted; the indigenous is devalued, supported by an educational system that places Europe and Europeans rather than Africa and Africans at its epicentre. Armed with an educational ethos of the state generated uncritically from the varying schools of Western anthropology and development studies, the African school system imparts to their students that their society is 'backward', 'developing', 'underdeveloped'; that 'women are, and have always been subordinate to men' and that their limited liberation has been achieved through the intervention of Western goodwill; that African extended family systems and

---

[138]Ibid.

kinship relationships are 'backward, impeding development and inferior to Western kin groups based on the nuclear family.'[139] Carter Woodson aptly captures the essence of this problem in a study that albeit focuses on African Americans. He argues that African intellectuals have largely been ineffective in dealing with their societies because they have been schooled in a system that valorises European existence while demonising theirs: 'The only question that concerns us here is whether these educated persons are actually equipped to face the ordeal before them or unconsciously contribute to their own undoing by perpetuating the regime of the oppressor.'[140] Jacob Carruthers, in a paper entitled 'The illusion of intellectual attainment,'[141] establishes the linkage between African mal-education in the Americas and African mal-education on the continent. Quoting from Julius Nyerere, the first post-conquest president of Tanzania, Carruthers shows how aware Nyerere was of the fact that the system of education inherited from the British colonial government failed to serve the future interests of his country: '[There] are basic elements in the [education] system which prevent... the integration of the pupils into the society they will enter, and which encourage attitudes of inequality, intellectual arrogance, and intense individualism among the young people who are to go through our schools.'[142]

While Nyerere is absolutely correct in his general assessment of the impact of the educational system on young Tanzanians, his specific evaluation of the problem is somewhat narrow and limiting. The *content* of our education as it currently stands and has stood since the advent of European conquest- states in Africa ensures that Western experiences and values are the norms towards which every living man, woman and child should and indeed do aspire. The question to ask therefore is: how does an African begin to approach his/her own human potential when either has very successfully been socialised by an educational system into consciously or unconsciously believing that one is culturally, intellectually and spiritually dependent on Western imported values?

---

[139]Niara Sudarkasa, 'The "Status of Women" in Indigenous African Societies,' in Ralyn Terborg-Penn et al, *Women in Africa and the African Diaspora* (Washington: Howard University, 1987), pp. 30 - 41.
[140]C. G. Woodson, *The Miseducation of the Negro* (Washington: Associated Publishers, 1969), p. xxxi.
[141]Jacob Carruthers, 'Black Intellectuals and the Crisis in Black Education,' in Mwalimu Shujaa, ed., *Too Much Schooling, Too Little Education* (Trenton: African World, 1994), pp. 39-41.
[142]Ibid.

The production of an educated class of individuals (to whose status, incidentally, the rest of society aspires) who are psychologically secure in the authenticity, uniqueness and integrity of their culture becomes quite remote. As a result of the overwhelmingly pervasive nature of European hegemony and racism, failure for the individual African is not limited to, or understood in the context of the self, but rather it is readily projected onto the group, the race. Today the chaos represented in Africa, in the wake of 40 years of the restoration of independence, stems from this mal-education. In Nigeria, for instance, where the military have been in power for most of this period (29 out of the 40 years), intellectuals have generally ensured the entrenchment of this arbitrary rule. They have given legitimacy to these undemocratically elected governments, presenting virtually no collective challenge (in-country) to these illegal regimes; they have acted as principal advisers especially in socio-economic policies often formulated in concert with the IMF/World Bank that have caused such hardships and devastation of life in Africa as we have already demonstrated.[143] Neo-colonialism and the perpetuation of social, economic and political structures that continue to serve Western interests, would never have been consolidated in Africa if alternative structures - designed to promote African indigenous institutions and interests - had been put in place. One of the most salient examples of this is gender where an egalitarian and advanced social construct of male-female relations has been labelled as 'inferior' and largely jettisoned, particularly among the middleclass. It should be recalled that on the eve of the restoration of independence, African countries were inundated with scholarships to study in the West. Many of them during the era (1960s/1970s) were trained in development studies departments which only a decade earlier would have been generally referred to as departments of anthropology or 'tribal' or 'primitive' peoples! The overwhelming majority of contemporary policy makers and professionals in Africa emerged from these schools which also had their replicas (Institutes of Development Studies) in several African countries. It is therefore not surprising that as the current grave social conditions of Africa continue unabated, critical African opinion is increasingly questioning the relevance to the continent of this immediate post-conquest educational project.[144]

---

[143]Herbert Ekwe-Ekwe, *Issues in Nigerian Politics Since the Fall of the Second Republic: 1984 - 1990* (Lewiston & Lampeter: Edwin Mellen, 1991), especially ch. 3.
[144]Ibid.

In *The African: His Antecedent, His Genius, and His Destiny*,[145] G. K Osai provides us with an apt illustration of how an uncritically transposed educational programme from Europe to Africa could be very damaging in its African application. He narrates the story of Jacobus Capitien, a young African born in the 18th century in what was then called Gold Coast (Republic of Ghana). Capitien was captured by slavers, acquired by a Dutch trader who found him to be exceptionally bright. Consequently, instead of confining him to the conventional slave's existence, he was recruited as the master's personal servant and traveled with him all over Europe. In order to demonstrate his position that Capitien was 'as intelligent as any European' (a frequent bone of contention), the Dutch trader enrolled him in university where he obtained the equivalent of a doctorate on a dissertation supporting the institution of slavery. Commenting on the use of such 'fine intellect' to further the subjugation of his own people, Carruthers observed:

Capitien was so successful and popular that he was sent back to the biggest slave factory in Africa, Cape Coast Castle, where he was made chaplain. Capitien's role was to pacify the slaves and get them resigned to their eventual fate. So distinguished was he in the performance of that role that he was buried in Cape Coast Castle amongst the Europeans who lived in that slave factory. The education of Jacobus Capitien continues to be the model for [African] education.[146]

Hence, Woodson's position which emphasises that 'with the miseducated [Africans] in control ... it is doubtful that the system would be very much different from what it is or that it would rapidly undergo change. The [Africans] thus placed in charge would be the products of the same system and would show no more conception of the task at hand than do the Whites who have educated them and shaped their minds as they would have them function.'[147] In other words, the current, very powerful European cultural values as taught by, and inculcated into Africans by the schools and the schooling process not only reinforce the myth of the 'superiority' of the European experience, but concomitantly negates the very basis of existence and humanity of every African man, woman, and most damagingly of all, child. As Cheikh Anta Diop

---

[145]G.K. Osai, *The African: His Antecedent, His Genius, and His Destiny* (New Hyde Park: University Books), 1971
[146]Carruthers, 'Black Intellectuals and the Crisis in Black Education,' p. 45.
[147]Woodson, *The Miseducation of the Negro*, p. 23.

has argued, 'the erasing, the destruction of the historical conscience also has been since time began part of the techniques of colonization, enslavement, and the debasement of peoples.'[148] When we turn our attention specifically to the issue of African women, the devastating effects of the mal-education of post-conquest Africa becomes evident. Through the 'appropriate' European cultural-based schooling of Africans, the structure of African society and the position of women therein become irrelevant, relegated to a position of political marginalisation of both thought and action in the ordering and maintenance of societal norms and values. Women 'now find themselves systematically excluded from any participation in the new set-up that has been hastily formulated by the intruding colonial powers.'[149] African women have, perhaps for the first time in their history, now lost out on their power base with the neutralisation of existing structures of social change and progress. It is perhaps most ironical that Sylvia Leith-Ross witnessed the intrinsic recognition by a group of African women of *their own importance as women* in their own right but she, herself, failed to recognise this glaring demonstration of independence. It is this failure that leads her to write: '[T]hat the wife resented being regarded in the light of a possession I very much doubt. She knew that in the last resort it was she who brought forth the children her husband craved for as much as she did ... But now her attitude may no longer be so satisfied. She is being taught that Christian marriage is based on love ... she is being told that she is not a chattel.'[150] Leith-Ross's inability to recognise that the women she interviewed *did not view* their position as one of a 'possession' simply because they were *not*, is extraordinary. Furthermore, Leith-Ross's apparent failure to realise that Igbo women's age-long independence in their society was fast receding as the process of the conquest state's socioeconomic programme of excluding women intensified, is indicative of the ignorance exhibited by these early 'scholars' on Africa. The illogicality of her recently-quoted comments could not be more evident when assessed alongside the following observation she makes in the same study on the independence of Igbo women. In what can only be described as an unguarded moment, her tone almost wistful, Leith-Ross comments: 'Yet one could not but be impressed but by that curious sense one so often had among Ibo women of private and independent lives, an existence of their own

---

[148]Cheikh Anta Diop, *Civilization or Barbarism* (New York: Lawrence Hill Books, 1991), p. 212.
[149]Lebeuf, 'The role of women in the political organizations of African societies,' p. 94.
[150]Leith-Ross, *African Women*, p. 125.

lived quite apart from home and husband and children.'[151]

Implications for future development

Presently in Africa, the implications for development are at once terrifying and exciting. This demands a total dismantling of a socioeconomic system which does not reproduce the value systems/achievement potential of African societies to be replaced by one which builds on the rich cultural heritage of Africa. On this subject, Jacob Carruthers has noted:

> If we are to save the African race, we [African] intellectuals... must, at the very least, Africanise ourselves ... The processes of Africanisation and transformation cannot be neatly separated into two stages - they overlap. Rather than continually struggling to make European systems more humane, we have to replace ... (sic) these ... with those that are African-centred.[152]

Adiele Afigbo's contribution to this issue is highly insightful. He asserts that operating from a conceptual context 'imbibed from the West,' which defines development as the 'total mobilisation of society for the increase of material well-being,'[153] women's contributions to societal development are assessed primarily in terms of their capacity to contribute physical and mental energy to the process, alongside men and in a manner similar to men:

> We are inclined to measure the importance of our women as a factor for success in development in statistical and quantitative term. Hence the concern of writers and speakers on the subject is usually with chronicling how many of our women are being 'educated' and to what level, how many are engineers, lawyers, medical doctors, permanent secretaries, professors, vice chancellors, ministers, business tycoons and so on.[154]

Afigbo argues that the weakness with this yardstick of analysis regarding

---

[151]Ibid., p. 118.
[152]Carruthers, 'Black Intellectuals and the Crisis in Black Education,' p. 118.
[153]Afigbo, 'Women as a Factor in Development,' p. 43.
[154]Ibid.

women's contributions to society is that 'it concerns itself with the exceptions which prove the rule rather than with the generality of womanhood.'[155] Herein lies the crux of the matter. Historical Igbo society was constructed in such a way as to allow distinct, institutionalised avenues for the broad sectors of women (and men) to make contributions to the ordering of society, the development of its values and norms, and the process of social change and progress on a *day-to-day* basis. Contemporary Africa's marginalisation of women is one symptom of the tragic fate of the 'inheritor' of a world-view that is, by and large, alien to its own very cosmology as has been established in this study. This world-view bears heavily on Africa's shoulders and the struggle to operate within an educational, political and social ethos that is diametrically opposed to its own seems insurmountable. So what do African women have to offer at this point in time? They will need to re-embark on the development, to the highest levels, of a moral/social/political consciousness and voice in society which will bring about a desperately needed reorientation and reconstruction of society.

The challenge for the future lies in a historical reconstruction that can impact on the social exigencies of the present. The task lies in achieving some equilibrium between the traditional role of women as the 'linch-pin of the family'[156] and those other roles which emphasise what is ultimately a measure of the economic value of womanhood. After all, '[t]he traditional power of African women had an economic and ideological basis, which derived from the importance accorded motherhood.'[157] In other words, motherhood with its many roles of childbearing, nurturing, character development, family cohesion and ultimately societal harmony and progress, needs to assume its traditionally highly-prized and much-coveted status. Within the role of motherhood lies the ultimate source of mental, intellectual, spiritual, social and physical human resource needed for development. To continue to disregard this in Africa would be to continue to undermine the very foundation of society itself.

---

[155]Ibid., p. 44.
[156]Ibid.
[157]Amadiume, *Reinventing Africa*, p. 112.

4

The Nwapa reclamation:
Efuru and *Idu*

In this chapter we shift our focus to a detailed examination of Flora Nwapa's writings – specifically, her first two novels, *Efuru* and *Idu*. Our purpose here is to examine the extent to which Nwapa's contribution to African literature constitutes an expression of a particular ideological stance embodied in the position of motherhood in African society and the role played by women in the transmission of cultural traditions from one generation to the next. We shall explore Nwapa's definition and characterisation of her own society and critically demonstrate how her writings are, to borrow from Ihechukwu Madubuike's observations on this genre of literary and sociological work in Africa, 'anchored in everyday happenings of society ... based on the tangible and the concrete through which we feel the pulse and the hidden movements of the society.'[1] Our contention is that Nwapa presents a vision of her world which is detailed in its specificity, capturing day-to-day life as expressed in the hopes and fears, the belief systems and values, the ambitions and aspirations of her people, and the relationship, indeed interplay between the personal and the communal, between the historical and the contemporary. *Efuru* and *Idu* are each novels principally about two women, their relationships with, and responsibilities to spouse and family (the immediate and extended) and the broader society. In each of these texts, we shall examine the roles that women play in society and establish how women, *themselves*, define or characterise the position of women in their community. Furthermore, we shall elicit what, if any, are women's aspirations in the overall context of the development and progress of their society. Nwapa clearly illustrates the power and confidence which women possess 'as upholders of tradition,' as Gay Wilentz has rightly observed

---

[1] Ihechukwu Madubuike, *The Senegalese Novel* (Washington: Three Continents, 1983), pp. 5 - 6.

– namely, passing on cultural values from generation to generation.[2] Efuru and Idu, the heroines in the novels are both 'economically secure and socially vibrant.'[3] Each of these characters and indeed other major characters in Nwapa's novels is pastiche, a composite of a number of real women that the novelist studies over time and which she configures into one character. The novelist vividly recalls the background that informs the construction of the characters in her work:

> From my childhood I lived among very strong women: my two grandmothers and their co-wives. They were strong women. In my native [Ugwuta] it was women who started trading with the foreign companies ... So the women gained economic power through trade before the men, and all this influenced my writing and that is why I project women as great achievers. I did not see women as second-class citizens.[4]

On the characterisation of heroine Efuru in particular, Nwapa notes: 'Efuru is so many women in one. I loved listening to stories. My mother would make clothes and many women came while she sewed. I think it must have been from there that I got the idea of how these women behave.'[5] It is therefore not surprising that all Nwapa's heroines in her novels and most of her short stories are traders/businesspeople. Even when they belong to other professions such as a school teacher as is the case of Ndidi Okeke in the short story, 'Daddy, Don't Strike a Match,' (*Wives at War*[6]), the novelist's emphasis in the development of the character has been to stress their entrepreneurial talents or initiatives. As soon as Ndidi, who lives in the northern Nigerian city of Kano, learns of the impending massacre of Igbo immigrants in the north, she goes to her local bank and transfers £2000 from her account to a deposit account in Enugu, the eastern town where her family would soon be returning to. For the journey home, Ndidi 'began to make preparations. She hired two lorries at a fantastic price and

---

[2]Wilentz, *Binding Cultures*, p. 4.

[3]Ibid.

[4]Flora Nwapa in an interview with Ezenwa-Ohaeto (1993), quoted in Umeh, 'Introduction: Historicizing Flora Nwapa,' p. 10.

[5]Flora Nwapa in an interview with Jane Bryce-Okunlola (1985), quoted in Jane Bryce-Okunlola, 'Motherhood as a Metaphor for Creativity in Three African Women's Novels: Flora Nwapa, Rebeka Njau and Bessie Head,' in Nasta, ed., *Motherlands*, p. 204.

[6]Flora Nwapa, *Wives at War and Other Stories* (Enugu: Tana, 1984).

packed everything, including her brooms'[7] In *Efuru*, we learn right from the outset of the novel that Efuru is a wealthy woman, 'distinguished.'[8] She trades in assorted goods particularly yams and fish up the River Niger and it is on crayfish that she makes a 'fortune' with her husband Adizua who joins the business after their marriage.[9]

Earlier on, Efuru had paid her own bride-wealth on behalf of Adizua because the latter did not have the money.[10] Idu, for her part in *Idu*, is another businessperson with a successful enterprise that incorporates partners in towns further away from hers. To stress the far-flung extent of Idu's business very early in the novel, we are introduced to partners Okeke and Okorie who 'had brought oil for her to buy. But they came late and were having to spend the night at her home because it was too late for them to return to their town.'[11] All considered, Nwapa's characters are based on the observation or study of real people who work and live in real historical/epochal references (Independent/ Pre-Conquest Ugwuta/Igboland, British-Occupied Ugwuta/Igboland/Nigeria, Liberation/ Reestablishment of Independence of Peoples in Nigeria/Africa, Post-Conquest Nigeria/Africa, Biafra War, Post-Biafra War) and set in real geographical references (Ugwuta, Enugu, Port Harcourt, Kano, Lagos, Onitsha, Benin). The key elements to the development of Nwapa's characters are therefore social and historical. 'I am an ordinary woman who is writing about what she knows,' Nwapa has insisted.[12] She adds: 'When I do write about women in Nigeria, in Africa, I try to paint a positive picture about women because there are many women who are very very positive in their thinking, who are very, very independent, and very very industrious.'[13] Nwapa's women are not ideal types nor exceptional women as C.L. Innes suggests,[14] but real women through whose lives the novelist has sought to interrogate two salient features in African history: the philosophical underpinning of motherhood as an overarching institution and ideology for social cohesion in Igbo/African society and the crucial role of women in the survival and transformation of the African

---

[7]'Daddy, Don't strike a Match,' p. 18.
[8]*Efuru*, p. 1.
[9]Ibid., pp. 20 - 21.
[10]Ibid., pp. 21 -24.
[11]Flora Nwapa, *Idu* (Oxford: Heinemann International, 1970), p. 10.
[12]Umeh, 'The Poetics of Economic Independence for Female Empowerment: An Interview With Flora Nwapa,' in Umeh, p. 668.
[13]Ibid., pp. 668 - 669.
[14]Innes, 'Virgin Territories and Motherlands,' p. 12.

family/community. As a result, Nwapa's success in both *Efuru* and *Idu* is unprecedently impressive. Ten years before the first sociological examination of the subject by any African scholar, she demonstrates in her novels, contrary to the European conquest historiography on Africa of the day, that Igbo women occupied a crucial independent space of political, economic and spiritual management of their lives that cohered to parallel male structures of social organisation in a dual-sex national complementarity of purpose and direction. Nwapa challenged and successfully laid to rest the lie in the conquest literature that Igbo women were a subjugated social group in independent, pre-conquest Igboland. Nwapa's enterprise is centrally rooted in the corpus of African history which, given the epoch, focuses on the theme of African reconstruction after the shattering decades of European conquest and occupation. Following Georg Lukács on his discussion on 'critical realism', Nwapa would agree that the 'ontological being' of characters 'cannot be distinguished from their social and historical environment.'[15] This would readily apply to her characters ranging from Efuru to Idu, Ndidi, Kate (*Never Again*[16]) and Amaka (*One is Enough*). Seen from this perspective, most of Nwapa's writing falls within the classification of 'critical realist' literary production. Even then, some of her work could be classified more appropriately within other schools of 'realism'. Roland Barthes has described as 'classical realism' literary work where the main task emphasised is the reading of social reality as objectively as possible.[17] For Barthes, realism is not so much the motivation toward social investigation but the urge to represent reality as much as it is – realistically, without any distortions. In that context, there is a consciousness of an awareness or conviction of what social relations and history prefigure this history which in Nwapa's case is the pivotal role of motherhood both as an institution and an encompassing ideology of social integration in Igboland/Africa. Seen from this context, her *Never Again* and *One is Enough* should be seen as work of 'classical realism'. Finally, Nwapa is concerned with the pursuit of the truth, historical truths, in her writing in the sense of the task earmarked by Bertolt Brecht : 'The demand for a realistic style of writing can ... no longer be so easily dismissed today ... The ruling classes use lies oftener than before – and bigger ones. To tell the truth is clearly an ever more urgent task.'[18] Nwapa was

---

[15]Georg Lukács, *The Meaning of Contemporary Realism* (London: Merlin, 1963), p. 19.
[16]Flora Nwapa, *Never Again* (Enugu: Tana, 1986).
[17]Roland Barthes, *Writing Degree Zero* (London: Cape, 1967).
[18]Bertolt Brecht, 'Popularity and Realism,' in E. Bloch et al, *Aesthetics and Politics* (London: Verso, 1980), p. 80.

once asked the following question by a critic: 'What do you think of Leopold Sedar Senghor and Ali Mazrui's statements that African women have always been liberated? In other words, is there any truth in the statement?'[19] Nwapa's reply is as precise as it is instrumental in her construction of the characters and the development of the plots in novels and short stories especially those set in the past such as *Efuru* and *Idu*: 'For me, yes!'[20]

As an undergraduate at the University College, Ibadan (1953-1957), studying History, English and Geography, Nwapa would have been appalled by the general anti-African content of the course curriculum which mainly valorised the European experience (especially pertaining to its conquest of Africa) both in literature and history. Particularly, Nwapa would have been unable to reconcile the curriculum's standard anthropological characterisation of African women with her knowledge of Igbo women independence and entrepeneural skills, in addition to her own family background of having three generations of very successful business women.[21] As her other compatriots who graduated at Ibadan during the 1950s (especially Chinua Achebe and Wole Soyinka), Nwapa's impetus to be a writer (and school teacher) must have been geared toward challenging this conquest historiography in order to tell the African story. In pursuance of this goal, therefore, Ernest Emenyonu has observed that Nwapa 'writes with a peculiar realism ... bring[ing] a feminine closeness and intuition into a theme.'[22] The use of language is of immense importance to this project. As Emenyonu further notes, '[o]ne would have to understand the language of Flora Nwapa's novels in order to appreciate her achievements.'[23] According to Emenyonu, this 'understanding' goes beyond one's basic ability of comprehension and communicating in Igbo. It 'includes both the Igbo world-view which [Nwapa] communicates and the way she reaches down to all her characters and communicates authentically at all their levels...'[24] Unlike any of her contemporaries, Nwapa's writings are steeped in the actual, everyday patterns of speech and communication of her characters - that is the totality of the expressed verbal and non-verbal ('Amarajeme shook

---

[19]See Umeh, 'The Poetics of Economic Independence for Female Empowerment,' p. 668.
[20]Ibid.
[21]Umeh, 'Introduction: Historicizing Flora Nwapa,' pp. 5 - 6.
[22]Ernest Emenyonu, 'Who does Flora Nwapa write for?', *African Literature Today*, No. 7, 1978, p. 31.
[23]Ibid.
[24]Ibid.

his head. He bit his finger and started shaking his leg again. Now tears were rolling down his cheek'[25]) language of people about whom she wrote. Both *Idu* and *Efuru*, in effect, read like English literal or near-literal translations of an original Igbo manuscript! The effect this achieves is to create a *real feel, an informed appreciation and understanding* of those issues of paramount importance to her and most African women, namely, the historical reminder/retention of their own autonomy and contribution to their world ('Efuru ... she was a remarkable women. It was not only that she came from a distinuished family. She was distinguished herself'[26]), the preservation of their families and the rejection of that which threatens these ('Prostitution is bad for our women ... Our woman of the Lake frowns at it, and that's why prostitutes of our town never profit by it'[27]); and the retention/strenghtening/longterm preservation of their own financial independence('a woman who holds her husband as a father dies an orphan'[28]).

Like Chinua Achebe's classic engagement in *Things Fall Apart*, Nwapa adapts, manipulates, or re-fashions the English language in her writing to capture, in very vivid form, the vibrancy and dialectics of Igbo life and world-view. Two examples from *Idu* are illustrative of this. Members of Adiewere's age-group arrive unannounced at the home of Idu and Adiewere, and Idu is suddenly faced with having to entertain these guests at very short notice and hurriedly sets out to provide for them, conscious of the importance of their relationship with her husband. Aware of the scrutiny to which her hospitality/generosity (represented in the quality and variety of refreshments) could be subjected she comments to her guests, in an attempt to deflect/pre-empt any possible criticism: 'My husband's age group, this is what I have brought. Drink it like that. Adiewere my husband did not tell me that you were coming, you would have seen it if he had told me. So don't be angry ... '[29] Here Idu is obviously being coy. Her statement, '[T]his is what I have brought. Drink it like that' deliberately attempts to minimise the extent of her generosity (belied by the array of refreshments put before the guests) which they heartily acknowledge by hailing her a great woman![30]. Elsewhere in *Idu*, Nwapa is vivid in capturing a son's resemblance to his father who is mentally ill as Idu learns

---

[25]*Idu*, p. 110.
[26]*Efuru*, p. 7.
[27]*Idu*, p. 39.
[28]Umeh, 'The Poetics of Economic Independence for Female Empowerment,' p. 670.
[29]*Idu*, p. 161.
[30]*Idu*, p. 161.

from the mother of the son in question:

He is my son. As you have seen him, you have seen his father when he was younger. His father vomited him out. But what a pity. He could have been like me. I have three other boys, they are all younger than this one and they are all like me. I thank God for that. But the eldest boy will be like his father. Soap cannot wash it.[31]

On some occasions, Nwapa even dispenses altogether with this deft tailoring enterprise to render her Igbo as literally as imaginable in the English. Hence, for example, the author's unmodified, directly-rendered translation from the Igbo to English in Ajanupu's conversation with Efuru (her niece in-law) in *Efuru*, 'So this is your eyes, Efuru. Trade does not allow you to see anybody these days' (a reference to Efuru's social unavailability due to pressure of work)[32] or in Ajanupu's other conversation with Ossai (her sister) when she comments, quite critically, 'You are just a woman for nothing. You can't see, you can't even hear smell'(Ossai is chided by Ajanupu for her apparent inability to detect Efuru's pregnancy).[33] Here, Ajanupu is alluding to a particular knowledge base expected of a woman of the age and experience of her sister (that is an ability to detect a pregnant woman through changing physical and behavioural patterns) which Ossai surprisingly does not display. 'You can't even hear smell' is a direct translation from Igbo to English as is the phrase in the preceding example 'so this is your eyes'. 'Eyes' of course does not refer to *the* eyes, but the individual, as a whole, whose absence is being felt.

The entire texts of *Efuru* and *Idu* are constructed in similar manner. These books take on the language, nuances, tone of the era in which Nwapa writes about. *Efuru* and *Idu*, set in Ugwuta of the 1930s, literally read as if they are written in Igbo and little wonder that the richness of these works can often be lost on the non-Igbo speaker. In her later books, we see again the language, tone, nuances of the era (this time, 1970s' Nigeria) captured vividly in the texts. Such was this vividness of Nwapa's fiction and the popular public response to it that during a social occasion in 1985, three years after the publication of *One is Enough*, someone approached the writer and said, pointing at a woman in the gathering, 'Look, the lady you wrote about in that story [Amaka, in *One is Enough*] is in this audience.' To Nwapa's apparent consternation, the woman

---

[31]Ibid., p. 122.
[32]*Efuru*, p. 27.
[33]Ibid.

came along to the author, shook her hands and said 'Mrs Nwakuche, I heard so much about this book. People say it is my story. I haven't read it; so I don't know whether it's my story.'[34]

New theatre

Nearly 10 years after the publication of *Things Fall Apart*, Nwapa is conscious of ensuring that *Efuru*, her first novel, does not merely retrace the grounds just trodden by Achebe's macro-history project. Instead, Nwapa chooses to interrogate the Igbo home or domestic life environment as her own contribution to the ongoing African literature of recovery and reconstruction embarked upon on the eve of the restoration of independence following the European conquest and occupation. Here, in *Efuru* (as well as *Idu*), the African story shifts, as it were, from *Things Fall Apart*'s preoccupation with the high drama of state politics, international politics and racism to the every-day drama of easily recognisable ordinary people (of equally no less importance as we shall demonstrate shortly) that focuses on life at home – in the family, the extended family, the market place (both in its immediacy and the extended spaces of travels to other towns and villages), the farm, essentially that site of the proverbial African community life. In the home, as Theodora Akachi Ezeigbo has shown, '[t]he figure of the mother looms very large in Igbo family life. It is the mother or the woman of the house on whom the foundation of the home squarely rests. Her abilities or inadequacies would affect the home positively or negatively.'[35] Nwapa chooses to concentrate on the home because it gives her the opportunity, as she states clearly in an interview (quoted earlier) to 'write about women ... because there are many women who are very, very positive in their thinking, who are very very independent, and very, very industrious.' Nwapa is aware of what Ezeigbo has described as the 'subtle but real power'[36] that Igbo women exercise in their household. For Nwapa, this power is based on the women's control of the 'pestle and the cooking pot.'[37] But it is in the financial and economic fields that the importance of Igbo women's independence has a more profound impact on Igbo society as Nwapa recalls in

---

[34]See Umeh, 'The Poetics of Economic Independence for Female Empowerment,' p. 667.
[35]Ezeigbo, 'Myth, History, Culture and Igbo Womanhood in Flora Nwapa's Novels,' p. 61.
[36]Ibid., p. 72.
[37]Ibid.

another interview, already referred to in this study:

> From my childhood I lived among very strong women ... [I]t was the
> women who first started trading with the foreign companies ... So the
> women gained economic power through trade before the men, and all
> this influenced my writing and that is why I project women as great
> achievers. I did not see women as second-class citizens.

So, by focusing on the home and the strategic role played by women in this
sphere of African life, Nwapa opens up a new arena, equally and crucially as
important as Achebe's earlier project, from where the African story of conquest,
recovery and reconstruction will, in addition, be told. In *Efuru* and *Idu*, Nwapa
not only demonstrates convincingly that women are the 'very embodiment of
African society and custodians of African culture,'[38] but she challenges head on
the corpus of colonialist historiography on the African conquest that has
ignored, marginalised, distorted or even demonised the role of African women
in society. Nwapa ends up creating what Elleke Boehmer has succinctly
described as 'highly verbalised collective women's biography.'[39] Surprisingly,
Bernth Lindfors refers to this achievement as 'dialogue [which] seldom rises
above the level of women's gossip'[40] even though the same critic acknowledges
a few years later in the 'Introduction' to a study on Chinua Achebe (jointly
edited with C. L. Innes) that Nwapa belongs to the 'School of Achebe' in
African fiction who has 'contributed something personal and unique to Nigerian
fiction.'[41] Surely what Nwapa has contributed to this fiction as well as Africa's
for that matter, as we shall demonstrate in this study, *cannot* amount to
Lindfors's derisive remark quoted earlier. For Eustace Palmer, there is an
intriguing conclusion on what he feels is the goal of Nwapa's writing in *Efuru*:
'Flora Nwapa ... wants to ensure that, whatever the subject matter, her novel
should embody the culture and spirit of her [people].'[42] If indeed this is
Nwapa's intention, it is not certain from Palmer's review of *Efuru* what exactly

---

[38]Amadiume, *Reinventing Africa*, p. 104.
[39]Boehmer, 'Stories of Women and Mothers,' in Nasta, ed., *Motherlands*, p. 12.
[40]Bernth Lindfors, 'Achebe's Followers,' *Revue de Littérature Comparée*, 48, 3, 4,
1974, p. 577.
[41]See C. L. Innes & Bernth Lindfors, eds., *Critical Perspectives on Chinua Achebe*
(London: Heinemann Educational Books, 1979), p. 6.
[42]Eustace Palmer, 'Elechi Amadi & Flora Nwapa,' *African Literature Today*, 1, 1968,
p. 57.

the problem is with this objective - in, or outside the novel. It will be difficult if any subject/component of Igbo life (or any other life for that matter) could be isolated from the very spirit and culture that imbues it with life, and informs and defines its essence. In this context, Adeola James reminds Palmer of the conquest historical background that led to the birth of contemporary African literature and argues that the African critic could therefore not afford to assess this literature 'from any vague or glib universal criteria.'[43]

Eldred Jones's criticism of Nwapa's work falls into the same class as Palmer's. 'What Flora Nwapa's novel lacks,' Jones writes, 'is a strong overall conception apart from the obvious urge to show how I[g]bos live.'[44] Implicit here of course is a criticism based on what Jones's thinks is the lack of a broad 'human nature'[45] or a 'universalist' reach in Nwapa's work as opposed to a more 'localised' focus on the Igbo nation's historical experience. But why should literary works be 'universal' in their capacity to be understood or for them to be acceptable? Posed another way, which literary works can be classified as universal? Who precisely decides on their universality? If Nwapa's project, clearly stated above, is to write about Igbo women, then that necessarily localises the focus of the goal of this literary enterprise on the Igbo just as Charles Dickens's *Hard Times* localises the focus of that literary endeavour on Victorian England or James Baldwin's *Just Above My Head* is a novel that examines the experience of African Americans during a particular epoch of American history. Yet, each of the three locally - or nationally - focused novels just cited has issues, themes or lessons that have implications far beyond their borders of focus. From Nwapa, the world learns, for instance, that women in Igboland, prior to the British conquest, enjoyed political and economic independence which was largely undocumented in both official state/academic conquest history of the area. Knowledge of this sort no doubt challenges and corrects, especially at a global/universal arena, the 'orthodox' scholarship of denial, distortion and demonisation that the world has so long regarded as factual. Dickens's stinging critique in *Hard Times* of the social conditions of working class Britons during the 19th century industrial revolution has a universal resonance applicable to the appalling working conditions that millions of people across the world still face. Similarly, the depressing picture of the

---

[43] Adeola James, 'Review of *An Introduction to the African Novel* by Eustace Palmer,' *African Literature Today*, 7, 1975, p. 150.
[44] Eldred Jones, 'Locale and Universe,' *Journal of Commonwealth Literature*, 3, 1967, p. 129.
[45] Ibid.

racist oppression of African Americans so graphically painted by James Baldwin in *Just Above My Head* is a crucial contributing feature to the haunting catalogue of the history of human subjugation and exclusion that the world has witnessed particularly in the past 500 years. In effect, for every conceivable piece of literature that has the 'locale' as its working focus lies a range of themes that have varying shades of the 'universal'. To be able to discern these constructs of the 'universal' is however dependent on how painstakingly critical the reader approaches the text. *But it remains, though, that the literariness of the text is not dependent on its universal implications or applications.* T. S. Eliot, a poet whose standard work usually incorporates a compendium of references and allusions across historical epochs and geographical outreaches has made the following observations on the subject of 'universality' which underscore our position on the subject:

Universality can never come except through writing about what one knows thoroughly ... And, though it is only too easy for a writer to be local without being universal, I doubt whether a poet or novelist can be universal without being local too.[46]

It remains of course that the clamour for 'universality' encountered in the Palmer and Jones's criticisms of Nwapa are echoes of the colonialist criticism of African literature that critics such as Gerald Moore and Charles Larson had established earlier on as some kind of 'benchmark of reference' in the assessment of African literature.[47] For these writers, 'universality' is synonymous with a European World definition and appreciation that supposedly transcends cultural or racial specificity and originality.[48] If African writers were

---

[46]T. S. Eliot, 'American Literature and the American Language,' quoted in Chinweizu, Onwuchekwa Jemie and Ihechukwu Madubuike, *Toward the Decolonization of African Literature* (Enugu: Fourth Dimension, 1980), p. 106.
[47]See Gerald Moore, *Seven African Writers* (London: Oxford University, 1962), Gerald Moore, *African Literature and the Universities* (Ibadan: Ibadan University, 1965) and Charles Larson, *The Emergence of African Fiction* (Bloomington: Indiana University, 1972).
[48]See, for instance, Larson, *The Emergence of African Literature*, p. 102, p. 106 and p. 230. On this subject, we should recall Chinua Achebe's observations made 25 years ago which could not have been more appropriate presently: 'I should like to see the word "universal" banned altogether from discussions of African literature until such a time as people cease to use it as a synonym for the narrow, self-serving parochialism of Europe, until their horizon extends to include all the world.' (See Chinua Achebe,

to accept these terms of reference, the literature that we have described as the African literature of recovery and reconstruction would not have been born. As Achebe has cogently observed, 'Most African writers write out of an African experience and of commitment to an African destiny. For them that destiny does not include a future European identity for which the present is but an apprenticeship.'[49] Finally, a comment on Adeola James's review of Nwapa's work. Contrary to Stratton's critique of leading African male writers and critics, the most contemptuous and dismissive review of Nwapa's work ever written was not carried out by a man, not Eustace Palmer nor Eldred Jones, but a woman – indeed an African woman. Despite pages and pages of text that Stratton expends in her book accusing the duo's reviews of Nwapa of amounting to 'crimes' of 'patriarchal criticism,'[50] not to mention the apparently more sinister 'phallic criticism,'[51] the most dismissive review of *Efuru* and *Idu* does not come from either man but from Adeola James. The conspicuous absence in Stratton's study of any reference to James's review which was published in a 1971 edition of *Africa Literature Today* is astonishing to say the least, especially considering the relish with which she quotes another edition of *African Literature Today* containing James's attack of Eustace Palmer's advocacy of 'objective and universalist' considerations in African criticism. It is surprising that Stratton would have been unaware of James's review of Nwapa published in a journal edited by Palmer with regular contributions by him as well as by Eldred Jones. It is obvious that her *manichaean* frame of analysis that pits African women (writers and critics) against African men (writers and critics) would have had to unravel uncontrollably if on this occasion she had quoted from Ms James's caustic review of Ms Nwapa's *Idu* and *Efuru*:

> Considering her performances in both *Efuru* and *Idu* one cannot help wondering what motivates Miss Nwapa beyond the elementary wish of everyone to be a writer. In her novels there is a complete absence of that ... impulse to write which "kicks you in the pit of your stomach". If this impulse is absent one expects, at least, to be compensated by other things such as beautiful narrative style, amusing and vividly described

---

'Colonialist Criticism,' in Achebe, *Hopes and Impediments*, p. 52.
[49] Achebe, 'Colonialist Criticism,' p. 50.
[50] Stratton, *Contemporary African Literature and the Politics of Gender*, especially pp. 81-86.
[51] See, for instance, ibid., p. 82 and p. 85.

incidents and powerful characterisation. All these are sadly missing in both *Efuru* and *Idu*.[52]

Ironically, there are facets of the above quote from James that could have literally come out of Eustace Palmer's 1968 review of *Efuru* which forms a prominent focus in Stratton's critique of African male authors. On the question of plot and characterisation, Palmer had in fact written: 'Nwapa, moreover, does not show any awareness of plot as the sum-total of events casually related to each other. Efuru is made up of a string of episodes some of which could have been usefully omitted.'[53] Thus, despite James's criticism of Palmer's 'universalism' preoccupation, the two at least have more in common on Nwapa than Stratton appreciates - with James distinctly more critical and dismissive of the novelist as we have indicated. Evaluating, essentially, the premise of Palmer's and James's attacks of Nwapa's work, it is clear that both critics share the same grounds on their views on the latter which invariably approximate to the standardisation of style, format, language skills (and usage) and reader expectations mapped out variously in the eurocentric 'universalist' prescriptions. On Nwapa at least, one just wonders what these two critics were arguing about in the pages of *African Literature Today* in 1975! More importantly though, what the example of James's and Palmer's criticisms of Nwapa show is that Stratton's attempt (and those of other contemporary colonialist critics that we have referred to in this study) to construct dichotomised groupings of African writers and critics based on gender is palpably farcical. If anything has been the source of division, or should we say site of contestation in the past 40 years involving African writers and critics, *women and men*, it has been on how to effectively respond to the very tragic history of Africa's humiliating conquest and occupation by a coterie of European states. The argument has centred primarily on whether the literature of this project should *insist* on an uncompromising African-centredness in its approach, or be more open or flexible to adhere to, to borrow, or be conscious or sensitive to the literary experience and practice of the European World especially, and those of people elsewhere in the world. We should stress the *flexibility* of the classification that follows because some of those who belong to the more eclectic school (for instance, Christopher Okigbo and Ngugi wa Thiong'o) have some of their works that are completely immersed in African-

---

[52]Adeola James, '*Idu*: Flora Nwapa,' *African Literature Today*, 5, 1971, pp. 152 - 153 .
[53]Palmer, 'Elechi Amadi & Flora Nwapa,' p. 58.

centredness.[54] Both men and women writers and critics belong to each of these two tendencies: prominent members in the African-centredness school include Nwapa (novelist), Achebe (novelist and critic), Zulu Sofola (dramatist), Ifi Amadiume (critic), Leopold Sedar Senghor (poet), Okot p'Bitek (poet), David Diop (poet) and Chinweizu (critic) whilst the other school of more eclectic practitioners includes Mariama Bâ (novelist), Buchi Emecheta (novelist), Christopher Okigbo (poet), Wole Soyinka (poet, dramatist, critic), Michael Echeruo (critic), Molara Ogundipe-Leslie (critic), Ngugi wa Thiong'o (novelist and critic), Bessie Head (novelist), Adeola James (critic), Ama Ata Aidoo (novelist, dramatist, poet), Eustace Palmer (critic), Dambudzo Marachera (novelist) and Eldred Jones (critic). Besides, the range of friendship and cooperation that exists between writers within and outside the tendencies especially those that clearly cut across gender identification question Stratton's gender manichaean construct – a point well illustrated by the working relationship involving no other pair than Flora Nwapa and Chinua Achebe at the beginning of the former's literary career in the mid-1960s. In an interview that Nwapa had given to *Africa Woman* in 1977 and quoted incidentally by another colonialist critic, Marie Umeh, the novelist recalled that Achebe influenced her 'a great deal.'[55] She had shown Achebe the manuscript of *Efuru* who 'quickly read' it, 'liked it, put a title on it, and sent it off to Heinemann for publication.'[56] Colonialist criticism of the Stratton, Umeh, Condé, Fido et al mode cannot ignore the implications of this revelation. If indeed Achebe has had this close attachment to *Efuru* as Nwapa herself recalls, including offering the choice of the novel's title, then there exists a strong affinity of shared interest on the subject covered in *Efuru* between its author and the author of *Things Fall Apart* (published eight years earlier) which much of the anti-male colonialist criticism on the subject has not been able to accommodate or perhaps is very much unaware of. In her comparative study of Nwapa, Achebe and Onuora Nzekwu, Carole Boyce Davies notes that 'unlike Achebe and Nzekwu she [Nwapa] often titles her works with the names of her heroines, indicating that she is telling

---

[54]See, for instance, Christopher Okigbo, *Labyrinths* (London: Heinemann Education Books, 1971) and Ngugi Wa Thiong'o, *Weep Not, Child* (London: Heinemann Education Books, 1964) and Ngugi, *The River Between* (London: Heinemann Education Books, 1965).

[55]See Umeh, 'The Poetics of Economic Independence for Female Empowerment,' pp. 667 - 668.

[56]Umeh, 'Introduction: Historicizing Flora Nwapa,' p. 7.

strictly of the woman's experience.'[57] If Davies's is an insightful observation which few will doubt it to be, then it underscores the importance of the *literary companionship* between Nwapa and Achebe that has existed for a very long time indeed – at least, since the eve of the publication of *Efuru* in 1966. Such companionship makes nonsense of the assumptions and the trajectory of the analysis on Achebe over *Efuru* found in the Stratton brand of colonialist criticism presently. It is therefore manifestly matronising at best but at worst racist for Stratton to band together the European colonialist characterisation of African women with that of Achebe and other African male authors.[58] Instead, the Achebe-Nwapa companionship is a celebrated example of contemporary Igbo dual-sex gender complementarity at work - this time at the site of artistic production. Yet, even if there wasn't this level of companionship between Nwapa and Achebe, there are no sentiments, views, themes, orientations, plots, characters, etc, that Nwapa expresses or develops in *Efuru* or *Idu* that justifies Stratton's use of these novels to attack Chinua Achebe (and other African male authors and critics).

Contrary to Stratton's claim, Nwapa *did not* in fact '[write] into *Efuru* what Achebe left out of *Things Fall Apart*,'[59] any more than Achebe 'wrote into' *Things Fall Apart* what Pita Nwana 'left out' in the latter's novel, *Omenuko* (an outstanding anti-British conquest novel of Igboland) which was published in 1933,[60] neither did Onwura Nzekwu 'write into' *Highlife for Lizards* (1965)[61] what Achebe 'left out' in *Things Fall Apart* nor indeed what Nwana 'left out' in *Omenuko*. In C.L. Innes and Caroline Rooney's contribution to this debate,[62] there is a teleological logic in the thrust of their argument which inevitably leads to the conclusion that whatever has followed Achebe's contribution to African literature[63] by African women writers constitutes the filling in of 'gaps' or 'missing pieces' in the latter's work. Innes and Rooney achieve this by situating

---

[57]Davies, 'Motherhood in the Works of Male and Female Igbo Writers,' p. 249.
[58]Stratton, *Contemporary African Literature and the Politics of* Gender, p. 83.
[59]Ibid., p. 87.
[60]Pita Nwana, *Omenuko* (London: Longman, 1933).
[61]Onuora Nzekwu, *Highlife for Lizards* (London: Hutchinson, 1965).
[62]Lyn Innes and Caroline Rooney, 'African Writing and Gender,' in Mpalive-Hangson Msiska and Paul Hylands, eds., *Writing and Africa* (London and New York: Addison Wesley Longman, 1997), pp. 193 - 215.
[63]Other leading African male authors such as Soyinka, Ngugi, Armah and Ekwensi have also been designated as writers whose works have 'gaps' that have been filled in by women writers in the last 40 years!

the contributions of Nwapa (and indeed other women writers such as Ama Ata Aidoo, Mariama Bâ and Buchi Emecheta) within the discursive compass of Achebe's main novels. This position which appears to define the role of African women writers as 'filling in the gaps' in Achebe's works (or any other male authors) or indeed 're-writing' him could be interpreted as sexist, especially coming from women critics. Some crucial questions need to be posed here to which this school of critics would need to respond: In the absence of the writings of Achebe, how would the works of Nwapa and other African women writers be assessed? Can the contributions of African women writers be assessed on their own terms without being subsumed within an Achebean problematic? If Chinua Achebe never wrote, what would be the assessment of these women's contributions to African literature? If the writings of these women are assessed independent of any other contributions to African literature, do any 'gaps' exist? What 'gaps'? Who will fill them?

Achebe's *Things Fall Apart* is undoubtedly one of the most outstanding literary successes of the Igbo/African World but it is not, and neither does it claim to be the definitive study of the reconstruction of Igbo history at the epoch of its focus, namely during the period of the British conquest and occupation of Igboland. No such study exists and none is ever likely to fill such a designation. This is an extensive and complex era of history that has already attracted several studies across a broad spectrum of intellectual endeavour including literature, sociology, history, economics, geography, archaeology, law, musicology and genetics. It will continue to attract more varied studies in the indefinite future. Seen in this context, *Omenuko*, *Things Fall Apart* and *Efuru*, each, in its own chosen patch of focus on this era of history, offers a *contribution* to this scholarship of Igbo Reconstruction. As we have indicated, Flora Nwapa's own contribution to this scholarship is immensely revolutionary. She launched a new theatre of discourse focusing on women centrally. It is important to recall that when Nwapa published *Efuru* in 1966, the so-called mainstream academic discourse on Igbo women and indeed African women at large was still defined, dictated and directed by the essentially racist and africophobist anthropological literature of the Evans-Pritchards of the Western World. It would take another 10 years before Kamene Okonjo, the Igbo sociologist, engaged in the first sociological treatise on the subject by an African woman,[64] a path-breaking study that anticipates Ifi Amadiume's *Male Daughters, Female Husbands* of the

---

[64]See Kamene Okonjo, 'The dual-sex political system in operation: Igbo women and community politics in Midwestern Nigeria,' in N.J. Hakim and E.G. Bay, eds., *Women in Africa* (Stanford: Stanford University, 1976).

1980s. In effect, subsequent studies engaged in this period of history will similarly continue with this contributory task of reconstruction and not just simplistically be content with 'filling in gaps' left in earlier works, especially those that may have achieved major successes such as *Things Fall Apart*. The fact is that Africans 'have tried to regain what is rightly theirs – a past composed of real and vulnerable people, their ancestors, not the figments of missionary and colonialist imaginations.'[65] For the challenge to the African author, the 'writing back ... to European texts'- component[66] of this historic enterprise is an important feature but definitely not central in the far elaborate and painstakingly *internally-focused* mission to reconstruct the 'shattered diamonds'[67] of a cultural heritage as Nwapa demonstrates convincingly in *Efuru* and *Idu*. Nwapa 'limn[s] out all sorts of debates blanketed'[68] in the interstices of Igbo women social existence to recreate a robust woman's world of independence, her social responsibility anchored on the importance of motherhood which is the bridge between the people's (past) historical heritage and the future generation (beginning with children),[69] the role of *uhamiri*, the water goddess that gives the entire societal architecture its spiritual investiture, and the dual-sex arrangement that guarantees the gender relationship of democratic participation and belonging.

Economic independence

In a quote from an interview already referred to in this study, Nwapa states categorically the legacy of the economic life of Igbo women: '... women gained economic power through trade before the men ... I did not see women as second class citizens.' The novel *Efuru* literally opens on this note of women's economic independence. Efuru, a successful business woman, elopes with and

---

[65]Margaret Laurence, *Long drums and Cannons* (London and Basingstoke: Macmillan, 1968), p. 9.
[66]Abdulrazak Gurnah, 'Introduction,' in Gurnah, ed., *Essays on African Writing: A Reevaluation* (Oxford: Heinemann International, 1993), p. xi.
[67]The metaphor is by Ivan Van Sertima, the African American historian, quoted by Amadiume, *Reinventing Africa*, p. 90.
[68]Toni Morrison, *Playing in the Dark* (London and Basingstoke: Pan Books, 1993), p. 4.
[69]Wilentz correctly identifies this responsibility as the women's role to pass cultural values from one generation to another. See Wilentz, *Binding Cultures*, p. 4.

marries Adizua who 'is nobody' and whose 'family is not known.'[70] Adizua is a poor man with no money to fulfil the customary marriage/bride-wealth obligations to Efuru and her family. Efuru, on the other hand, comes 'from a distinguished family'[71] but she herself is distinguished in her own right, an important feature of Igbo sociological heritage aptly illustrated in *Things Fall Apart*: '... among these [Igbo] people a [person] was judged according to his worth and not the worth of his father.'[72] Efuru refuses to engage in farm work with her husband, preferring instead to channel her energies in the direction of trade where she excels. 'They [Efuru and her husband] were the first to discover the trade that year ... Four trips gave Efuru and her husband a huge profit.'[73] 'Adizua was not good at trading. It was Efuru who was the brain behind the business. He knew this very well...'[74] The importance of trade in Igboland cannot be overemphasised. Nina Mba, in her study of the politics of African women, recalls:

> Trade ranked next in importance to agriculture in Igboland, but some were far more important as centres of trade than others. The riverain areas had been the meeting point for traders from the delta and the Igala traders from the north; with the coming of the Europeans in the nineteenth century, places like Aboh, Asaba, Onitsha, and Oguta [the town in which both Efuru and Idu are situated and Nwapa's own birthplace] became very important and lucrative trading centres. In these areas, women had largely controlled local trade and participated actively in long-distance trade.[75]

In *Idu*, the importance of this business venture and the central role that women play in it is unequivocal as Uzoechi and Nwasobi (friends of Idu's sister-in-law, Ogbenyanu) recall:

> 'Does she know how to trade, then?' Uzoechi asked. Nwasobi laughed. 'No, she does not know how to trade. That is why we say she has no sense. A woman who does not know how to trade in our town is a

---

[70]*Efuru*, p. 7.
[71]Ibid.
[72]Achebe, *African Trilogy*, p. 20.
[73]*Efuru*, p. 21.
[74]Ibid., p. 36.
[75]Mba, *Nigerian Women Mobilized*, p. 30.

senseless woman. She is not a woman at all...'[76]

Within this context of Efuru's business acumen, her decision to elope with Adizua becomes less unremarkable and more explicable than it may have initially appeared. She is confident that it is only a matter of time before she/they obtain the funds needed for her bridewealth and the fulfilment of her societal and family expectations. Indeed soon after her commencement of trading, she amasses enough wealth to pay a visit of propitiation to her father. The position of trading and indeed its capacity to challenge the primary role of agriculture in Igboland is important to stress. Efuru refuses to go to work on the farm with her husband, noting, 'if you like, go to the farm. I am not cut out for farm work. I am going to trade.'[77] The financial mechanism through which much of this trading is maintained is a clearly identifiable credit system operated by the women, offering lines of credit to one another. Lines of credit appear to be not only monetary but commodity-based also, as is demonstrated in the exchange between Ajanupu and one of Efuru's debtors, Nwabuzo. Ajanapu adamantly refuses to leave Nwabuzo's house until the latter pays off her debt to Efuru. As in contemporary society with its lines of credit, Efuru's world also has cash-flow problems. Thus, Efuru recalls: 'I am so busy ... our trade is bad. People don't pay their debts, and so when I return from the market I go to collect these debts and have no time for anything else...'[78]

In both *Efuru* and *Idu* we note the obvious control that women and others in their respective communities have over their economic activities. Idu is highly independent, as independent as she is successful. She maintains her own network of suppliers and has a business relationship with them (including entertaining them in her home) that is clearly not dependent on her husband, Adiewere. Both Okeke and Okorie are Idu's business partners and 'had brought oil for *her* to buy' (emphasis added).[79] In fact, both 'were having to spend the night at her home because it was too late for them to return to their town.'[80] It is clear that it is with Idu that business is being transacted. Finally, and perhaps of particular significance, we note in both novels that the vast amount of visible wealth in the form of infrastructure are owned by women through their association with *uhamiri*, the lake goddess. On this, the respected *dibia*, or

---

[76]*Idu*, p. 29.
[77]*Efuru*, p. 10.
[78]Ibid., p. 45.
[79]*Idu*, p. 10.
[80]Ibid.

diviner, recalls: 'Look around this town, nearly all the storey buildings you find are *built by women*' (emphasis added).[81] If economic power provides access to greater political power for Igbo women, then it is clear, by implication, that these women were very much involved in the political affairs of their societies. Yet, as we have already indicated, Igbo politics did not operate in this isolated and institutionalised manner but rather was interwoven with the social exigencies of the day involving the general public of men and women as we shall demonstrate now.

Political roles

What political roles do we discern from *Efuru* and *Idu*? What political role does Nwapa ascribe to her characters and are they credible roles given what has been demonstrated in this thesis about the political roles played by women in historical Igbo society? The Chambers Dictionary defines politics as pertaining to governance – encompassing the nature of the state, issues of rights (individual, collective, etc.), character of leadership, representation, policy, control, organisations/political parties, territoriality and relationship with other states, etc. On the surface, an uncritical textual analysis of *Efuru* and *Idu* could suggest very limited political roles for women. On the contrary, the dynamics of politics in Ugwuta, as well as elsewhere in Igboland as we have argued, is a much more diffused process, always transcending centralised, institutionalised forms of involvement, representation, decision-making and governance. In effect, this is the politics of the 'anti-state state' as Herbert Ekwe-Ekwe has aptly described it.[82] The very art of day-to-day living and more specifically the societal/ communal activities as well as structures that support the community's lifestyle are all by their very nature political phenomena. One of the central themes of Nwapa's writings is an examination of the relationship between the individual and the community that defines and empowers its individual members (individually and collectively) with a mandate for a complementary and supportive co-existence. It is this flexibility in Ugwuta social relations that enables Efuru to opt to trade rather than join her husband on the farm. We observe, most interestingly, certain roles undertaken by women, indeed seen as obligatory by women, in ensuring the maintenance of societal complementarity -

---

[81]*Efuru*, p. 153.
[82]See Ekwe-Ekwe, *Africa 2001*, p. 3.

that is, a world which operates in co-existence with the male. Igbo society's demands for children as the singularly most important outcome of any marital relationship and the shared involvement of society, male and female, in promoting the achievement of this goal presents us with a classic example in *Efuru*. The case of Efuru's second marriage to Eneberi is highly illustrative. The couple still have no child. Efuru's harshest critic of this state of affairs is embodied in the person of a community elder and village gossip, Omirima. But Omirima is by no means alone in her expression of these views as her discussion with Efuru's mother-in-law shows: '...Your daughter-in-law is good, but she is childless. She is beautiful but we cannot eat beauty. She is wealthy but riches cannot go on errands for us...'[83] Other women also deliberate on this affair with the conviction that it is not only their *right* but in fact their *duty* to comment on and assist in the resolution of Efuru's plight which for them now has serious societal implications: 'The important thing is that nothing has happened since the happy marriage. We are not going to eat happy marriage. Marriage must be fruitful. Of what use is it if it is not fruitful. Of what use is it if your husband licks your body, worships you and buys everything in the market for you and you are not productive?'[84] Elsewhere in the book, similar sentiments are expressed, clearly indicating the primacy of children over any material possession: 'What is money? Can a bag of money go for an errand for you? Can a bag of money mourn you when you are dead? A child is more valuable than money...'[85] These observations lead to the repeated dispensation of the same piece of advice from a series of sources – namely, that Eneberi should marry a second wife. So, from as varied a source as the well-meaning Ajanupu, Efuru's aunt-in-law from her previous marriage, to the vicious Omirima, the consensus is that an additional wife must be found for Eneberi to overcome the problem of childlessness in the household. As Amede, Eneberi's mother puts it, 'My daughter-in-law should be productive. We are productive in our family.'[86] For the Igbo, women's role as child bearers (discussed in greater detail later on in this chapter) is a crucial political role precisely because it ensures that women have a direct influence in determining the continuation of societal norms and values. This, in turn defines and shapes the character of society. As a result, Ada Mere has argued that women are the 'most primary and

---

[83]*Efuru*, p. 163.
[84]Ibid., p. 137.
[85]Ibid., p. 37.
[86]Ibid., p. 139.

constant agents of child socialisation.'[87]

What the above illustration in *Efuru* underscores is that child bearing in Igboland is crucial in all marriages for the continuation of the family lineage. The undermining of this particular cultural norm in the form of alleged barrenness in Efuru potentially threatens society's very existence. Thus, the quest for the well-being of the whole of society becomes the basis of the political existence of society itself, or what J. A. Sofola has described as the 'altruistic moral belief that all human species exist for one another's benefit.'[88] It is in effect the society's means of ensuring that differences among society's members do not become so disparate as to become unjust. Societal expectations govern the line of action or decisions undertaken by the people in formulating and pursuing individual goals. To this extent individualism is readily 'subverted' to accommodate the good of all. Yet, even on this all important subject of motherhood, the example of Efuru shows that the individual is not boxed into an impossible position if she is unable to attain this goal. *Uhamiri*, the most revered goddess of the lake is herself childless, having 'never experienced the joy of motherhood' in a society that regards motherhood with such high esteem.[89] Why then do women worship *uhamiri* even though the goddess cannot give them a child? Unlike Maryse Condé's incorrect assertion that Efuru's experience indicates that '[n]o happiness can be achieved for a woman unless in childbearing,'[90] the correct answer to this question provides the insight into the flexibility in-built in Igbo society which gives women the opportunity to negotiate alternative options of social fulfilment in the event of not attaining the overarching goal of motherhood. The guarantor to this dispensation is of course the goddess *uhamiri* herself who is beautiful, wealthy, childless *but* happy. No wonder we learn at the end of the novel that the beautiful, wealthy and childless Efuru 'slept soundly that night.' She *happily* identifies herself with the qualities of the revered goddess of her people despite or rather because of her inability to achieve the status of motherhood. In spite of Efuru's inability to fulfil one of the most 'primordial' of functions as an Igbo woman, she is still lovingly accommodated in her society; in spite of Efuru's obvious failure to contribute towards the biological continuation of the lineage or society, the flexibility nevertheless exists in her society for her to pursue

---

[87]Ada Mere, 'The Unique Role of Women in Nation Building,' quoted in Wilentz, *Binding Cultures*, p. xix.
[88]Sofola, *African Culture and the African Personality*, p. 69.
[89]*Efuru*, p. 221.
[90]Condé, 'Three Female Writers in Modern Africa,' p. 134.

some other career course and forge a destiny that in effect precludes the very destiny society prescribes for her - by virtue of her womanhood. Similarly in *Idu* it is acknowledged that Ojiugo, Idu's closest friend, has committed adultery - a most serious violation of societal norms in Igbo society. She becomes pregnant by her husband's best friend, considered as an abomination in society. Yet, her society accommodates her as hers are mitigating circumstances - she has finally acted upon a discovery made two years earlier that 'her husband [is] not a man.'[91] The inherent flexibility and tolerance of this society is underlined in Adiewere's comments: 'People told her but she did not believe it at first, but eventually she herself discovered. She wanted a child. Do you blame her when she went to a man who could give her one?'[92]

Flora Nwapa is not alone in her portrayal of the political role of motherhood in Igbo society. It is thus useful to examine briefly how other leading Igbo writers address this subject. Onuora Nzekwu's *Highlife for Lizards*[93] clearly accepts that motherhood constitutes a political role in society. Agom, the main protagonist in the novel is plagued by infertility for many years in her marriage, leading her husband to marry a new wife. In the meantime, in a sequence of events reminiscent of Efuru's experience in *Efuru*, Agom embarks on business where she amasses huge wealth and uses the proceeds to finance her involvement in the politics of liberation of her land, takes expensive titles, and becomes a member of the leadership of the women's councils. To crown her entrepreneurial success in later life, Agom succeeds in getting pregnant and ends up having three children of her own. This unexpected development of being a mother in her life radically transforms Agom's position in society, as she becomes a focus of goodwill and prestige by all and sundry including especially those who knew of the untold misery that afflicted her when she was childless. Whilst his position on the role of motherhood in Igboland is almost identical to Nwapa's, Chinua Achebe would probably not describe child bearing as a 'duty' nor indeed a 'political role' in society. Instead, motherhood for Achebe has a more revered, spiritual reference – *nneka, mother is supreme*, is the name that defines this position best as Uchendu, the maternal uncle of Okonkwo, the hero in *Things Fall Apart*, is keen to state. The occasion is very important, coming in the wake of Okonkwo's enforced exile from his home in Umuofia to Mbanta, his mother's land, as punishment for his accidental murder of a kinsperson's son during a funeral. Okonkwo's crime is against *ani*, the

[91]*Idu*, p. 112.
[92]Ibid.
[93]See Nzekwu, *Highlife for Lizards*.

earth goddess, the most revered in the Igbo pantheon which oversees fertility and guarantees the 'female principle' corpus of the 'dual-sex' gender relationship of society. Given the obvious urgency at stake, Umuofia's quick punishment of Okonkwo is a propitiation to *ani* which is clearly aimed at re-establishing the tilted balance that had occurred in the governing female-male duality as a result of the murder. Buchi Emecheta's position on the subject is interestingly different from those of the three writers just discussed, but especially that of Nwapa's, the only woman in the trio. For Emecheta, motherhood does not receive the critical adoration that Nwapa, Achebe and Nzekwu have expressed on the subject. In *The Joys of Motherhood*, a novel whose title Emecheta derives from an identical set of words in one of the closing sentences in *Efuru*, the author challenges head on the dominant facets of Igbo people's attitude to motherhood. Nnu Ego, the heroine in the novel whose Igbo name translates to 'the millionaire' in English, contemplates suicide following the death of her four-week old child. Despite the agonising irony implied, Emecheta in fact gives the title, 'The Mother,' to the first chapter of the novel even though Nnu Ego is no mother at this stage of the story; besides, there is the added sad revelation that Nnu Ego had in fact been divorced from a previous marriage because of her presumed state of barrenness. By employing the term 'mother' to caption such a chapter, Emecheta is of course alluding critically to what appears as the existentialist quest by the Igbo woman to become a mother in order to satisfy social obligations. Furthermore, Emecheta is ridiculing the universal Igbo reverence for motherhood: '[S]he is to cook and bear the children and look after you and them...'[94] She signals her intention to pursue this goal of ridicule by re-working the Igbo belief in reincarnation to ensure a problematic outcome. In Emecheta's formulation, Nnu Ego is revealed as a slave in her previous life, owned by none other than Agunwa, the previous wife of her own father, and was buried alongside Agunwa when the latter died.[95] In a dramatic feature of Nnu Ego's slave status that clearly goes against the grain of the Igbo ethos on the established sequence of reincarnation which only involves people with proven blood relation, the slave had threatened just before she was entombed in Agunwa's grave to return to the world as the *daughter* of the latter's husband (Nnu Ego's father). This decision was aimed as retaliation for her death sentence. The slave returns to earth and the event is confirmed by a respected dibia or diviner who insists that the returnee is indeed Nnu Ego![96]

---

[94]Buchi Emecheta, *The Joys of Motherhood* (New York: George Braziller, 1979), p. 71.
[95]Ibid., p. 23.
[96]Ibid., p. 27.

For Emecheta, the message is clear: whilst the process of the slave's self-directed reincarnation has enabled the slave to change the source or origin of her birth (now the daughter of the husband of her owner in the previous life), the slave's status has still not discontinued but has now moved into a new life, a new generation. 'God,' Nne Ego asks, 'when will you create a woman who will be fufilled in herself, a full human being, not anybody's appendage... When will I be free?'[97] As far as Emecheta is concerned, the reincarnated Nnu Ego, the woman or the wife or the mother, is no less enslaved to her societal pressure and demands for motherhood than in her previous life's societal demands and expectations as the slave of Agunwa. To underscore the point, Emecheta's choice of names for the main protagonists of her formulation of the 'unchanging oppressed woman' could not be any more ironical: the meaning of Nnu Ego (as stated above) for a female in the circumstance is haunted by its materialist implications whilst the meaning of Agunwa, 'longing for a child,' does not really fit in with being a slave owner nor indeed one who at death is buried with an 'accompanying' human being.

As we've seen Nwapa's position on the political role of motherhood in Igbo society is, broadly speaking, shared with Nzekwu and Achebe, but is in contrast to that of Emecheta. Nwapa would find Emecheta's parody of motherhood perhaps amusing especially the ironical interplay between the names/characters and their status in society. But the premise of this parody, namely, that motherhood is defined as 'to cook and bear the children and look after [husband and relations],' would be unrecognisable to Nwapa. Indeed, as we have shown in this study such a premise is unhistorical in Igboland. On the contrary, motherhood is the *embodiment of the political, economic, and cultural heritage and survivability of society.*

This is why, to return to *Efuru* and *Idu*, Efuru and Idu as well as Ojiugo, who are mothers/communal mothers and successful business people in society are highly political figures in themselves, conducting such political acts as conflict resolution - dispensing advice to all members of the community (both male and female); materially and emotionally providing support to individuals and families facing major life challenges; achieving status and wealth quite independently of their spouses and in effect acting as 'role models' for all of society. In the case of Efuru, she is a priestess of a powerful deity. Efuru is clearly the brains behind the business she runs with Adizua, her first husband - a situation which the entire community including her own mother-in-law

---

[97]Ibid., pp. 186 - 187.

acknowledges. The birth of Efuru's baby and consequently the time taken by her away from her trade leads to a slow down in the pace of business. Returning to the business means that help must be found to take care of the baby. Ossai, her mother-in-law, presents Ogea the daughter of Nwosu, her cousin, as the solution. Nwosu has recently been under severe financial difficulties. A combination of natural disaster (he has lost all his yams in a flood) and the pitiless extraction of taxes by the occupying colonial force threaten to leave him destitute. In response to Efuru's search for a maid, Nwosu makes a proposal: 'Please ask *her* to take my daughter as a maid and give me ten pounds. At the end of the year we shall give her ten pounds plus four pounds interest and take our daughter' (added emphasis).[98] Thus it is clearly established that the principal actor behind this negotiation is Efuru and not her husband. Efuru, however, does not at any point in time *behave* in a manner that portrays to the wider community that she is the initiator and sole-negotiator of the transaction. To the visiting Nwosu Efuru responds, 'My mother-in-law told me about your daughter. My husband has just gone to the back of the house. He will soon be here. A woman has no say in these things.'[99] Efuru's behaviour is that of a woman possessing great humility and tact. Her husband is made to partake of, and participate fully in these consultations and negotiations. As a result of her status, family background and wealth, she has been approached to provide critically needed help in an emergency situation. She has provided not only material but psychological support in desperate times. She has done so, however, in a manner that ensures that the standing and position of her husband as the 'head' of the household is not undermined, marginalised nor in any way compromised. This seeming contradiction between the accepted and expressed/demonstrated norm with regard to the practicalisation of male and female roles in Igbo society is a fascinating and often confusing feature of the society not easily understood by those unfamiliar with the nuances of the culture. Nwosu and Nwabata, his wife, renege on this agreement, failing to provide Efuru with either the money or yams and thus subsequently avoid contact with her. However, it is to Efuru that they once again return in desperation when faced with yet another emergency. The same Efuru who at the very least expresses a view point that 'a woman has no say in these things' chastises and places the overwhelming blame on Nwabata, for this state of affairs: '[Nwosu] you have not done well ... Why have you behaved so

---

[98]*Efuru*, p. 38.
[99]Ibid., p. 39.

childishly? And Nwabata, you have not done well. You have the greater blame. *You should correct your husband, for what do they know after all'* (emphasis added)?[100] This is a clear collective reference to the strengthening, supportive and intuitive role that is ascribed to womanhood. Nwabata's obvious failure in expressing these traits and thus playing this role within her own household is seen as a crucial factor in the resulting and continuing crisis.

Through her family contacts and friendship with Dr Uzaru, the Western-trained medical doctor, Efuru creates numerous opportunities for medical consultations, advice, treatment and support in general for members of her community as in the cases of Nwosu,[101] Nnona[102] and Ossai.[103] She is the personification of generosity and largesse, making time to listen to the numerous challenges faced by those who seek her help and advice, a situation which leads Ogea to comment, 'If you continue giving people money in this way, they will take advantage of your generosity and worry you all the more.'[104] It is to her compound that the village children are consistently drawn for many meals and it is undisputed that she is a *true mother* to the village in spite of her youth. It is also to her compound that the community congregate for one of the most important functions of the day, namely, story telling[105] - one of the most pleasurably of ways to communicate cultural values, traditions and morals. Efuru's high degree of responsibility towards members of her community is evinced when she loses her child, Ogonim. 'Efuru was well known in the town and so she had many sympathizers. She herself had given generously to her friends who were bereaved so these friends also gave to her generously.'[106] Sympathy for Efuru is therefore heart-felt and widespread. Mourners recall: 'A good woman who greeted you twenty times if she saw you twenty times in a day. A woman with a clean heart, and who respects her elders. God, please give her the strength to bear this loss.'[107] Quite clearly, Nwapa is using Efuru's bereavement and the effusive public sympathy in response to remind her readers of the overriding importance of the pervading cultural tenet of one being their sister's/brother's keeper. Efuru has been exemplary in her generosity to other

---

[100]Ibid., p. 169.
[101]Ibid., p. 97.
[102]Ibid., p. 129.
[103]Ibid., p. 158.
[104]Ibid., p. 172.
[105]Ibid., p. 105.
[106]Ibid., p. 77.
[107]Ibid.

members of society including those who are not necessarily close relations. Given that this value of support for others rests principally on personal initiative and responsibility in its actual practice, and considering the very diffused nature of politics in Igboland, Nwapa no doubt regards this form of support for others as a political act that impacts positively on society both individually and collectively. Furthermore, it is important that there is public recognition at this stage for Efuru's success as a businessperson and the generosity that has flowed as a result. Such public goodwill will later on act as a supporting buffer for Efuru when it becomes generally known that she can no longer become a mother after the death of Ogonim.

In *Idu* both Idu and Ojiugo are important individuals that remind us of Efuru. Ojiugo is 'prosperous ... [has] a lot of will-power ... [is] very generous ... and ... [is] by nature cheerful.'[108] Idu is equally a generous woman. Uzoechi and Nwasobi, two community social commentators, not only reflect on Idu's generosity but also praise the adorable nature of Idu's relationship with her husband, Adiewere. In a reply to Uzoechi's complimentary remarks on the couple, Nwasobi observes:

'It is not only [their marriage], it's their kindness. Do you know what, when two people live together, one gradually begins to behave like the other?'
'What do you mean?' asked Uzoechi.
'You know Adiewere was not all that magnanimous before he married Idu. Now the two of them are about the kindest couple I know in this town.'[109]

Here, Nwapa highlights what she considers is the inherently powerful role of women to shape/define both the home and societal environment, almost always exerting considerable influence over their spouses and the decisions affecting the immediate and extended family. Like Efuru, Idu is an important woman in the community. Her home is quite literally a centre for advice and support[110] while she herself is the agent of goodwill comforting Amarajeme, Ojiugo's husband, when Ojiugo leaves him for another man. Yet, Idu makes no attempt to disguise the loyalty she feels towards her friend Ojiugo as well as the respect she has for her controversial decision. Not only does she react positively to

---

[108]Ibid., p. 35.
[109]*Idu*, p. 3.
[110]Ibid., p. 69.

people's difficulties when she is consulted, she also takes an equally proactive stance when problems are brought to her attention. Her encounter at the beach with the young boy exhibiting early signs of mental illness leaves her determined to visit the boy's mother and offer help, in spite of her friends' caution not to have anything to do with 'them, people like that.'[111] Idu is determined that 'something must be done'[112] and that the condition of the child should not be allowed to deteriorate further. Similarly, Idu responds admirably by offering to adopt the son of her business partner Okeke soon after the latter is found murdered. Idu pledges to support the child to complete his education. Just as with Efuru, Idu's home is the main place for the evening gathering of young people for story telling and other folklore activity. Idu herself plays an important part in the proceedings with her ability to tell stories which children particularly love.[113] Ada Mere's earlier quoted assertion that women 'are the most primary and constant agents of child socialisation' in Africa is aptly demonstrated.

Motherhood

There is little doubt from our analysis of both *Idu* and *Efuru* that motherhood is the single most important role for a woman in Igboland - as is fatherhood for a man. In this society, motherhood remains the ultimate manifestation of being female and children are viewed as blessings directly from goddesses and gods.[114] For Amadiume, the spiritual foundation of this sociological dispensation entrenches motherhood in the consciousness of the people. '[This conveys] a very clear message about social and economic justice ... couched in a very powerful goddess-based religion [and] a strong ideology of motherhood.'[115] In *Idu*, the underlining importance of this sociological heritage comes from the following rumination by one of the principal characters in the novel: 'What we are all praying for is children. What else do we want if we have children?'[116] The strong theme of motherhood runs through *Idu* and *Efuru*, detailing the varied components of this role - from child bearing and rearing,

---

[111]Ibid., p. 117.
[112]Ibid.
[113]Ibid., p. 151.
[114]Ibid., p. 38.
[115]Amadiume, *Reinventing Africa*, p. 101.
[116]*Idu*, p. 150.

nurturer, companion, provider, educator and the role of the (African) extended family. The intense desire for children is powerfully communicated in both novels. There is a deeply touching, heartfelt, almost spiritual yearning for children that female as well as male characters in the texts exhibit. This feeling appears to transcend the highly politicised role of women as the 'means' through which the propagation of society occurs and the concomitant complementary role of men in assisting this process. Rather, Nwapa conveys what she reckons is a deeply-felt reverence in the Igbo for the sanctity of children and the capacity of human beings to reproduce themselves under the benevolent guidance and care of the goddesses and gods of the land with the presence of *uhamiri*, a constant reminder: 'When a woman is good, God, our ancestors, and the Woman of the Lake all look at her stomach, not at the head, but at her stomach.'[117] It is 'dreadful [to be] denied the joy of motherhood.'[118] This feeling is voiced quite passionately by the principal characters in both Nwapa's novels. The conversation between Idu and Ojiugo in chapter 4 of *Idu* is particularly illustrative of this feeling. As they lament their seeming fate of childlessness, there is a constant reference to the fact that the goddesses are in control of their destiny and as such the capacity to be 'blessed by a child' is constantly open to them.[119] Idu's pregnancy brings great joy to her and to her friend Ojiugo. There is hope, great hope not only for Ojiugo but for every woman that they will experience the 'joy of motherhood'. For Efuru, her own opportunity also comes with joy! 'Is this happening to me or someone I know,' she reflects with almost total disbelief, 'Is that baby mine or somebody else's? Is it really true that I have had a baby, that I am a woman after all...'[120] The baby's birth is a normal delivery and we glimpse the tendency of women here not to express physical pain at childbirth, since 'if you cry or shout you will continue crying and shouting each time you have your baby.'[121] In further conversations by women who have come to congratulate the new mother and child, Nwapa creates more insight into other spheres of Igbo cultural life that add more colour, tone and rhythm to our understanding of the society. The following set of conversations are interestingly vivid:

'Yes, all is well. My daughter has had a baby.'

---

[117]Ibid., p. 42.
[118]*Efuru*, p. 165.
[119]*Idu*, p. 37.
[120]*Efuru*, p. 31.
[121]Ibid.

'Oh, Orisha, thank you. What did she have?'
'She had a baby girl.'
'Good, Orisha, thank you. Efuru is hot. It was only yesterday that she danced with her age-group and came back late. Who ever thought that she was going to have a baby in the night,' one of them said.[122]

'How many children have you, Ajanupu?'
'Hush, we don't ask people how many children they have. It is not done. Children are not goats or sheep or yams to be counted. I will tell you. I conceived eight times, one died of convulsion.'[123]

Nwapa also highlights the richness of traditional African natural herbal remedies to many illnesses and conditions as well as their limitations: from Efuru's high level of water retention during her pregnancy ('"Every morning and night, you warm it [the herbs] over a slow fire, put some palm wine in it and drink"... Efuru kept to the instructions religiously. The medicine worked ... her legs and feet were no longer swollen.')[124] to her inability to produce enough breast milk for her baby ('"It is simple. When I had my first baby, the same thing happened to me. You have to drink plenty of palm wine..." She chewed some palm kernels which she used in rubbing her breasts. "This will help," she told her kindly ... Efuru was all right. Her breast was full.'),[125] and finally to the saving of Ogbenyanu from almost certain death when she miscarries following a haemorrhage ('Nwasobi crushed the leaves on her palm, put some drops of water in it, made it into a ball and asked Ogbenyanu to open her mouth. She opened her mouth and Nwasobi put the stuff, drop by drop into her mouth. She rubbed palm kernel on her body and asked her to lie down ... "I don't think there is any more danger now."')[126] - all are done within the contours of local knowledge, understanding and ingenuity. And these worked for the Igbo during this particular historical period with all its obvious limitations as evidenced in the high levels of infant and maternal mortality that are constantly mentioned in the narratives in both *Efuru* and *Idu*. Both Efuru and Idu lose their mothers at childhood. The reflections of a friend who calls on Efuru to console her over the premature death of her own daughter sums up the situation: 'I conceived

---

[122]Ibid., p. 32.
[123]Ibid., p. 33.
[124]Ibid., p. 29.
[125]Ibid., p. 33.
[126]*Idu*, p. 18.

eight times. All died before they were six months old.'[127]

Companionship

Companionship for the African woman is certainly one of the most important criteria by which her success as a wife is judged in Igbo society. Being a good companion would entail exhibiting qualities such as confidante, helper, friend, lover and peace-keeper in the family. Her input in planning for the needs and general progress of the family very often presents as the voice of wisdom shedding light on the situation, the cautioning hand restraining impetuous decisions, the deciding factor in what often amount to complex intra-familial and economic situations. Indeed Ogbenyanu, Idu's sister-in-law is an example of the crisis that can result in a family when one does not marry 'a sensible girl.'[128] Ishiodu's reckless behaviour is attributed directly to his own stupidity. However, Ogbenyanu, his wife, is equally criticised. She is indeed criticised even to a greater degree because she is a woman, a mother with an inherent maturity and intuition that should act as a restraint on her husband and steer him and their affairs along the correct way. Instead, Ogbenyanu 'collaborates' in Ishiodu's stupidity and the entire family suffer as a result. It is this same sentiment that we see raised in *Efuru* when Efuru, in condemning Nwosu and Nwabata for their irresponsibility in dealing with her loan to them, berates Nwabata even more for failing to act as *that* restraining and indeed corrective hand. Nwabata ought to know her duties and she has failed in carrying them out!

Both Efuru and Idu are the perfect companions. They are fully aware of their responsibilities as wives, as companions and the entire community appreciate them for it. It is interesting to note that even in the case of Efuru who marries two irresponsible men, the community never blame her for both husbands' aberrant ways, precisely because they are aware that she has fulfilled her duties and played her role to the utmost. As her aunt-in-law tells her 'everybody in our town knows that you have been a faithful wife. Everyone knows that you are a good woman and what is more they love and respect you.'[129] In the case of her first husband, people are astonished that a woman of such standing in the community has agreed to marry him. The discussion between some of Adizua's

---

[127]*Efuru*, p. 74.
[128]*Idu*, p. 29.
[129]*Efuru*, p. 58.

farming colleagues is illuminating: 'How [Efuru] agreed to marry him remains a mystery to everyone.'[130] 'I give them three years. By then the woman will know her husband too well to want to stay with him any longer.'[131] Because Adizua's irresponsible ways are already known, and because it is clear that Efuru has done everything to support him and her marriage, even to her own detriment, she is completely exonerated from all blame in the failure of the marriage.

Educator

As we have already shown, the mother plays a crucial role in socialising and educating the child - from birth to the stage of its acceptance into the adult world. During this period the child is socialised into the communitarian way of life. It is here that the child's feelings of belonging to the family and community are imbibed and solidified. Sanctions and rewards for quality of behaviour are also readily applied in order to ensure that the foundations of acceptable behaviour are clearly understood and firmly laid. There is and remains no greater medium for the transmission of cultural mores than through folklore; and both *Idu* and *Efuru* present us with examples of the operationalisation of this technique. Efuru's compound is the gathering point for all the village children on moonlit nights. When she herself is not directly involved in narrating the tales, she is the organiser of these events. The story related by Eneke[132] reinforces the highly valued trait of respect for parents and receptivity to advice from elders in general. The character in this story is an extremely beautiful daughter and the only child of a very wealthy woman. The young girl's mother leaves strict instructions that her child is not to leave the house while she goes to the market. The child disobeys and ends up with an unsolicited and undesirable husband from the spirit world. She is saved from this unsavoury future by the kindness of one sister who devises a clever plan to rid her sister of the spirit husband. In this story three important themes are evident. First, the tragic consequences of disobeying a parent are made obvious and it is clear that this behaviour is one upon which the society frowns. The story is particularly relevant to Efuru who herself has disobeyed her father, or, at the very least, not involved him in her choice of spouse and has ended up with an unsuitable

---

[130]Ibid., p. 11.
[131]Ibid., p. 12.
[132]Ibid., pp. 105 - 111.

partner and unhappy marriage.[133] The message is that while the ways of one's people and the traditions which they uphold may not be perfect, the wealth of wisdom and insight which they have acquired over time compels one to pay attention to their advice. Efuru's independent and dynamic personality has earned her the respect and admiration of her community. However, she pushes this admirably independent and fighting spirit too far. She fails to tap into a rich and age-long mechanism for minimising failed marriages - *the involvement of families and the investigation of the intended partner's family and personal background*. She pays the consequences in her husband's treatment of her only to discover that 'it is in the family... [His] waywardness is in his blood and you can do nothing about it.'[134] Second, through the story, the children learn that the Igbo have a four-day week and that the days of the week are *Eke, Orie, Afo and Nkwo*. These are represented as the names of the beautiful girl's four sisters. Third, the issue of responsibility towards and support for the family is highlighted. The audience is disgusted at the three sisters who refuse to help in this crisis situation and are full of admiration and praise for the last sister Nkwo who, in spite of her fear and the risk to herself, helps her sister to get rid of her spirit husband. The moral of the story in *Idu* is 'that no matter how poor a mother may be, a mother is a mother.'[135] This delightful story is told to a compound full of children, again on a moonlit night and emphasises the virtues of patience and perseverance. Mmegbudi, the youngest of 10 wives of the king is maltreated and abused by all nine older wives and the king himself, on advice from these wives. Mmegbudi endures the abuse, biding her time and is presented with unsolicited help along the way in her quest to survive. She becomes pregnant (all the other wives remain barren) and gives birth to a son whom the rest of the wives attempt to claim as their own. The mothers are put to the test by the king in an effort to discover who the real mother is. The young boy is asked to eat only the food of his mother. All the other wives labour over the preparation of elaborate and expensive dishes, a luxury that is denied Mmegbudi who must content herself with scraps and bones from the market, served in an earthenware pot. In spite of the impressive array presented by the nine wives, the young boy selects his true mother's food, humble as it is, unhesitatingly. The young wife is vindicated as the king drives away all the other wives from his palace and she happily assumes her rightful position in the palace. Nwapa employs this story to illustrate, once again, the powerful role of

---

[133]Ibid., pp. 8 - 9.
[134]Ibid., p. 61.
[135]*Idu*, p. 153.

the mother and the unconditional love and support between mother and child that is the norm in Igboland and indeed the rest of Africa.

Extended familyhood

The extended family among the Igbo strictly speaking is defined as a group of individuals related closely or distantly through blood or marriage. It operates as a community of individuals willing to assume responsibility and concern for its members. The primary and most important role of the Igbo/African extended family is in its function as provider of social support. This is played out in minute detail in *Efuru* and *Idu*. Here, Nwapa problematises the efficacy of this institution by compounding its membership to include those whose very character/activities could undermine the aspirations and goals of the family in focus or indeed those of society as a whole. So, in Nwapa's formulation, not only does the extended family have leading characters who admirably assume their responsibility, but there are also members who are aberrant, irresponsible and non-likeable individuals. In *Idu*, Ishiodu, Idu's brother-in-law, and his wife Ogbenyanu both typify the weak links in the extended family structure. Ishiodu is a lazy, idle, non-enterprising individual who is as different from his brother (Adiewere) as day is from night. The vast differences in character lead a family friend to observe 'whether it can be the same God who created both Adiewere and his brother Ishiodu...'[136]

Another observer is equally critical: 'How can a man merely exist, eating and not thinking of tomorrow, and what is more relying on his only brother for everything.'[137] Ishiodu is unable to farm successfully because he consumes the yams seeds. He is equally incapable of trading in the town, confining his activities to merry making with his friends and plunging, not only himself, but, by implication, Adiewere and Idu into great debt. It is Adiewere who arranges his marriage for him and assumes the entire cost. It is Adiewere who has built the house in which he lives with his family and it is Adiewere who virtually supports him. Both Adiewere and Idu give him money to start a business that never materialises, and purchase three canoes for him all of which are 'lost' in mysterious circumstances. They have also on two occasions bailed him out of jail. In other words 'Ishiodu, Adiewere's brother, [is] a ne'er-do-well,'[138] a man

---

[136]*Idu*, p. 3 .
[137]Ibid., p. 30.
[138]Ibid., p. 14.

who is so much a reminder of Unoka in *Things Fall Apart* who 'was lazy and improvident and was quite incapable of thinking about tomorrow.'[139] Even when Adiewere is seriously ill, Ishiodu is still incapable of providing the most minimal of support, such that Adiewere is driven to comment that 'I said long ago that a person who has you has nobody.'[140] Herein lies the seeming contradiction in this Africa's age-old support for the extended family system: it is clearly the case that every character trait exhibited by Ishiodu is despised by the same humanity whose cultural ethos it is that a kinsperson should be given support. Nwapa is hinting at the potential for abuse of such a legendary social security system and the consequences thereof. The refocusing in emphasis required in this system, Nwapa appears to be insisting, is that while it ensures that the individual is not alone and isolated, roaming aimlessly in a void but the ready recipient of love, care, responsibility and justice from the family/community at large, the individual must himself/herself be an active contributing agency to the success of the structure. As we shall soon demonstrate, such is in fact the importance of Nwapa's critique of the extended family that she configures the salient features of her observations on the subject as the overarching perspective to end her novel, *Idu*.

Spiritual

As earlier discussed, the spiritual life of the Igbo, like most Africans, is inextricably linked with their everyday existence. The role of women in the divination/spiritual life of Igbo society is clearly evident in Nwapa's works. The social mores of society are anchored in the spiritual world, and adherence or violation of these incur simultaneous blessings or curses from beyond the physical world. Indeed throughout this chapter it has been extremely difficult to isolate the spiritual from the sociopolitical and economic existence of the literary characters created by Nwapa. It is the thread that intricately weaves together Igbo social existence, defining the parameters for acceptable social mores. As we have shown, following Wendy James's conclusions on her study of African women, 'there is a deeper and historically more enduring level at which the nature and capacity of women are given primacy in the definition of the human condition itself.[141] An important reminder of this heritage is evident

---

[139]Achebe, *The African Trilogy*, p. 18.
[140]Ibid., p. 140.
[141]James, 'Matrifocus on African Women,' p. 60.

in *Idu*. Adiewere's 'sudden' death leaves his wife Idu devastated and she is determined to die with him: 'I am going with my husband. Both of us will go there, to the land of the dead ... [W]e shall continue our lives there. It will even be better there.'[142] Idu cannot and will not reconcile herself to the death of Adiewere as both couple have had an extremely happy and supportive relationship in which they have lived as if 'God gave them to each other.'[143] Their lives and fate appear very similar to those of Ogbuefi Ndulue and Ozoemena, his wife, in *Things Fall Apart* who both 'had one mind.'[144] Ndulue 'could not do anything without' informing Ozoemena. Such is their companionship that it does not completely come as a shock that on the same day that Ndulue dies, Ozoemena also dies. Similarly, Idu, herself, dies, having lost the will to survive Adiewere's death. Idu's death obviously adds to the unexpected tragic end that characterises *Idu*. After all, everyone in society accepts that Idu's marriage to Adiewere is a success: the couple have a son and Idu is pregnant with a second child. In effect, Idu's life as a woman has been completely fulfilled. Or has it?

If we are to analyse this closing scene of *Idu*, Idu's behaviour appears as a serious indictment, if not a rejection of the norms of society, especially those that underpin motherhood. The welfare and overall future interest of her child, indeed her children (for she is expecting a new child soon), for which Idu deeply longed and craved for so many years seem to recede from any critical judgement by her as she speculates on how to cope in the wake of the death of Adiewere. To put it bluntly, it appears that as we get to the end of *Idu*, Idu's desire for the companionship and love for husband is in great contention with that of motherhood. That Idu herself dies suddenly in her sleep whilst trying to resolve this dilemma has been taken on by a number of critics quite mistakenly, in our judgement, as evidence of the triumph of the quest for a happy, harmonious marriage over motherhood. Ada Uzoamaka Azodo believes that Idu's death represents an affirmation of the importance of 'soul love which can exist between two married people.'[145] Gay Wilentz is unambiguous in her reading of the implication of the death of Idu: 'Nwapa [is] privileging the bond

---

[142]*Idu*, pp. 210 - 211.
[143]Ibid., p. 2.
[144]Achebe, *African Trilogy*, p. 64.
[145]Ada Uzoamaka Azodo, '*Efuru* and *Idu*: Rejecting Women's Subjugation,' in Umeh, ed., *Emerging Perspectives on Flora Nwapa*, p. 179.

of husband-wife over mother-child.'[146] Yemi Majola arrives at a similar conclusion. She argues that Nwapa is challenging women to cherish and 'preserve' a successful marriage 'built on love like the marriage of Adiewere and Idu' even though she questions the artistic judgement of Nwapa's conclusion,[147] a point she shares with Adeola James's explicitly dismissive review of *Idu*.[148] Theodora Akachi Ezeigbo pursues this issue of authorial artistic choice by posing the following question: 'Is it aesthetically valid given the importance attached to motherhood in Nwapa's recreation of [African] traditional society ... that [Idu] would will herself to die to follow her dead husband?'[149] For Carole Boyce Davies,[150] Theresa Njoku[151] and Chidi Ikonne,[152] Idu's shocking death is attributed to avoiding marrying her husband's brother, the discredited Ishiodu, as dictated by 'traditional mores.'[153] The Ishiodu 'factor' just referred to by the last set of critics cited above is of course the most tempting but the least convincing of the possible explanations for Idu's death. Throughout the novel, Idu maintains deep and open contempt for Ishiodu (and his wife Ogbenyanu) who she feels is lazy, un-enterprisingly dependent on her (and Adiewere) and a disgrace to the enlarged or extended family. This is definitely not the kind of person that Idu would wish to marry, even in the name of tradition! Idu and indeed all other characters created by Nwapa have been adept in the way they employ the immense flexibility that exists in Igbo culture to advance whatever goals that they have targeted upon including deciding who they get married to, who their friends are, their occupation, and the character and range of their supportive work in the community. Ishiodu himself is fully aware that no traditional precepts could force Idu to marry him. In fact he acknowledges this, albeit implicitly, when he calls at Idu to demonstrate the

---

[146]Gay Wilentz, 'Not Feminist but Afracentrist: Flora Nwapa and the Politics of African Cultural Production,' in Umeh, ed., *Emerging Perspectives on Flora Nwapa*, p. 148.

[147]Yemi Mojola, 'The Works of Flora Nwapa,' in Henrietta Otokunefor and Obiageli Nwodo, eds., *Nigerian Female Writers* (Lagos: Malthouse, 1989), p. 23.

[148]James, '*Idu*: Flora Nwapa,' p. 152.

[149]Theodora Akachi Ezeigbo, 'Traditional Women's Institutions in Igbo Society: Implications for the Igbo Female Writer,' *African Languages and Culture*, Vol. 3, No. 2, 1990, p. 159.

[150]Davies, 'Motherhood in the Works of Male and Female Igbo Writers,' p. 252.

[151]Theresa Njoku, 'The Mythic World in Flora Nwapa's Early Novels,' in Umeh, ed., *Emerging Perspectives on Flora Nwapa*, p. 122.

[152]Chidi Ikonne, 'The Folk Roots of Flora Nwapa's Early Novels,' *African Literature Today*, No. 18, 1992, p. 103.

[153]Njoku, 'The Mythic World in Flora Nwapa's Early Novels', p. 122.

purely symbolic gesture of interest of 'being available as a prospective husband' of his late brother's wife. Idu recalls the encounter: 'Ishiodu came to put the thread round my neck this morning ... I just looked at him, he put the thread on and left. He was not sure of himself ... What I am saying is that it will not happen.'[154]

There and then, this possible option in Idu's future relations is *decidedly blocked* by Idu herself. Whatever the expectations or pretensions on the part of anybody in society, Idu is in no way pressurised to get married to Ishiodu – not even from Ishiodu himself, unlike Tamsir who in a similar situation in *So Long a Letter* audaciously lays claim to Ramatoulaye his brother's wife.[155] A mourner at Adiewere's wake-keeping summarises the position: 'Marry Ishiodu? She will not ... She will prefer to stay as I see her now. She won't agree to marry any other person.'[156] Quite clearly, Ishiodu does not feature as a motivating factor for Idu's decision to 'will herself to die' after Adiewere's death. We should now examine the other plausible explanation proffered by critics (mentioned above) to explain Idu's death, namely that this represents the author's judgement, made very late in the day, to repudiate the saliency of the heritage of motherhood in African society. Ernest Emenyonu's discussion on the subject is vital in our examination.[157] Emenyonu rejects the assertion that Idu's death is far-fetched, and therefore artistically flawed. He argues that critics who have come to this conclusion have done so because of their unfamiliarity with the Igbo concept of 'tragedy'. 'Tragedy in the Igbo is not,' Emenyonu argues, 'in the feeling that nothing goes right for the individual, but in the fact that any success he attains is followed sooner or later by a bigger and more terrible misfortune.'[158] There is a notion of love centrally inculcated in the concept of *ume* which stresses that the 'love between two individuals can be such that one can die without the other.'[159] Emenyonu traces the origin of this Igbo world-view of tragedy to the

---

[154]*Idu*, p. 216.
[155]Mariama Bâ, *So Long a Letter* (London: Heinneman Education Books, 1981) pp. 57 - 58.
[156]*Idu.*, p. 214.
[157]See Ernest Emenyonu, 'Who does Flora Nwapa write for?' *African Literature Today*, No. 7, 1978, pp. 28 - 33.
[158]Ibid., p. 31.
[159]Ibid., p. 30. Another variant of this notion of love called *di uwa* is explicit in indicating that given the love that exists between a couple, if one dies, 'the other must surely die.'(See A.C Izuagha, 'Oguta and the Novels of Flora Nwapa: A Biographical Approach,' quoted in Ezeigbo, 'Myth, History, Culture, and Igbo Womanhood in Flora Nwapa's Novels,' p. 73.) It is equally applicable to the kind of analysis we have

phenomenon of *ume* and shows that this is a theme that has since been a feature in the work of Igbo writers including Chinua Achebe, Cyprian Ekwensi, John Munonye, Pita Nwana and Onuora Nzekwu. Achebe's engagement with *ume* in the characterisation and career of Okonkwo in *Things Fall Apart* is perhaps the best known in the genre. It should however be noted that in her study of Achebe's *Arrow of God*,[160] Molly Mahood transposes the discourse on *ume* across two historical epochs that are not too dissimilar on the nature of the emergency faced by the Igbo - from the acute concerns of Ezeulu, the Umuaro philosopher-priest who contemplates gravely on Umuaro's range of responses to the late 19th century/early 20th century unfolding British conquest and occupation of Igboland ("'And our fathers have told us that it may even happen to an unfortunate generation that they are pushed beyond the end of things, and their back is broken and hung over a fire. When this happens they may sacrifice their own blood.'"[161]) to the options open to the Igbo who for 20 years, beginning from the late 1940s to the 1960s, are in the vanguard of the struggle for the liberation of Nigeria from British rule but who from 1966-1970 are confronted with the tragedy of pogrom and war by their fellow Nigerian compatriots.[162]

Nwapa is of course the first Igbo woman author to confront the phenomenon of *ume* and contrary to some of the views of the critics quoted above, she has in fact used the concept to principally reinforce her position of the overriding importance of motherhood in Igboland, and, specifically, *the monumental responsibility that society must itself assume in propagating this role*. We have already discussed earlier that motherhood is not a singularly referenced concept, but is a collective responsibility in Africa. We shall in the concluding section of this study return once again to this concept, i.e. motherhood in this communal definition and emphasis, when we discuss Africa's on-going response to the HIV/AIDS emergency. In Nwapa's adaptation of the concept of *ume* in *Idu*, one is dumb-struck by the tragedy that strikes in the household of the admirably successful couple, Adiewere and Idu, who literally have 'everything going for them' - a child and a new one expected, successful businesses flourishing in Ugwuta and beyond, supportive work for the extended family/community – when Adiewere dies unexpectedly. Idu is shocked and devastated after the death

---

conducted here with the other variant.

[160]See M.M. Mahood, *The Colonial Encounter* (London: Rex Collins, 1977), pp. 37 - 64.

[161]Achebe, *African Trilogy*, p. 457.

[162]Mahood, *The Colonial Encounter*, pp. 63 - 64.

and does not recover from her grief as she dies a month after Adiewere. For Nwapa, Idu's death ensures that this tragedy plays itself out and this is profoundly intelligible in the context of *ume* and therefore not an outlandish artistic device. Nwapa also works through the love construct in *ume* as it applies to Adiewere and Idu.

A review of the text shows that Adiewere does not invoke the love that he has for Idu and thus entreat her to 'accompany him' in death so that they can continue to share their love beyond this life. This is the most dramatic expression of love for Idu that Adiewere displays, i.e. not insisting that the yet-unprepared Idu should die with him. Idu's response hauntingly reflects on the 'selflessness' of Adiewere's gesture but she refuses to accept it: 'Weep for what? Weep for Adiewere? That is not what we agreed on. He has cheated me. We did not agree that this will happen ... I am going with him ... I am going with him.'[163] Yet, by 'willing to die' in response to Adiewere's death, Idu indeed acknowledges the 'selflessness' of the husband's love for her ('I am coming to meet you there, and we shall continue our lives there'[164]). The couple's engagement in this intricate dynamics of love and death is not played out in a restricted space of husband and wife but impinges overwhelmingly on the family, especially the extended family/community or the society given the individual reference and responsibility to the latter as we have repeatedly shown in this study. For Nwapa, also as we have demonstrated in this study, motherhood is the foundational basis of Igbo societal existence. It follows therefore from this premise, and herein lies the crucial contribution that Nwapa is making on our understanding of *ume*, that even on such an emotional and very personalised subject as love and loving, the decisions and challenges that individuals or couples take impact strategically on society. It is therefore imperative that society always strengthens the connecting links or chords that bind members together to respond to or cope or sustain the consequences that make up the spectrum of such individual decisions. It is precisely because of this that Idu maintained unwavering criticism of Ishiodu's laziness which she correctly felt was a weak link in the operation of their extended family. Nwapa is therefore alerting society that it must ever be prepared *in advance* to take up the responsibility, especially as regards motherhood in all its ramifications, to preserve its essential interests even in the event of *ume* striking and affecting its most illustrious and successful. In that event, society would be in the position

---

[163]*Idu*, p. 210.
[164]Ibid.

to take over the responsibilities bequeathed by the dead with the pain but dignity that precede Idu's funeral: 'She has kept her word. She has followed her husband to the land of the dead. Come let's prepare her properly for the journey.'[165]

---

[165]Ibid., p. 218.

5

Transition: the Biafra war

War is a terrible thing. It does not end when the last bomb is dropped nor when the air raids cease and the mangled bodies of civilians and soldiers alike no longer present a common sight. War does not end when the dusk-to-dawn curfews are lifted and the roadblocks are dismantled, nor does it end when orphanages are thrown open to well-meaning citizens and thousands begin the heart-wrenching task of locating relatives and friends. No, war goes on well beyond this point in time. Indeed this is a different kind of war. It is a war of recovery. It shifts from the battlefield of physical violence manifesting as total mayhem to the battlefield of emotional violence in a long and tortuous effort to recover self, dignity, humanity, and to lay the pain and the loss to rest. It takes courage and strength of purpose, conviction and support of the kind difficult to conceive or acutalise. It is inconceivable that a people are ever able to fully recover from war once they have been touched by it. Rather it is a degree of recovery that is attained, and this is in direct proportion to one's level of preparedness (spiritually, culturally and emotionally) before one encounters this tragedy. But this, in itself, is surely a contradiction - for how is one ever prepared for war? ... Flora Nwapa focuses variously on these themes of war in the following publications: *Never Again*, a novel, and *Wives at War and Other Stories* and *This is Lagos and Other stories*,[1] both of which are collections of short stories. The war that Nwapa writes about is of course the Biafra War which still retains the haunting reference as Africa's most brutal armed conflict which cost the lives of 2.5 million people. In addition to the three texts above, Nwapa contributes a story to Chinua Achebe et al, *The Insider: Stories of War and Peace from Nigeria*.[2] Her contribution, 'The Campaigner,'[3] is not strictly

---

[1] Flora Nwapa, *Wives at War and Other Stories* (Enugu: Tana, 1980).
[2] Chinua Achebe et al, *The Insider: Stories of War and Peace from Nigeria* (Enugu: Nwankwo-Ifejika, 1971).
[3] 'The Campaigner,' in ibid., pp. 73 - 88.

about the war but instead provides some acute insight into the grave political situation in Nigeria immediately preceding the conflict. In this chapter, we shall examine Nwapa's writings on the Biafra War vis à vis three other literary representations of the war: Buchi Emecheta, *Destination Biafra,*[4] the only other African woman novelist on the war; Isidore Okpewho's *The Last Duty,*[5] a novel whose principal and most influential character is a woman, and Chinua Achebe's 'Girls at War'[6] which again has, as the central theme, the impact of the war on young women.

Prior to the outbreak of the war in July 1967, there was a series of massacres of Igbo people in the northern region and elsewhere in Nigeria in May - September 1966 following a military coup d'etat in January 1966 that overthrew the post-independence civilian government. By October, the massacres had taken a toll of 80,000 - 100,000 killed.[7] Two million surviving Igbo had also returned to the eastern homeland from the rest of the country. Igboland, with its population of 12 million then (current population: 30 million), has the second highest population density in Africa after the Nile valley. It was to this population that the desperately traumatised survivors of the northern massacres returned. The resettlement implications for the administration of General Odumegwu Ojukwu's government were enormous. It is testament to the remarkable nature of Igbo, indeed African, extended family system that the welfare needs of these refugees were absorbed, with *no* external aid whatsoever - not even from the central Nigerian government. With the return of the refugees, many of whom were professionals, the pressure on the Ojukwu government to secede from Nigeria as a result of the pogrom was unrelenting. Christopher Okigbo, the renowned poet, not only underscored the urgency of the public demand for the declaration of Igbo independence from Nigeria, but the power and the role of 'ordinary' women to influence events in their society when he stated in a major rally: 'If Ojukwu does not declare secession, we will organise twenty thousand market women to lynch him.'[8] On 30 May 1967, almost one full year to the day since the Igbo massacres in the north began, the Igbo declared themselves independent of the Nigerian Federation under the

---

[4]Buchi Emecheta, *Destination Biafra* (London: Allison & Busby, 1982).
[5]Isidore Okpewho, *The Last Duty* (London: Longman, 1976).
[6]Chinua Achebe, 'Girls at War,' in Achebe, *Girls at War and Other Stories* (London: Heinemann Educational Books, 1972), pp. 98 - 118.
[7]Ekwe-Ekwe, *Conflict and Intervention in Africa*, p. 12.
[8]Quoted in Billy Dudley, *Instability and Political Order*, (Ibadan: Ibadan University, 1973), p. 177.

name of the republic of Biafra. Five weeks later, the federal government declared war on Biafra. The Biafra War lasted for 30 months. The federal government received massive military aid from most of Europe, especially Britain and the Soviet Union, while Biafra recieved little more than humanitarian sympathy from the international community except the diplomatic recognition accorded it by Tanzania, Zambia, Côte d'Ivoire and Gabon. By the end of the conflict 2.5 million Biafrans were dead, the overwhelming number of them through starvation.

It is to this nightmare that Nwapa turns her attention in her writing of the period. Once again Nwapa focuses very specifically on the role of motherhood, including 'communal motherhood,' during a time of heightened emergency in the lives of her people. In addition to examining this theme we shall assess how the other key supportive and enabling roles of women in society that we have discussed elsewhere in this study (economic, political, spiritual) feature during this period of war. We shall also use these same criteria in our comparative discussion of the other 'war literature' mentioned above, namely those by Emecheta, Okpewho and Achebe. It should be stressed right from the outset that it is difficult to draw comparisons and contrasts between Nwapa's work on Biafra with either Okpewho's or Emecheta's for a very specific reason. Both latter novels do not strictly fall within the theatre of the war itself. With the exception of Achebe's 'Girls at War' which like Nwapa's contributions, clearly deals with aspects of the war, Okpewho's and Emecheta's both take place outside the specific realm of the war. Okpewho's *The Last Duty* gives insight into the impact of the war on the lives of key characters from a Nigerian village located near the Biafran frontier, while Emecheta's *Destination Biafra* focuses on the political environment immediately preceding and surrounding the war, without providing the reader with a real sense of what it was to live with the war in Biafra on a day-to-day basis.

Economics

Nwapa uses the three Biafra War-focused stories in *Wives at War and Other Stories* ('Wives at War,' 'Daddy Don't Strike the Match' and 'A Certain Death') and *Never Again* as the backdrop to portray and critically evaluate the role of women in the mobilisation and general sustenance of the war effort, confirming in reality the burgeoning power and influence of women in the new republic to which Okigbo had alluded in the quote above. In 'Wives at War,' the dramatic confrontation between a delegation representing three leading

Biafran women's organisations and the Biafran foreign minister over a question of women's representation in a major diplomatic mission abroad is a graphic reminder of this role. The women are upset that in this delegation supposedly sent to London at the request of Queen Elizabeth to discuss her country's support for federal Nigeria in the war, the Biafran government has not consulted with the leaderships of the women's organisations but has instead sent an 'unknown group of women,'[9] handpicked by officials, to represent the interests of Biafran women. Clearly, the authentic leaders of the women's organisations feel that they should be the ones to convey to the British head of state the strong feelings in Biafra about the British intervention in the war: 'The war would have ended long ago but for the British, who are supplying arms to Nigeria. If it had been between us and Nigeria, the war would have ended ages ago. The British, they are causing all these troubles. You wait until we win. We will deal with the British.'[10] Apart from the opportunity to highlight the role of women generally in the war including the sphere of diplomacy, Nwapa is also using this incident to hint at the case of nepotism and elitism in decision-making that she detects at this stage in the Biafran struggle. The first spokesperson for the women's delegation is blunt in her protest to the minister:

> Your offence is that you by-passed us. Without the women, the Nigerian vandals would have overrun Biafra; without the women, our gallant Biafran soldiers would have died of hunger in the war fronts. Without the women, the Biafran Red Cross would have collapsed. It was my organisation that organised the kitchens and transport for the Biafran forces. You men went to the office every day doing nothing, busy but doing nothing.[11]

A second spokesperson is no less blunt, reminding the minister that women supported the Biafran resistance right from the outset:

> Right from the word go, we organised the women for a real fight. We asked for guns to fight the enemy ... Did not women and girls fight in Vietnam? ... We knew Nigeria would fight us, so we must be prepared. Now after all we did ... you had the impudence to send an unknown handful of women to represent Biafran women. It is most unfair. I have

---

[9]'Wives at War,' p. 12.
[10]*Never Again*, p. 19.
[11]'Wives at War,' p. 13.

never seen anything like this before...[12]

The foreign secretary, as indeed any senior Biafran official, is well aware of the crucial role being played by women in food procurement and is undoubtedly conscious of not alienating women as the resistance intensifies. He emphatically denies the allegation of the mission to England: 'I swear by my mother that the Biafran government received no such request from ... the Queen or from any other prominent woman in the world. What you heard is absolutely untrue.'[13] In the end, the women leave the foreign ministry apparently reassured. The minister is obviously sensitive to the potential implications in Biafra of the charges made by the women especially on the subject of nepotism in the new republic which Biafran propaganda often stresses is a major vice in the Nigerain federation. It is a subject that also attracts the attention of Eddie Iroh in his *Forty-Eight Guns for the General* where he is critical of the preferential treatment in the allocation of essential goods and services enjoyed by a European combat brigade that is recruited to fight for Biafra at a time when Biafrans themselves, combatants and non-combatants alike, have ever diminishing access to these facilities. This brigade, notes Colonel Chumah, the brave Biafran field commander, takes few risks and is generally reluctant to fight despite its evident privileges in the republic.[14] Instead, '[it is our people who are] fighting for our lives, for our parents, for our new nation.'[15] In the same breath, S.O. Mezu's *Behind the Rising Sun*,[16] is a stinging attack on the activity of Biafran diplomats (based in Europe) responsible for the purchase of arms for the resistance. The ostentatious life style of the diplomats, ever jetting around the world, is in stark contrast to the scarcity, frugality and deprivation back in Biafra. But, even more seriously, the weapons being purchased by the group rarely arrive in Biafra when they are urgently needed but are diverted to other destinations by the web of tricksters involved in the hazards of the clandestine arms trade. Such growing criticism of nepotism and ineptitude involving some public officials as the war intensified soon compelled the Biafran leadership to publish the popular Ahiara Declaration, a declaration of citizenship rights, ethics and responsibility overseeing holders of public office in the new republic.

---

[12]Ibid., p. 14.
[13]Ibid., p. 15
[14]Eddie Iroh, *Forty-Eight Guns for the General* (London: Heinemann, 1972), p. 13
[15]Ibid., p. 69
[16]S. O. Mezu, *Behind the Rising Sun* (London: Heinemann, 1972).

The strategic and prominent role played by women in buying food and other essential 'survival items' for Biafra from across Nigerian frontlines in either Nigerian territory proper or from occupied parts of Biafra during the war has been studied in a number of historical studies on the conflict.[17] The critical economic roles of women in Igboland which we see in *Idu* and *Efuru* are once again made evident in 'Wives at War' and *Never Again*. Thus, even in times of societal upheaval and acute emergency, as one of the spokespersons of the women's organisation states above, or as Kate, the heroine and principal character, reminds us in *Never Again* ('Some of [the women] cooked for the soldiers, others traded with the enemy on the borders'[18]), women are centrally involved in the economic life of the nation. In Biafra, this economic activity is called *afia atak*, or 'attack trade' - an allusion to the immense danger surrounding this enterprise.

It should be recalled that as part of the federal strategy at the early phases of the war to limit the possibilities of a protracted Biafran resistance, it attacked and captured the prinicipal food producing provinces of Biafra. This created the serious food shortages in Biafra that would come to be associated with the conflict world-wide. Besides international relief supplies to aid the refugees displaced by the fighting, Biafra made strenuous efforts to procure food for its population locally through two methods. First, bands of traders regularly crossed the federal lines into Nigerian territory (hence, 'attack trade') to buy food and other essentials for sale in Biafra. Secondly, several farmers who had abandoned their farms at the advance of the Nigerian army often re-crossed the federal lines to return to work their farms (in occupied territories), albeit clandestinely, and sell their harvested produce back in Biafra. A significant proportion of these extremely brave cross-border traders were women. As a result of the obvious harzards associated with these trips across Nigerian lines, elderly women, or young women or indeed men disguised as elderly women, were most frequently involved in these operations. It has been estimated that without the steady stream of these 'food couriers' throughout most of the 30-month duration of the war, the horrendous extent of the starvation-related deaths quoted above would have been worse.

Never Again is a moving narrative of the attempts at survival of an entire community of family and friends in the face of war-time realities. It is set in Ugwuta (the Biafra lake-side town, which is also the site of both *Efuru* and *Idu*)

---

[17]See, for instance, Herbert Ekwe-Ekwe, *The Biafra War, Nigeria and the Aftermath* (Lewiston & Lampeter: Mellen, 1990), pp. 87 - 89.

[18]*Never Again*, p. 16.

which is captured by Nigeria but re-taken by the Biafrans just 24 hours later. The story revolves around Kate and her husband Chudi, their family, and friends. It is powerfully vivid in its portrayal of the love, support and trust as well as the fears, denials, the disillusionment and betrayal that such environments give rise to. It focuses distinctly on the central role played by women in both organising and firmly supporting the family in the face of the emergency of war. Kate is strong, very practical and well organised, with the sole aim of seeing her family survive the war. As Ugwuta is threatened, Kate is preparing for the evacuation of the town in keeping with the Biafran strategy of moving the bulk of their civilian population away from a town threatened by the Nigerian advance. The people of Ugwuta would soon embark on what Cyprian Ekwensi has described in his own Biafra War novel, *Survive the Peace*, as the 'march of the thousands': 'it was as if this was happening in another world. Refugees were marching three deep, thousands and thousands of them.'[19]

The weariness of war, the mounting casualties, the abandonment of invaluable property as yet another town is evacuated, and the threat of starvation are now contributing to the immense feeling of uncertainty for the future as the women of Ugwuta contemplate a new place of refuge away from their beloved land. Kate retrieves her highly prized pieces of quality fabric and jewellery (coral beads, gold trinkets, stacks of wrappa with intricate embroidery) which she has owned virtually throughout life and is prepared to 'sell them' if necessary 'to buy food.'[20] 'I was determined not to see my children suffer. I would sell all I had to feed them if I had to.'[21] Obviously, there is a deep sense of anguish as she reflects on the political situation since the beginning of the Igbo massacres in Nigeria: 'I have never known hunger all my life ... No, the Nigerians should not have fought us. We had left Lagos for them. They should have left us in peace in our new found Biafra.'[22] As the authorial voice reflects in Chukwuemeka Ike's *Sunset at Dawn*, the quest for survival is uppermost in everybody's consideration, perhaps the most discernible facet of the philosophy of the resistance presently.[23] The Woman of the Lake which features prominently in both *Efuru* and *Idu* is once again placed at the centre of Ugwuta's spiritual life as the town braces itself for an imminent military attack. There is confidence that Ugwuta will be protected from the invasion by

---

[19]Cyprian Ekwensi, *Survive the Peace* (London: Heinemann, 1976), p. 23.
[20]*Never Again*, p. 49.
[21]Ibid., p. 27.
[22]Ibid., pp. 49 - 50.
[23]Chukwuemeka Ike, *Sunset at Dawn* (London: Fontana, 1976), p. 16.

uhamiri, the lake goddess: 'The Woman of the Lake would not allow it. She had never allowed the conquest of Ugwuta by water or by land or by air.'[24] In order to ensure that Ugwuta does not fall to the enemy, a *dibia* (a diviner, a seer) is brought in to offer the appropriate sacrifices, including a white ram. The commander of the Biafran forces defending Ugwuta shares in the belief of the power of *uhamiri*. Kate herself is hopeful that the sacrifices will ensure a positive respnse from a benevolent goddess because the consequences of the fall and possible occupation would be devastating: 'If Ugwuta could be threatened, then that was the end not only of the war, but of the world.'[25] Ugwuta is indeed attacked by the Nigerians and is successfully defended by the Biafrans - an outcome that is attributed to none other than *uhamiri*. The quest for survival beyond the successes of Ugwuta's defence also projects into the future concerns of all the survivors of the resistance as the authorial voice in *Sunset at Dawn* solemnly reflects after the formal end of hostilities in January 1970: 'No sign of the Biafra Sun. Not even at noon. Hibernating, like a migratory bird? Gone with the soul of Biafra? Or just Disappeared...'[26] Thirty years later, in the year 2000, it appears that the 'hibernating' Sun is breaking through the clouds: the Igbo have formally demanded the payment of 8.7 trillion naira (approximately $US9 billion) from the Nigerian state as reparations for the death of 2.5 million Igbo people killed in the Biafra War and the preceding massacres in northern Nigeria, and the Movement for the Actualisation of the Sovereign State of Biafra (MASSOB), its renaissance cultural organisation, give notice of their intention to re-establish the Biafran Republic.[27]

Kate's determination to survive the war with members of her family strikes a familiar resonance with the preoccupation of Mr Okeke and his wife Ndidi in 'Daddy Don't Strike the Match' (*Wives at War*). Mr Okeke is a dedicated and brilliant Biafran scientist involved in constructing home-made weapons for Biafra as the resistance finds arms importation both costly and difficult to procure. Ndidi on the other hand strives to maintain a semblance of a rapidly-receding family lifestyle, including a degree of both mental and physical security. She and her family are part of the Igbo 'returnees' from the Nigerian federation. They have, until lately, been domiciled in Kano, northern Nigeria, where Ndidi is a school teacher. In a quick reminder of *Efuru* and *Idu*, she is

---

[24]*Never Again*, p. 7.
[25]Ibid.
[26]Ike, *Sunset at Dawn*, p. 9.
[27]*New Events* (Lagos), 28 December 1999, *The Hallmark* (Lagos), 29 December 1999; *Body & Soul* (Lagos), 9 January 2000.

another successful and independent woman whose 'husband did not control her finances. Whatever she earned she spent on herself and her children.[28] Just prior to the onset of the Igbo massacres, Ndidi is alerted by an informed European friend of the impending pogrom. She is strongly advised to return to Igboland at once with her family for their safety. Ndidi and her husband take the warning seriously and plan to leave for the east to escape the massacres. In the meantime, Ndidi transfers £2000 from her savings in her bank in Kano to Enugu to help with the family re-location. Like Kate, Ndidi is determined to sell her five pieces of prized *abada* material to feed her children should the need arise.[29] Ifeoma, the youngest of the Okeke children, is a highly intuitive and spiritual child who foretells an impending accident in her father's laboratory.[30] Sadly, her warning is not taken seriously and a tragic accident which claims her father's life occurs just at the time Mr Okeke successfully achieves a scientific breakthrough in his weapons development programme.[31]

Unlike the Okekes, Ebo and Bisi, the 'returnee' couple in 'Wives at War' whose home used to be Lagos prior to the Igbo massacres, have a harder task in their resettlement effort in Biafra. Here, there is the absence of the foresightedness in financial management similar to Ndidi's. Besides the financial consideration, it is clear however that Bisi, who is Yoruba, finds resettlement in Biafra onerous because of her unfamiliarity with the new cultural environment, not to mention the prevailing war conditions. Bisi soon suffers a mental collapse and is sent abroad for recovery, thanks to the position of Ebo who now works in the Biafran military intelligence. For Nwapa, the pre-war marriage in Lagos of Ebo, an Igbo, and Bisi (a Yoruba), is a potent symbolism of the immense potential and possibilities of a successful federation incorporating Nigeria's several nations and nationalities: 'The marriage was blessed by three sons in quick succession. Bisi was a devoted wife ... Ebo was also a good husband who did all in his power to see that his family was well provided for.'[32] The Igbo massacres and its interconnectedness with Bisi's inability to adjust to the social conditions of war-time Biafra and her mental collapse amount to the dramatic collapse of this symbolical alliance. A similar case of the emergence and collapse of the symbolical 'unity' in the Nigerian multinational state underscores the otherwise troubled plot of Kole Omotoso's

---

[28]'Daddy Don't Strike the Match,' p. 18.
[29]Ibid., p. 19.
[30]Ibid., p. 28.
[31]Ibid., pp. 29 - 30.
[32]'Wives at War,' p. 1

The Combat. In this case, the symbol of 'unity' is a child named Isaac whose father, Ojo Dada, has a friend called Chuku Dede. Both Dada and Dede are close friends who call each other 'brother and friend'. One day, though, Dede runs over Isaac with his car. But in what is obviously a serious weakness in the novel's plot, it is not evident why Dede shows no remorse for the tragedy, not even to Dada, his friend, except of course Omotoso could be hinting, and in that case acceding to an important Biafra political position during the conflict that those in Nigeria who destroyed the basis of 'unity' in the federation cared very little for the character of this state in the first place.[33] Dada insists that his friend takes responsibility for the murder of Isaac: 'You must apologize for it or else I am not going to live in the same house with you ... Or else you must accept my challenge to a single combat.'[34] Dede refuses to show any remorse and Dada is left with no other course of action than to challenge him to a combat. The murder of Isaac symbolises the Igbo massacres and therefore the death of the Nigerian federation while the Dede-Dada combat is a reference to the raging Biafra War.

Political

In 'A Soldier Returns Home' and 'My Soldier Brother,' two stories in *This is Lagos and Other Stories*, Nwapa focuses on the effect of the (1966) massacres of Igbo military officers in the Nigerian army. The July coup is essentially an opportunity for the organisers of the massacres to extend the killing fields of the 3-month old mayhem within the civilian population to murder hundreds of Igbo officers across the country's military bases. 'A Soldier Returns Home' charts the journey of Okay (an Igbo military officer) from his base in Kaduna (northern Nigeria) back to Igboland after he is warned of the impending massacre by his Hausa driver. Okay embarks on this journey on a goods train driven by Mr Okoye, an Igbo who is also escaping from the pogrom. In this story Nwapa raises the absurd nature of the tragedy of the Hausa-Fulani attacks on the Igbo. Long-term friendships, associations and partnerships suddenly seemed to count for very little, giving way to a deep-seated rage, resentment and hatred in the Hausa for their Igbo sisters and brothers. Mr Okoye desperately wishes to find out, but without sucess, those factors that could have turned

---

[33]See, for instance, Ekwe-Ekwe, *The Biafra War, Nigeria and the Aftermath*, pp. 119 - 125.
[34]Kole Omotoso, *The Combat* (London: Heinemann, 1972), p. 15.

neighbours against one another: 'It couldn't be the people I knew so well, not the people whom I had lived with all those years were guilty of the murder, arson, rape. Not them, I kept telling my wife.'[35] Yet, it is a Hausa who is responsible for alerting Okay of the impending danger, enabling the latter to embark on his present flight to safety! Even though the informer displays an extraordinary act of courage and love in the process, Nwapa is in effect alluding to the premeditated planning that must have gone into the execution of the pogrom.

Such a state of affairs however contains the very contradictory characteristics which ironically create the opportunities for those Igbo who depart the north early enough, just prior to the outset of the tragedy. This is why both the driver (here) and Ndidi's friend (the Kano-based European in 'Daddy, Don't Strike the Match') are aware of the mayhem beforehand and accordingly inform their friends. Equally, in 'My Soldier Brother,' rumours of the impending massacres in Lagos alert Adiewere, an apparent reincarnate of the much-admired Adiewere in *Idu* and now a student at the University of Lagos, to flee Lagos for Biafra where he joins the resistance and is mortally wounded. The narrator of the story, Adiewere's younger brother, follows in his much loved brother's footsteps and is determined to 'get ten heads of the enemy before they got [him].'[36] Nwapa here addresses the waste of human life, and especially the innocent, young, and non-implicated life. First, Adiewere dies, and the odds against his younger brother staying alive are indeed enormous. It is ironic that this opposition to such wanton loss is voiced through Monica, the family aunt, known and disliked by the family for her gossip and trouble-making. A character much like Onyemuru in *Idu*, she is given her due respect as an elderly aunt of the family and tolerated. It is Monica who in her grief over the loss of Adiewere (her nephew), raises perhaps the most important theme of Nwapa's contribution to the Biafra War literature - the questioning of the justification for such human loss, the importance of the cause notwithstanding. In response to a sympathiser who attempts to comfort Adiewere's father by pointing out the fact that 'Adiewere died an honourable death... [so] that you and I and all of us here might live,'[37] Monica counters: 'I am tired of people coming here and talking rubbish. What death is honourable? Death is death. A good and intelligent boy died and [they] say he died honourably. The sooner

---

[35]'A Soldier Returns Home', p. 100.
[36]'My Soldier Brother,' p. 117.
[37]Ibid., p. 116.

they stop talking of honourable death, the better.'[38] The silence which greets this outburst is indicative of one of two things. Either Monica touches a sympathetic but mute cord of assent among the mourners, or she has been completely ignored and side-lined for her 'distasteful' intervention. These dual possibilities raise the contradiction Nwapa is keen to convey - the unacceptability of the brutality of an imposed hegemonic order on any humanity by others and the unacceptability of war as the all too often readily-adopted means of resistance or liberation from this situation. In *Never Again*, she delivers her most incantatory statement on the subject:

> Why, we were all brothers [and sisters], we were all colleagues, all friends, all contemporaries; then without warning, they began to shoot, without warning, they began to loot and rape and to desecrate and more, to lie, to lie against one another. What was secret was proclaimed on the house tops. What was holy was desecrated and abused. NEVER AGAIN.[39]

The political role of women in Nwapa's writings on the Biafra War highlights another shift in Igbo women's reference points from traditional to the more recently created infrastructures of the contemporary state. The historical role of Igbo women both as initiators or champions of political/societal change, particularly in crises times as illustrated through Nwapa's varied characters, has become somewhat muted and the powers of its supportive political structures decidely diminished. We have illustrated from the historical evidence presented in earlier chapters of this study that those powerful women's groups would have been involved not only in those decisions about what roles and activities to participate in with regard to the war effort itself, but also in the decision to embark on war in the first place, in a manner similar to the roles played by their forebears. It is indeed a testament to the greatly eroded power of these traditional structures that their presence was only quite marginally demonstrated in the former. To begin with it is significant that the Biafra War cabinet itself did not have one female member nor an adviser of any category or capacity - not even for the perfunctory women affairs! 'Wives at War' provide illuminating insight in this regard. Dignified and influential women's indigenous institutions such as the *omu* or the *umu ada* societies do not feature in any of

---

[38]Ibid., p. 117.
[39]*Never Again*, p. 70.

these stories. They have now been replaced by nondescript groups such as the Busy Bee Club (B.B.C).[40] The reflections of Biafra's foreign secretary (who is male) on women's groups during that confrontation in 'Wives at War' is a case in point: 'Why could not the women organise themselves in one body and have just one leader? Why must every one of them want to lead? In this world there [are] leaders as well as followers. But here in Biafra each one of them [wants to] form her own group...'[41] These remarks are a pointer to a society operating from a philosophy in direct contradiction to its own well-established cultural world-view. Igbo society as a whole, noted for its autonomous and decentring village political authorities is structured, politically, along extremely democratic lines.[42]

It is therefore sadly indicative of the distortions and contradictions that have occurred within Igboland that a prominent member of the administration of a war cabinet (at war, ironically, because of the sustained Igbo rejection of hegemonic domination of others) wonders why there is not one single women's group, with clearly defined leaders and followers. The stated 'fractious nature' of the relationship within the (existing) Biafran women's organsiations[43] clearly attests to the fact that the philosophical world-view of the Igbo, defined for generations by a complementarity of social existence, has been displaced by a philosphy that is based on competition and an intolerance for that which is different or indeed reflects a diversity of opinion. The Igbo philosophical world-view celebrated in both *Idu* and *Efuru* clearly appears to have become subverted. The critical remark here stems not from a desire to minimise the very valuable work undertaken by groups such as B.B.C. during the Biafra War, but rather to highlight the underutilisation and marginalisation of women's talents as well as their own created organisations in Africa in the wake of the European post-conquest era.It is to highlight the tragedy of Africa which, in the decades following the restoration of independence, failed to reconfigure its structures to adapt to its use those desirable currents and processes of societal change and human progress while retaining its own organically-evolved and authentic culturally-rooted references. It is to highlight also the failings of political, economic and educational systems that have served more to create chasms and strictures in society rather than to inform, uplift and build on those structures that enhance the greater understanding and cooperation among peoples in a

---

[40]See 'Wives at War,' p. 12.
[41]Ibid., p. 11.
[42]See ch. 2 of this study.
[43]'Wives at War,' pp. 11 - 13.

multinational state.

Just as in 'Wives at War' where Nwapa uses part of the plot of the story of the marriage between Ebo, the Igbo and Bisi, the Yoruba, as a symbolism to interrogate the success or otherwise of the construction of a successful multinational state, Isidore Okpewho's *The Last Duty* similarly pursues this theme but here the plot is situated in Nigeria rather than Biafra, and the sexes of the leading protagonists are reversed: the woman Aku, is Igbo and she is married to Oshevire, an Ijo from the west Niger delta (which is part of Nigeria) where they both live in the town of Urukpe with Oghenovo, their 5-year old son. As the 1966 Igbo massacres rage elsewhere in Nigeria, Aku decides to continue to live with her family in Urukpe rather than return to Igboland across the Niger. She remains steadfast in her decision to remain in Urukpe even after the Nigerian army takes over the administrative control of the town as the Biafra War gets underway, brutally killing several Igbo residents (who like Aku have decided not to flee to Igboland) in the process. Besides this grave emergency, Aku's life in Urukpe is now thrown into even greater danger by the sudden arrest of her husband by the new military authorities. Oshevire is falsely accused by his local business rival, Chief Toje, of being a Biafran collaborator and he is sent to prison for three years. Chief Toje's main motive for falsely implicating his business rival is because 'I felt that Mukoro Oshevire stood in my way.'[44] With Oshevire out of the way, Chief Toje, even though impotent, now wants to seduce Aku. But Aku is not attracted to Chief Toje's sexual attentions even though she benefits from his financial support. Undeterred, Chief Toje piles up the pressure on Aku employing the services of his handicapped newphew. As it stands, to borrow from Kadiatu Sesay's apt observation, '[t]he odds are stacked high against Aku.'[45] Unwanted though the sexual attentions remain, both uncle and nephew manage to activate 'dormant' sexual desires in Aku. Unable to have them fulfilled by the impotent Toje, Aku turns to Odibo who willingly assumes this role. Her relationship with both men leads to a brutal fight over her which leaves both men close to death. Meanwhile, Oshevire is proven innocent of Toje's false allegations of sabotage and is set free. He returns home to learn what has transpired in his absence from Major Ali, the commander of the army unit in Urukpe. He is, predictably, completely distraught and devastated by the 'dishonour brought upon [his]wife -

---

[44]Ibid., p. 11.
[45]Kadiatu Sesay, 'Ekwensi and Okpewho on the Nigerian Civil War,' *African Literature Today*, No. 9. 1978, p. 101.

and on [his] household...'[46] In what can only be described as an act of ablution, Oshevire undertakes to purge both his home (by setting fire to it) and ultimately himself (by setting himself up for certain death at the hands of the occupying soldiers) of this shame. The wife and son who sustained him throughout his period of incarceration are tragically unable to see him through what is clearly this most difficult time. Aku and her son, at the centre of this tragedy, end up widowed and fatherless and her future prospects in Urukpe highly untenable.

Okpewho's portrayal of Aku in particular as well as other characters are thought-provoking. Aku whose Igbo name literally means 'wealth,' could be a reference to the oil-rich, potentially wealthy Biafra. Her perception that she is fully integrated into Urukpe society and her subsequent decision to remain with her husband's/*her* people when all other Igbo people have fled, leaves her terribly exposed and extremely vulnerable. Like Biafra itself, Aku's presence within the 'fold' (Nigeria) is one that is overtly untenable. She is increasingly powerless and unsupported by other members of the 'fold'. Indeed she is viewed with outright hostility from the community as she discovers even when she goes to the market to shop. This is not to suggest that her sisters across the border in Biafra, as depicted in Nwapa's *Never Again* or *Wives at War*, do not experience some difficulties and challenges. On the contrary. In the latter cases however, the women do derive a level of mutual support and empowerment that have evolved out of a *commonality of shared experiences and goals*, especially when one such goal is survival in the wake of Igbo massacres and the on-going war. Aku's honourable decision to remain in Urukpe with her husband and thus 'vindicate the course of justice'[47] ultimately leads to the destruction of all that she cherishes most with major implications for a subsequent generation represented by her son, Oghenove. Ultimately she has no recourse but to leave Urukpe as life has clearly become untenable under prevailing conditions. Just as the collapse of the Ebo-Bisi marriage of multinational/multicultural state symbolism ('Wives at War'), Aku's valiant struggle to ensure that her marriage to Oshevire survives to sustain this symbolism collapses with dreadful consequences for all those around. Just as Bisi departs from Biafra in this last act of signification for a failed enterprise, Aku abandons Nigeria to return to her home in Biafra where her right of belonging would not be a subject for contestation. Interestingly, both Nwapa and Okpewho arrive at the same conclusion on this crucial subject of the 'unity' of the Nigerian federation even

---

[46] Okpewho, *The Last Duty*, p. 237.
[47] Ibid., p. 33.

though each lived on either side of the frontline - Nwapa, in Biafra and Okpewho in Nigeria. In foreclosing all options towards a 'united' Nigeria by making Aku's return to her own homeland inevitable and indeed desirable, Okpewho is no doubt indicating his aversion to the Igbo massacres in Nigeria and the subsequent federal Nigeria military offensive against Biafra.

Yet, for an African woman and mother as Aku is, there remain certain shades of her character which are highly suspect and disturbing. Not only is she coerced into a relationship with a man whom she must know is her husband's business rival, but she becomes sexually involved with this man's nephew and allows the latter to make love to her while her five-year-old son is asleep beside her! Here Okpewho typecasts Aku as being driven by pent-up sexual desire that is kindled by the caresses of a man whose attention, we are repeatedly told, is unwelcome. This is definitely not a characterisation of a woman who abandons her 'principles and trade[s] in sex in order to gain essentially commodities'[48] as Florence Stratton incorrectly asserts. So, if this uncontrolled sexual desire leads Aku to a momentary loss of 'sanity and caution,' she nonetheless continues, following this occasion of indiscretion, to pursue this dual relationship with both uncle and nephew. It could be argued that such behaviour could be attributed to the 'madness of war' during which people become uncoupled from traditional norms and mores and where the quest for survival takes precedence over everything else. Even then, the plot surrounding the rampant sexual encounters between Aku and the uncle and nephew duo with scant regard for her son is voyeuristic, if not nihilistic. It is therefore difficult to accept the authenticity of Aku's character in this very regard, especially in a society where the spiritual/moral as well as physical well-being of the mother and relationship to her child/children is of paramount importance within the family, which in turn has immense consequences for the wider society.[49] Even whilst facing the three-faceted acute crisis in an increasingly hostile society of waiting for the return of a husband detained on trumped-up charges by the military, community rejection, and financial deprivation, an African mother would have still been able to judge that Aku's amazingly lax sexual proclivity in *The Last Duty* is an abomination - against *ani*, the earth goddess! It would be extraordinary if Aku herself is not aware of this. In effect, this is an unsuccessful attempt by Okpewho to project onto the African woman/mother what he, Okpewho, thinks is the *method* to solve a crisis that is indeed serious. Okpewho's failure occurs

---

[48]Stratton, *Contemporary African Literature and the Politics of Gender*, p. 122.
[49]Cf. Ch. 2 and 3.

precisely because in his characterisation, Aku's general behaviour and her response to the challenges in which she finds herself is not informed by the wealth of values which such an African woman would have drawn on - even in a crisis situation. Aku, as the wife of a rich businessman, is not an 'ordinary' person. There is no indication whatsoever in the text that the family has suffered a sudden financial collapse as a result of the detention of her husband by the military, even though it would not be inconceivable that some downturn or stagnation in the family business could occur as a result.

Given her social background which in this case is very similar to Kate (*Never Again*), Ndidi ('Daddy, Don't Strike the Match') and Bisi ('Wives at War'), it is equally inconceivable that Aku would be without some savings or have access to some property or indeed valuables (clothes, jewellery, household luxury items) to sell to provide for food and other essentials for (just) herself and son Oghenove if the need arises as she awaits Oshevire's freedom. Unlike Kate or Ndidi for instance, we do not encounter those very engaging motherly declarations of 'I will not allow my children to starve... I will sell those wrappa if necessary...' or 'I will sell my coral beads... my gold necklace... to ensure that my family survives' or 'I'm sure selling those wedding wrappa will fetch enough money to buy food to survive' etc., etc., from Aku as she contemplates how to overcome her state of deprivations. Besides, it is surprising that Okwpeho does not have in his plot any *nzuko umu nwanyi*, the ubiquitous Igbo womens's organisations found in every conceivable village or town, where Aku would readily appeal to for help to survive the deprivations that constitute her current emergency. No *nzuko umu nwanyi* would allow its member to drift into the kind of desperation that Aku finds herself!

If Okpewho does not explore the rich African cultural heritage that would have ensured that Aku, whose Igbo name means 'wealth' as we have indicated, emerges from the crisis of social depreviation without the humiliation of being sexually violated by Chief Toje and his nephew Odibo, could there be some other message that the author is seeking to convey in this most implausible of plots? In C.L. Innes's essay on the use by some African (and Irish) male writers of the principal woman character in the novel, poem, or play as metaphor for the oppressed occupied/betrayed country or land,[50] she notes the following: (a) the woman character in question is often 'allegorized'[51] as the subjugated country the author is writing about; (b) this central character or a close relation of hers -

---

[50]Innes, 'Virgin Territories and Motherlands,' pp. 1 - 14.
[51]Ibid., p. 11.

her mother or grandmother for instance - is often portrayed as the custodian of the people's culture; (c) this central character may have tried prostitution; (d) this central character 'awaits or seeks (sic) a true male partner to rescue her'[52] and (e) the liberation of this heroine 'depends upon her partner becoming truly a man, taking on his manly responsibilities, and that involves also an acknowledgement of and reconciliation of the women's [heroine] complicity[53] in the prevailing emergency.

A quick interrogation of whether the *Last Duty* fits into this genre of writing shows that it really does not, despite two perspectives of the novel's plot that appear to correspond to or reflect upon Innes's formulation. First, Aku's sexual encounters with Toje and Odibo amount to some form of prostitution, and secondly the resolution of Aku's plight hinges on the release of her husband, Oshivere, from military detention. Whilst Aku is a central character in the sense that her fate invariably impacts on the other leading male characters in the novel, her character is not robustly nor fully developed to depict or acquire a coherent allegorisation of a subjugated, conquered, or betrayed homeland, even though some of her experiences attest to occasional or partial flashes of the Igbo massacres/Biafra. Aku is therefore not a Ramatoulah in Ousmane Sembene's *Xala*[54] for instance nor Wanja in Ngugi wa Thiong'o's *Petals of Blood*[55] nor indeed Wariinga in Ngugi's *Devil on the Cross*.[56] The main symbolism of her character in *The Last Duty* only exists in her *relation* to Oshivere, namely the possibilities of the viability of the multinational Nigerian state which is foregrounded by their marriage. In that context, the character shares the same metaphor depicted by the Ebo-Bisi couple in Nwapa's 'Wives at War'. As an Igbo, Aku's social ostracism and sexual humiliation at Urukpe as well as the collapse of her marriage (following the death of her husband soon after his freedom) and departure for Biafra signal the death of the Nigerian federation. Finally, the response of Oshivere to the developing saga after he regains his freedom from military detention is clearly not that of a liberator of his humiliated wife! He learns of the sordid details of what has happened to Aku and son Oghenove during his incarceration and makes no effort to challenge and destroy the agency that created the emergency in the first place - Chief Toje. Neither does he even wish to meet Aku for a crucial opportunity between

---

[52]Ibid.
[53]Ibid.
[54]Ousmane Sembene, *Xala* (London: Heinemannm 1976).
[55]Ngugi wa Thiong'o, *Petals of Blood* (London: Heinemann, 1977).
[56]Ngugi wa Thiong'o, *Devil on the Cross* (London: Heinemann, 1982)

husband and wife to discuss and seek reconciliation after the trauma of such tragic events. Husband, wife and son never meet again as a family. Instead, Oshivere sets the family house on fire. Next he embarks on what is surely a suicidal mission by running past a near-by military check-point without stopping when challenged by the guards. The guards respond by shooting him dead. In the process of embarking on what is clearly an exercise of ablution for the humiliation of his wife and family, Oshivere ends up committing suicide, itself an abomination in African cultural existence.

In the end, as a result of what happens to Aku, this principal woman character in *The Last Duty*, tragedy is visited upon all other male characters around her - Oshivere, her husband, Chief Toje and Odibo. Singularly, she alone is the most influential factor whose fate, particularly in the wake of her sexual violation in the unfolding drama, impacts invariably on all those around her. This is a clear allusion that Okpewho makes to the centrality that the woman/motherhood-principle plays in African societal relations as we have stressed in this study. On this ground at least, we observe some similarity between *The Last Duty* and Chinua Achebe's 'Girls at War'. 'Girls at War' is a story about a presumed loss of ideals, vision and hope that occurs among Biafra's young women as the impact of the Biafra War (including gross internal inequities in access to essential basic goods) begins to be felt, and the instincts of survival, featured so vividly in Nwapa's varied contributions, take precedence over 'the state'. It is a 'presumed loss of ideals' because the moral defeat that seems to have occurred afflicts only the women in 'Girls at War,' leaving the men despairing over 'what a terrible fate to befall a whole generation! The mothers of tomorrow.'[57] Gladys is an idealist young woman who leaves school at the beginning of the Biafra War, wishing to sign up for the militia. She is refuses entry but ends up instead working for the civil defence. Reginald Nwankwo is a senior official with the ministry of defence who has three chance encounters with Gladys. The first occurs at the beginning of the war when Gladys is eager to play a meaningful role in the Biafran cause and defence. He next meets up with her as the war intensifies. She has been recruited to oversee a military checkpoint searching vehicles moving between districts. By the time they meet for the third time, at the height of the war, Nwankwo observes that Gladys's personality has changed drastically. She is no longer the bright-eyed idealistic young woman Nwankwo met on previous occasions. Now she wears a 'high-tinted wig and a very expensive skirt and low-cut blouse. Her shoes,

---

[57]Achebe, 'Girls at War,' p. 114.

obviously from Gabon, must have cost a fortune. In short ... she has to be in the keep of some well-placed gentleman, one of those piling up money out of the war.'[58] The moral decline that is presumed to have occurred solely affects Gladys and women like her. It does not seem to be extended to the men - not even to the 'well-placed gentleman' nor indeed Nwankwo himself who subsequently embarks on a onenight sexual encoutner with Gladys! Here, Nwankwo the principal character, subscribes to the opinions of the European who in a drunken fit storms: '[E]verything here stinks. Even these girls who come here all dolled up and smiling, what are they worth? Don't I know? A head of stockfish, that's all , or one American dollar and they are ready to tumble into bed.'[59] The men with whom these women apparently 'tumble into bed,' remain exonerated. Or, so it seems.

What indeed is Achebe attempting to convey about the war and its moral impact on society through this story? A number of very specific criticisms are made in this story about this newly emerging state for which so much sacrifice has already been made. The sexual licentiousness and corruption of powerful male officials within Biafra and the perpetuation of practices that have familiar registers in the discredited Nigerian federation is here underscored. Achebe never quite makes us privy to the thoughts of Gladys throughout all her interactions with Nwankwo, nor her surname for that matter! This is in contrast to the detailed analysis of the thought processes that occur on the part of Nwankwo in his association with Gladys. But perhaps the attempt is to demonstrate the nondescript nature of Gladys and women like her in the newly emerging nation. In other words the attempt is to demonstrate to the reader the 'superior', patronising, and self-righteous attitudes that are once again being carried over from a dysfunctional Nigeria into a new nation attempting to define, at least philosophically, a different sort of destiny, internal and external interrelationships. That this philosophical goal does not actually translate into behavioural and attitudinal changes in Biafra is apparent in Nwankwo. The absence of an honest and informed discussion about the roles both men and women have played in creating the non-functional societies that define contemporary Africa is testament to Biafra's failure to address this issue. During their second meeting, when Nwankwo is stopped at a road checkpoint by this young and obviously committed woman, he reflects on the possibility that a 'different' sort of African woman is emerging. Yet, it is a reflection that

---

[58]Ibid., pp. 103 - 104.
[59]Ibid., pp. 110 - 111.

is heavily tinged with ridicule for these women and the role they could play in the reconstruction of a new state, belittling and thus reducing this most sacred of women's roles (*i.e. motherhood*) to a travesty of itself. Hence, 'the prime joke of the time among his friends was the contingent of girls from the local secondary school marching behind a banner: WE ARE IMPREGNABLE!'[60]

These reflections of Nwankwo capture, in much the same way as Nwapa depicts the musings of the Biafran foreign secretary in his confrontation with the women's groups, a cynical, disrespectful, condescending and heavily patronising attitude by male public officials towards women. It is significant that such an attitude by male public officials towards women does not appear in Nwapa's earlier works (*Efuru* and *Idu*), nor does the historical and sociological evidence provided earlier on in this study substantiate the presence of such attitudes by the broad sectors of the male population towards women. As we recall in 'Wives at War,' the Biafran foreign secretary is patronising in both speech and attitude during his meeting with a delegation of women of the new republic. The women have come to protest over an allegation that government had sent a team of non-representative women to England to discuss the British military support for Nigeria with Queen Elizabeth. The minister denies the allegation, and then adds, with obvious condescension, 'I'd advise you to go home and continue the good work. Soon we are going to have women guests from abroad.'[61]

This attitude of condescension, no doubt more disguised on the part of the foreign minister than Reginald Nwankwo, is not unnoticed by the women. It is only Nwapa's women, however, who have a response to it: 'You wait until the end of this war. There is going to be another war, the war of women ... When this war has ended we will show you that we are a force to be reckoned with.'[62] In contrast, Achebe's women remain mute in the presence of this barrage of insults on womanhood. The Igbo dual-gender complementarity of relationships and existence (discussed extensively in earlier chapters) has been seriously eroded by the time the Biafra war occurs. It has been argued that Biafra's energies at this time were being directed at responding to the acute emergency of defending its people, their homeland and their right to define and control their own destiny. Consequently, internal contradictions were shelved in the face of such devastating and destructive externalities.[63] While one can easily

---

[60]Ibid., p. 100.
[61]'Wives at War,' p. 15.
[62]Ibid., p. 13
[63]See Ekwe-Ekwe, *The Biafra War, Nigeria and the Aftermath*, especially ch. 5.

concede to the logic of this argument, it nonetheless begs the question, for the attempt to silence the Igbo voice within Nigeria and to deny a humanity its right to self-determination led to the tragic and irreparable loss that resulted from Biafra. The Igbo recognised this 'disequilibrium' and were both outraged and indignant at this violation of their own cultural and social norms of political and social autonomy. It is ironic then that the leaders of this same society, who were by this period all men, were unable to acknowledge the internal as well as external violations of another social norm - gender complementarity. In effect, the violation of the grounding of the woman/motherhood-principle in Biafra was a grave error with incalculable consequences considering the sheer range of crucial decisions that the country's leadership were faced with during such an unprecedented emergency.

Destination Biafra is the only other Biafra-related war novel written by a woman, although unlike Nwapa, Buchi Emecheta, its author, was not actually present in either Nigeria or Biafra during the war itself. *Destination Biafra* revolves around the quest of Debbie Ogedemgbe (Oxford-educated daughter of one of Nigeria's most corrupt and corrupting politicians) to participate fully in the building of a new post-conquest country by joining and using the army as the primary vehicle. The symbolism of a military career, as a male preserve, is not lost on the reader. However, the selection of this particular career as one of the very few options which Debbie sees open to herself, generates considerable grounds for concern if she and her friends symbolise the so-called newly emerging African female. As her mother comments, 'we all want freedom for women, but I doubt we are ready for this type of freedom where young women smoke and carry guns instead of looking after husbands and nursing babies.'[64] That women's roles have never been defined in its totality in Africa as 'looking after husbands and nursing babies,' and that carrying guns and smoking could in any fashion be depicted as liberatory, even symbolically, clearly demonstrates the cultural distortions that both Debbie Ogedemgbe and mother Stella represent. One is here inclined to speculate that Emecheta may have been nodding approvingly to a dominant corpus of 1960s/70s 'development discourses' in western academia which, in responding to the spate of military coups across the Southern World (Latin America, Africa, Asia), stated that the military 'was an agent of modernisation' in these parts of the world.[65]

---

[64] Emecheta, *Destination Biafra*, p. 108.
[65] See for instance, S.E. Finer, *The Man on Horseback* (London: Pall Mall, 1962) and Samuel Huntington, *Political Order in a Changing Society* (New Haven: Yale University, 1968).

It is surprising that it does not appear extraordinarily far-fetched to Emecheta in her plot conception of *Destination Biafra* that Debbie, an officer of the Nigerian military who participates fully in the anti-Igbo could d'etat of the era (see below), cannot be a credible candidate to embark on a diplomatic peace mission to help reconcile the two protagonists of the Biafra War - represented by Abosi, the leader of the Biafran independence movement and Momoh, the military head of state of Nigeria. It is equally naive to anchor Debbie's 'credibility' as a peace envoy on the premise that she is neither 'I[g]bo nor Yoruba nor Hausa, but simply a Nigerian.'[66] The fundamental legalistic subject in contention in the war is that of competing or conflicting notions, desires or allegiances of sovereignties: Nigeria Vs Biafra. In the circumstances it is amazingly foolhardy for anyone to expect a Nigerian, an army officer for that matter, to have succeeded in a journey to Biafra aimed at persuading the leadership to discontinue the independence struggle on the premise that they are neither 'I[g]bo nor Yoruba nor Hausa, but simply a Nigerian.' (Equally, it would have been inconceivable that the Nigerian leadership during that period would have been persuaded of the desire for Biafran independence if an apparent peace envoy from Biafra had arrived in Lagos claiming that he was 'neither Igbo nor Ibibio nor Ijo, but simply a Biafran'!) In a multinational state such as Nigeria, there is no such thing as 'simply a Nigerian' that is *not preceded* by one's primary reference to their constituting nation or nationality in the federation - Angas, Birom, Efik, Gwari, Hausa-Fulani, Ibibio, Igbo, Ijo, Itsekiri, Jukun, Uhrobo, Yoruba, etc, etc. As a result, contrary to Stratton's reading of the situation, Debbie's designation in the novel as someone from the Itsekiri nation 'rather than being Igbo or Yoruba or Hausa' does not confer her with any kind of 'neutrality' over the political issues at stake over Biafra just because the Itsekiri have a relatively small-sized population (about 1.5 million).[67]

Based on their legitimate objective interests, the Itsekiri, as a people, as a nation, supported the Nigerian federation during the conflict. Thousands of them fought against the Biafrans. Besides, the Itsekiri are cousins of the Yoruba, another nation that was in the forefront in the war against Biafra. Furthermore, it should not be forgotten that the Nigerian military officer modelled on Momoh in the novel is indeed Yakubu Gowon who is Angas a nationality in northern Nigeria whose population (about one-half of a million)

---

[66]Emecheta, *Destination Biafra*, p. viii.
[67]Stratton, *Contemporary African Literature and the Politics of Gender*, p. 123.

is even smaller than the Itsekiri's and who were actively involved in the military campaign in Biafra particularly in the infantry regiments. No constitutent nation in Nigeria, 'big' or 'small,' played a *disinterested* role in the Biafra War. On the contrary. The fact that Gowon's preference for the Nigerian federation was not any more endearing to the Biafrans despite his being Angas is indicative of the very marginal relevance of the size of these Nigerian nations and nationalities in deciding whether to support Nigeria or Biafra's sovereignty claims and aspirations.

Primarily, Debbie's mission to Biafra, as we have already hinted, is to convince Abosi to withdraw the declaration of Biafran independence and reintegrate into the Nigerian federation.[68] She embarks on the trip to Biafra starting from Lagos, via Benin, and it is here that she is repeatedly raped by Nigerian soldiers who are convinced that she is a Biafran sympthiser and not a federal soldier as she claims. She ultimately reaches Biafra following several most harrowing experiences that leave her coping with repeated episodes of physical and psychological abuse. In Biafra, Debbie fails to convince Abosi to abandon Biafran independence. Instead, in a twist in the story, she agrees to fly to England to promote the cause of Biafra. She mounts an effective campaign to demonstrate to British public opinion 'the reality of Biafra' and expose the devastating effect of British military intevention in the conflict, a clear reference to the concerns of the Biafran women's organisations in Nwapa's 'Wives at War'. She however decides against Abosi's other request to procure weapons for Biafra and fly these back to the republic aboard a Red Cross emergency relief aircraft. Impressed by her performance, particularly on this score, Momoh recruits Debbie once again to return to Biafra to 'convince' Abosi to renounce Biafran independence or in the alternative assassinate him - blow up his plane, as she indeed unsuccessfully attempts, underscoring the mindset that foregrounds the mindless violence that would haunt the African political scene in subsequent years as Rwanda, Uganda, Sierra Leone and Liberia gravely demonstrate. But with the unexpected collapse of the Biafran resistance and departure of Abosi from the country, Debbie's mission to Biafra is no longer necessary. With the war now over, she decides to remain in Nigeria to participate, yet again, in the 'healing and shaping' of the country's future.

Destination Biafra is perhaps the most troubling and unconvincing piece of writing on the Biafra War. Not only is the lead character quite unrealistic, but the actual interpretation of historical events is often naïve, plainly misleading,

---

[68]Emecheta, *Destination Biafra*, p. 123.

daft, farfetched or just untrue. If assessed solely as an effort at imaginative writing, the outcome is even worse. The plot does not enjoy any sustained sense of purpose nor coherence but relies on a hotchpotch trail of themes and events, often outlandish, often contradictory. If Emecheta's goal is to paint a portrait of utter mayhem to depict the tragedy of the Igbo pogrom and the resultant war, hers appears more irrational a construct than the real events, the horrendous outcome of the latter notwithstanding. Ironically, one needs to understand the Biafra War in order to appreciate the failure of *Destination Biafra* and not the other way round. The contradictory turmoil that bedevils this text begins right at the outset. Debbie Ogedemgbe, the lead character is supposedly highly embarrassed and distressed at her parents ostentatious display of wealth. Stella Ogedemgbe, her mother, makes her money through 10 per cent kickbacks paid to her Swiss account on various contracts entered into with foreign suppliers.[69] The women who inhabit the world of the Ogendemgbes constitute an extremely small minority of leeches who live off their husband's/father's/society's wealth. Theirs is a community of ill-gotten wealth and rampant greed. They are unrecognisable among the independent and hardworking Efurus/Idus of the early Nwapa writings and even the Kates/Ndidis/Bisis of the later Nwapa period despite its emergency of war. Less than 50 years in existence, the Ogedemgbes of the African World are yet an aberration from the (African) norm but no less dangerous for they have earmarked huge estates of the collective national inheritance to which they lay claim.

The Ogedemgbes are a reminder of Chief Mrs Deide (suitably and impressively titled - no doubt, some affiliate of Chief the Honourable M.A. Nanga, M.P. of Chinua Achebe's *A Man of the People*!), the character in Nwapa's 'The Campaigner' which is also set in the context of Nigeria's ostentatious politics of the early 1960s. Chief Mrs Deide is an influential politician, a position she inherits from her late husband. With all the appropriate connections made though marriage, she is well equipped to enter the field of politics defined essentially by duplicity, embezzlement and the trading of sexual favours. Just as we find with the Ogedemgbes, Chief Mrs Deide's world no longer valorises the hard work ethic and industriousness that enrich the world of Efuru and Idu. In this new era of post-conquest Nigeria, devoted and hard work is equated with suffering: '[I]n Nigeria these days, when one worked hard, it was said that one suffered. Hard work meant suffering. Few people worked

---

hard, so those who worked hard, who were compelled to work hard, suffered.'[70] The duplicity is rife and reflective of a widespread incipient greed: 'Money wins elections, only money. Have you tried to buy him over?'[71] and 'Chief Mrs Deide knew he was lying, and that the Hon [Honourable] was lying too. She too lied. None trusted the other. The bigger the lie, the better you got on with party members.'[72] Nothing is sacred anymore, and the concept of an 'act of abomination' that the Efurus and Idus would invoke to sustain responsibility, transparency, and probity in public life no longer exists for Chief Mrs Deide and her cohorts. They will stop at nothing to realise their political goals. They defame, they bribe, and even murder - all without any consideration to societal reference points for accountability and honour. 'Old ways' have given way to the 'new' with economic gain subverting all traditional societal norms that have for generations developed a self-regulating social and spiritual system that has had at its focus the integrity of the individual, family and community. Debbie Ogedemgbe is fully aware of this state of affairs and does not miss any occasion to vocalise her protests. Yet, she herself participates fully in both the display and the consumption of the era with panache:

> That evening at the state banquet the Ogedemgbes as usual surpassed everyone in their turn-out. There was such a big show of wealth, and the women came in the latest lace designs. Stella Ogedemgbe and her newly qualified daughter (Debbie) wore shoes heavily decorated with real gold.[73]

And yet Debbie apologetically and rather naïvely remarks to comments made by Alan Grey, her English boyfriend, about her elegant participation in the independence day celebrations: 'I had no choice ... my father bought [this] car costing almost ten thousand pounds just to drive through that crowd. Oh, I feel so guilty about it all.'[74] Similarly, 'Debbie [feels] like laughing despairingly whenever her mother mention[s] the word "greed". Could she be so blind as not to see that all of them, especially her family, were equally guilty of that greed?'[75] This same woman who vociferously voices her opposition to the greed

---

[70]'The Campaigner,' p. 81.
[71]Ibid., p. 85.
[72]Ibid., p. 84.
[73]Emecheta, *Destination Biafra*, p. 39.
[74]Ibid., p. 40.
[75]Ibid., p. 49.

and corruption of politicians and the system as a whole, continues to partake directly in the spoils through her own lifestyle. She decides to join the army 'to help the Nigerian army - not as a cook or a nurse, but as a true officer.'[76] In spite of the murder of her father by the military during a coup d'etat, Debbie accepts the invitation to enlist from the *same* military. Soon, despite her relative youth and inexperience, she is allowed to lead a surprise arrest and attack on Igbo officers during the course of yet another coup d'etat! She bellows at these officers as she leads her platoon to arrest them: 'Everyone stand up and put your hands on your head!'[77] What gives this 'new breed' of Nigerian woman some pleasure is a sense of power and accomplishment which her position as a military officer gives her over these men. In another occasion, she arrives at the officers' mess and 'scream[s] at the bemused men sitting around at the Ikeja mess ... [her] large eyes sparkled with excitement and fear.'[78] Guilt-ridden that she has been the prime mover in securing the arrests, and subsequently the deaths of these innocent Igbo officers, she nevertheless admits that 'I did enjoy making those men obey me.'[79] Theodora Akachi Ezeigbo is very much enthused by the militarist character of Debbie when she writes: 'Emecheta ... subverts male dominance by making Debbie Ogedemgbe not only an assertive and independent woman but also a soldier.'[80] Yet, it appears that Ezeigbo is not too sure about the militarisation of the feminine because later in the same study, she does a complete volte face by agreeing with the anti-war position vocalised by aunt Monica in Nwapa's 'My Soldier Brother': 'The young officer's [Adiewere] subsequent death justifies her opposition and affirms her perception of soldiering as a dangerous and destructive profession and war as needless and senseless.'[81]

The point remains that power for Debbie and her contemporaries is *control over* men. Little value or importance is attached to womanhood *per se*, motherhood or marriage, nor are these ever defined in terms that do not connote restriction, powerlessness, and drudgery of existence. This is aptly demonstrated when in considering her options for the future Debbie states: 'I would like to stay in the army ... I don't want to go back to civilian life, and don't talk to me

---

[76]Ibid., p. 45.
[77]Ibid., p. 79.
[78]Ibid.
[79]Ibid., p. 93.
[80]Theodora Akachi Ezeigbo, 'Vision and Revision : Flora Nwapa and the Fiction of War,' In Umeh, ed., *Emerging Perspectives of Flora Nwapa*, p. 484.
[81]Ibid., p. 486.

about gettng married. *I'm in no mood to start breeding*[82] (emphasis added). The emergence of this 'modern,' very much culturally alienated African woman is here confirmed, an outcome cheered on exuberantly by Ada Uzoamaka Azodo:'As long as women's primary role and responsibility continue to be wifehood and motherhood, men continue to take advantage of women's biology to oppress them.'[83] In very similar vein, Debbie equates the enormous multifaceted task of motherhood with a single word 'breeding.' This she does in spite of the fact that she has spent days in the presence of strong mothers such as Mrs Madako, mother of three, whose husband has been shot by the Nigerian soldiers; or the young mother Dorothy who takes on the breast-feeding of the orphaned new-born. It is theoretically conceivable that Debbie would 'marvel at the resources of these women'[84] and yet be repelled by their motherhood - *the primary factor that identifies and unifies these women, particularly in an African context.*

Most ironically, the capacity for resourcefulness of traditional African womanhood vis à vis the greatly diminished capacity of this 'newly emerging' African female is not lost on Debbie herself: '[I]t struck her that African women of her age carried babies like this all day and still farmed and cooked; all she had to do was walk, yet she was in such pain.'[85] So, the same Debbie who participates in the anti-Igbo coup in which hundreds of Igbo officers are murdered (part of the ravages of the nation-wide Igbo massacres that would lead to the declaration of Biafran independence) would, in one of the innumerable absurd twists in the plot of the novel, soon lead a delegation (on behalf of the regime formed by officers who carried out this coup) to Biafra in an effort to persuade the leaders of the new republic to abandon their independence from Nigeria. Equally unconvincing is Debbie's relationship with Alan Grey. They are lovers, yet theirs is a stilted formality of speech which revolves around constant accusations by Debbie especially about Alan's role in the conflict but also that of Britain in the staging and manipulation of events leading up to, and fuelling the on-going war. Debbie's anti-imperialist declarations in the circumstance are so farcical that they are best a desperate device by the author to rescue a novel gasping for life and meaning as the end approaches. The rescue however fails to materialise and the Debbie-Alan relationship does not qualify as 'a kind of allegory of the imperialistic rape of her [Debbie's, that is!]

---

[82]Emecheta, *Destination Biafra.*, p. 93.
[83]Azodo, '*Efuru* and *Idu*: Rejecting Women's Subjugation,' p. 177.
[84]Emecheta, *Destination Biafra*, p. 213.
[85]Ibid., p. 191.

country'[86] as Katherine Frank generously asserts. In the meantime, Debbie's rounds of anti-imperialist denunciations are followed by more rituals of love making with Alan as she always appears 'somehow ... to allow Alan to make love to her...'[87]

Destination Biafra is replete with instances of the constant derision of women: 'In other words you think I'm weak because I am a woman'[88]; 'Your family and his were friends for a very long time, and of course you were both at Oxford, although you are a woman'[89]; 'Don't meddle in things bigger than you and don't forget, my dear, that you are a woman'[90]; 'Why, she is only a woman holding a gun.'[91] There is a continuing state of competition, indeed hostility amongst the men and women in Emecheta's novel, graphically stated in the words of Debbie: 'You men make all this mess and then call on us women to clear it up.'[92] It would appear that Emecheta's female characters grow in strength and resourcefulness in direct proportion to the diminution of their husbands. Mrs Madako, wife of one of the murdered Igbo men and mother of four, gives way to an earlier passivity, becoming more assertive after her husband's death, including taking control and calming a 'hysterical companion' whose husband has also been murdered. She observes to her companion: '[I]n the process of letting your husband provide for you, you have become dumb and passive. Go back to being yourself now.'[93] This is a most grotesque interpretation of the emotional and spiritual union created in typical 'familyhood.' Clearly, the empowering reservoir of the African spirituality that Nwapa would invoke in interrogating circumstances of this nature are lacking in Emecheta's.

Indeed *Destination Biafra* makes extremely little reference to the spiritual. Apart from an occasional exclamatory reference to God,[94] the world of the Ogedemgbes is strangely devoid of the acknowledgement of the presence of a spiritual component to their lives. The one clear reference to the presence and power of God is made by Stella Ogedemgbe when Nigerian soldiers capture

---

[86]'Frank, Women Without Men: The Feminist Novel in Africa,' p. 27.
[87]Emecheta, *Destination Biafra*, p. 114.
[88]Ibid., p. 95.
[89]Ibid., p. 123.
[90]Ibid., p. 129.
[91]Ibid.
[92]Ibid., p. 114.
[93]Ibid., pp. 213 - 214.
[94]Ibid., p. 108.

their party on its way to Benin. Having failed in her attempts to stop the rape of a pregnant Igbo woman, she admonishes, 'She is pregnant - don't you people fear God?'[95] The attempt here is of course an appeal to the men to reject this act of abomination which is sure to attract dire repercussions. She is ignored, an act indicative of the degree to which society has strayed from its cultural origins, again most vividly illustrated in Debbie Ogedemgbe herself, epitome of a 'reconstructed' African womanhood! So, in the 'reconstructed' gender relations of the new age, *Destination Biafra* has apparent sympathy with the sentiments expressed in Katherine Frank's 'Women Without Men,' the implication being that women are liberated through the removal, and in this instance, the tragic murder and loss of their spouses. This theme runs thoughout *Destination Biafra* - the competitive, non-complementarity of roles that exist between women and men, with women occupying a most disadvantaged position in all female/male associations. It is a position which sits quite precariously in the face of the established evidence and which is in direct contrast to Nwapa's perspicacious reading of this history. As Nwapa has shown, women continue to demonstrate the strength and central role they play in families *alongside* their men despite the obviously acknowledged erosion of traditional values and women's roles in recent history. Kate (*Never Again*) and Ndidi ('Daddy, Don't Strike the Match') are salient examples of this legacy.

In conclusion, Nwapa's main contribution to the Biafra War literature is three-fold: (a) she condemns the massacres of Igbo people in northern Nigeria and elsewhere in the federation that led to the declaration of Biafran independence, and war; (b) she demonstrates the immense contributions that Igbo women made in the war and (c) she questions the recourse to war to achieve even legitimate causes such as the right of a people to declare their independence. On Biafra and on the subject of conflicts and conflict resolution, Nwapa extends the dominant themes of motherhood central in her writing (mothering, nurturing, up-building) to offer a means of an inclusive politics of participation that values differences while respecting autonomy. In effect, she offers the philosophy underlining the age old norm of dual-sex complementarity as the basis of politics in contemporary Africa - for gender relations as well as co-existence within multinational states.

---

[95]Ibid., p. 133.

6
Post-war

Besides her books for children which we examine later on in this chapter, the remainder of Nwapa's published novels/short stories is contained in three texts - *One is Enough, Women are Different*, and *This is Lagos and Other Stories*. Each of these books signals a decided shift in the power relationship between men and women in society, the beginnings of which we witnessed in her 'war literature'. The focus here is on male-female relationships, in the wake of the dismantling/ breakdown and the disintegration of traditional norms and values. But as we have argued earlier on in this study, the disintegration of social mores, so vividly apparent in several stories contained in these books which we are about to examine, has their origins in the historical period preceding the era of Nwapa's writings on the Biafra War and subsequently. As we have shown, the European conquest of Africa adversely affected the status and role of women in African society. The manifestations of social disequilibrium and distortions, so well captured by Nwapa in her writings, would appear to be the culmination of this phenomenon in society. In this chapter we shall examine the roles played by the women in the post-Biafra War epoch focusing on, in particular, women's economic and political involvement. Nwapa's writing of the period will be compared with Ama Ata Aidoo's novel, *Changes: A Love Story*,[1] which similarly details the conflicting emotions and roles which contemporary African women increasingly face.

Economics

She had made her mark in business. She was a woman to be reckoned with.[2]

---

[1]Ama Ata Aidoo, *Changes: A Love Story* (London: Women's Press, 1993).
[2]*One Is Enough*, p. 1.

No more appropriate quote exists to begin an examination of the economic roles of women depicted by Nwapa during this period. Amaka is the principal character in *One is Enough*. She has been married for six years to Obiora and has supported him both emotionally and financially throughout their marriage ('It was she who bought the car and presented it to her husband ... So Amaka ... went to the bank, withdrew all the money she had and gave it to her husband, and told him to buy a Peugeot 504.'[3]). She has however not been able to become pregnant. In a move supported by his own mother but unbeknown to Amaka, Obiora marries a second wife who bears him two sons. This action is reminiscent of the background to the plot in Mariama Bâ's, *So Long a Letter* where Modou Fall, the husband of Ramatoulaye, the heroine of the novel and mother of their 12 children, decides to marry a second wife in secret with his mother's encouragement. Ramatoulaye is distraught and devastated over the 'betrayal' of her husband, an action she finds inexplicable after 25 years of marriage and 'after having borne twelve children.'[4] Equally, Amaka is devastated over her own experience of 'betrayal' especially coming after she herself had earlier suggested to Obiora, *a la* Efuru and Idu, to marry a new wife and have children as a means of overcoming her assumed state of 'barrenness'. Obiora had during that occasion 'not welcome[d] the idea,'[5] implying that he was not, at least not then, unduly troubled by their childlessness. At the centre of this feeling of 'betrayal' in each couple is of course the action of Modou Fall and Obiora who each embarks on marrying another wife without openly discussing with their wives as is in the tradition.[6] 'All of this has to be negotiated openly [to] win the first wife's consent, observes Rashidah Ismaili Abubakr in her essay on *So Long a Letter*.'[7] Similarly when Amaka confronts Obiora about the news of his secret wife and sons, Amaka's question is poignant enough: 'Why didn't you talk to me about it?'[8] The crucial element of trust between husband and wife/wives which is embedded in the working of the African polygenous marriage system, Nwapa is no doubt stating here, has

---

[3]Ibid., pp. 15 - 16.
[4]Bâ, *So Long a Letter*, p. 39.
[5]*One is Enough*, p. 5.
[6]Cf. Jane Bryce-Okunlola, 'Motherhood as Metaphor for Creativity in Three African Women's Novels: Flora Nwapa, Rebeka Njau and Bessie Head,' in Nasta, ed., *Motherlands*, p. 205.
[7]Rashidah Ismaili Abubakr, 'The Emergence of Mariama Bâ,' in Gurnah, ed., *Essays on African Writing*, p. 26.
[8]*One is Enough*, p. 18.

dissipated considerably since the era of the Efurus and Idus. This is what is at stake here and not Katherine Frank's mistaken assertion of an attack on what she terms the 'intolerable prospect of polygamy'[9] nor Florence Stratton's predictable gripe about the African male: 'Amaka soon discovers that a woman has no "home she [can] call her own" unless she builds a house for herself, and that loving and cherishing a man means subjugation, self-abnegation, and humiliation.'[10] On the contrary, to emphasise the point, Efuru shows that when trust and openness are central in the deliberation on this subject between wife and husband, the wife may not be averse to her husband taking a new wife if the former considers this important in the 'general interest of the family.'[11]

When Obiora and his mother decide it is time to move the second wife into the marital home, Amaka is confronted and informed of this decision by her mother-in-law in the most humiliating manner. The latter's principal reason for Amaka's treatment is that her daughter-in-law is unable to bear her son, and thus the lineage, any children. Additionally, Obiora's mother accuses Amaka of not contributing in any significant degree to the advancement of Obiora either materially or otherwise. This charge is untrue as Amaka runs her own business through which she has purchased the family car and through which she consistently supplements the food budget.[12] In reflecting on the historical evolution, or more appropriately, the degeneration of her people's social norms and mores, Nwapa vividly captures one of the key themes of this research – namely, that historically Igbo women have always been industrious and economically independent, in control both of their own means of production and the manner of its dispersion:

In the good old days, a wife took the praise for her husband's success in life. Alas, it was no longer so, *for the pattern of life was changing ...* Times changed and men began to assert their masculinity over their industrious wives. Men made fun of husbands, at drinking places, whose wives were well-to-do ... And they spat to show their disgust (emphasis added).[13]

The viciousness to which Amaka is subjected in her own home by both

---

[9]Frank, 'Women Without Men,' p. 21.
[10]Stratton, *Contemporary African Literature and the Politics of Gender*, p. 100.
[11]Cf. *Efuru*, p. 50, p. 53.
[12]*One is Enough*, especially ch. 2.
[13]Ibid., p. 17.

husband and mother-in-law causes her to flee her marriage and Onitsha, the not-too-traditional town in eastern Nigeria where she lives,[14] for Lagos. Once again, Katherine Frank mis-judges what exactly is the sociological implication of Amaka's departure. She argues that it amounts to her losing the 'feminine impotence or powerlessness of the traditional African woman.'[15] On the contrary, Amaka leaves her marriage precisely because the Igbo age-old *extensive range of functioning feminine independence guaranteed in marriage* is in serious crisis as a result of an ill-managed 'modernity' of post-conquest Africa that is unsure of its goals and priorities. On this score, Elleke Boehmer is correct to note that 'Nwapa's women characters are concerned about bearing children and being good mothers, yet their lives are not defined solely through their maternal function ... In Igbo society ... it is in trade as much as in marriage and childbirth that women obtain power.'[16]

Thus, in this novel Nwapa not only addresses the issue of women's economic independence, but also deals with the social disequilibrium created in society with regard to women's access (especially for Igbo women following the Biafra War) to these means of economic independence. In Lagos, Amaka is introduced to the corrupt world of 'contract work'. It is this era that sets the scene for Nigeria's subsequent reputation as one of the most corrupt societies in the world. 'Contract work' as in most societies around the world involves the awarding of contracts - in this case government contracts to potential suppliers. In the example of Nigeria however, the contract items may or may not be required as they may have already been supplied. Amaka, for instance, is awarded a contract of half a million naira for building a wall around some military barracks.[17] She arrives at the barracks to assess what is needed for the job only to find that the wall has already been constructed. She discovers, to her astonishment, that the reality is that she will be paid 25 per cent of the contract amount (in spite of the fact that she has done absolutely no work) while the balance is returned to the officer who has awarded the contract! She is merely a conduit for siphoning off public funds by corrupt officials. Another feature of this contract process is that sexual demands/favours often accompany each transaction.

---

[14]What makes Onitsha, the town that has for the past 50 years been the site of west Africa's largest market a 'traditional world' in Katherine Frank's conception (Frank, 'Women Without Men,' p. 21) is frankly beyond comprehension!

[15]Frank, 'Women Without Men,' p. 22.

[16]Boehmer, 'Stories of Women and Mothers,' pp. 17 - 18.

[17]*One is Enough.*, p. 77.

Nwapa presents a most illuminating and sympathetic picture of the economic plight of many young Igbo women in the aftermath of the Biafra War. These women who came from a culture which expected and valorised their women's economic independence were now faced with huge financial responsibilities of supporting families (often in the absence of a father/husband who had been killed in the war) in a society that remained hostile to their people and their cause, but where the abuse of power, money and morality had now become commonplace. That these women exploited these channels in order to survive and contribute to the reconstruction of their society is common knowledge, not only among the Igbo but other nationalities in Nigeria also. Atrocities had been witnessed, abominations had occurred, families and the very basis of family life had all but been destroyed. Indeed the boundaries of acceptable or appropriate behaviour had long since been violated. All that remained was a determination to survive the trauma and rebuild that which could be salvaged. In the Nigeria to which they returned, 'corruption, graft and greed could not have been more blatantly institutionalised in the workings of the country's economy.'[18] Edwin Madunagu, the mathematician and social critic appropriately describes this era as the 'political economy of state robbery.'[19] Since these women had been subjected to levels of abuse and corruption, hitherto unimaginable by them, they now fully exploited the new order of the day! New parameters of 'social interaction' had been drawn up and Biafra's young Lagos women demonstrated themselves extremely capable of adapting to the new rules of the game. Nwapa displays compassionate insight into the motivating factors behind the seeming corruption in these women lives:

> Overnight the girls in Biafra had been let loose. Their villages had been sacked, their relations killed, they had escaped with sisters or brothers and had fallen on the mercy of Biafran officers ... One could not blame the girls. They had to survive. At the end of the war, they had to 'survive the peace'. That meant that they had to start all over again, away from it all. So Lagos was fertile ground: no brother, no sister, no cousin to say to the girls '[e]nough is enough ... Go home to your parents.' For one thing, there was no home to go to. The war took care of that. The war destroyed family life as the girls knew it.[20]

---

[18]Herbert Ekwe-Ekwe, *Issues in Nigerian Politics Since the Fall of the Second Republic* (Lampeter: Mellen, 1991), p. 14.
[19]Quoted in *ibid*.
[20]*One is Enough*, p. 58.

With the help of Ayo, her sister, it is with this 'new generation of [business] women'[21] that Amaka makes contact when she arrives in Lagos. They have formed their own exclusive club which consists of 10 women - six of whom are widows and the rest divorced. It is significant that they have all been involved in the Biafra War-time 'attack trade'. Husbands and, most tragically of all, children had been lost. Indeed it was not uncommon for multiple child deaths to occur in one family. That the lives of these women had been touched in the most tragic of ways is obvious. Now 'all they cared for was themselves and their children if they had any.'[22] This club acts as a most effective network which keeps its members abreast of information on the most current and lucrative contracts, the key contact people responsible for these, and how to get to them. In other words, society's power brokers are tracked and monitored for the benefit of the club members! These women are ruthlessly calculating and quite ingenious in the skill with which they gather, manage and disseminate information for the economic benefit of their club members. Indeed, it is easy to draw broad similarities, at least as far as the mode of operation is concerned, with traditional women's groups and associations as discussed in earlier chapters of this study. Both have as their ultimate goal the advancement of women in their community; both have memberships that are exclusively female, and both provide critical emotional/psychological and other forms of support to one another. Amaka exploits this network, becomes extremely wealthy within a very short space of time and becomes the envy of her friend, Adaobi.

Adaobi, a civil servant lives with her fellow civil servant husband Mike in an affluent part of Lagos. Yet 'nothing [house, furniture, etc] was theirs except for the clothes, cooking utensils and children's toys. They hadn't even finished paying for their cars.'[23] Amaka's success leads Adaobi in particular to question the degree to which she has become complacent about her family's economic security and future. Adaobi realises that she is 'living in a fool's paradise,'[24] especially in the wake of the uncertainty of life under a military dictatorship which is entrenched in Nigeria's affairs. She feels she has been neglectful in her obligations to her family and decides to correct this potentially costly oversight in spite of objections from her husband. She engages Amaka's assistance. Through Adaobi's contacts in the civil service she secures contracts for Amaka and they share the profits. In this way she is able to build a three-bedroom

---

[21]Ibid., p. 49.
[22]Ibid., p. 50.
[23]Ibid., p. 63.
[24]Ibid.

bungalow for her family without Mike's knowledge - and, as it turns out, this construction of a new family home occurs fortuitously as Mike is soon retired from work following yet another military coup. Amaka's mother who is at first quite scornful of her daughter's entire handling of her marital situation, comes to greatly respect her newly found wealth. She herself (i.e. Amaka's mother) is a successful business woman, albeit not on Amaka's scale of wealth. This character presents a very interesting analysis of past cultural norms which underscore the historical authenticity of the position that Igbo women were *actively* encouraged by their own society to pursue and maintain a financial standing quite independent of their husbands. Indeed, Amaka's mother, in this story suggests that women's economic independence was more highly valued than finding and retaining a husband! The importance of the husband as far as the establishment of a cohesive family unit, the continuation of the lineage, and the maintenance of societal norms as a whole in Igbo society cannot be disputed historically. With the passing of time, however, and the alterations in the balance of roles and power between men and women, the importance of husbands appears to have diminished, not however (as Nwapa illustrates through Amaka's mother's reflections) at the expense of children or wealth:

'What do you ... think was the reason why our prosperous mothers went out of their way to marry wives for their husbands? ... They did not want to sacrifice their trade or economic life by waiting on their husbands and ministering to their every need.'[25]

Consequently, they participated wholeheartedly in marrying young wives for their husbands so that they could, understandably, devote much needed time and attention to their businesses. And it worked for this generation of women. The historical evidence supports Amaka's mother's assertion about the degree of prosperity of this earlier generation of Igbo mothers. So wealth was and remains both an important aspiration and criteria of success among Igbo women. And children? The philosophy stipulates that this wealth is acquired primarily for the advancement of the children of the family, in particular, and the family as a whole. Children have remained paramount in the ordering of priorities, hence Amaka's mother's advice to her daughter (Amaka) that while she may be justified in being without a husband, as long as she remains childless she cannot afford to completely terminate her relationship with men! Subsequently, when

---

[25]Ibid., p. 118.

Amaka does become pregnant, the paternity of the child is at first neither questioned nor is it of particular interest. This marks a decided departure from Igbo age-old norms where the sanctity of family life, as expressed through marriage, was paramount. However, Amaka's mother cautions her daughter who, in her new found financial and other freedom, is reluctant to marry the father of her children when he does propose: 'You have your own house ... You will be financially independent of him ... You will be free. But now you have two lovely boys. *The boys need a father ...* You have nothing to lose. You have much more to gain' (emphasis added).[26] Once again, the paramount importance of children and their needs in society come to the fore. Amaka who clearly does not love Izu, the father of her children, is urged to marry him not out of any societal or cultural obligation, but rather out of a need to ensure that the well-being of these children is ensured - both in the short but particularly in the long run. Amaka eventually chooses not to marry Izu, in spite of tremendous pressure from her family (and initially from Izu himself) signalling perhaps a shift in women's thinking about the degree of disadvantage they are willing to endure in what are increasingly becoming disadvantaged positions within marriages. She believes she is more than adequately equipped to cater for all their material needs, and she has no intention of severing links with her children's biological father. Yet the constraints on her life, as experienced in her first marriage, leave her quite content to remain single as long as she can become a mother. In effect, as Jane Bryce-Okunlola has correctly noted, there remains the 'retention of the centrality of motherhood [now] combined with the decentering of the role of wife...'[27] So powerful is this theme of women's economic independence throughout all of Nwapa's writing that the frontispiece of *One is Enough,* which is an Hausa proverb, reads 'A woman who holds her husband as a father, dies an orphan.' Indeed it is obvious that Nwapa's position is that the historical legacy of African women as a whole and Igbo women in particular is a dual legacy of motherhood and economic independence. These dual levers have provided women with the means and scope to participate fully in shaping the direction of their society. This legacy has neither been sustained in the recent history of the people not does it adequately inform the priorities of contemporary life. It is this inheritance that women should once again seek to reclaim in the reconstruction of their society.

---

[26]Ibid., p. 139.
[27]Bryce-Okunlola, 'Motherhood as Metaphor for Creativity in Three African Women's Novels,' pp. 207 - 208.

Changing social orders and the impact on male-female relationships

One is Enough interrogates the rapidly changing societal norms and values following the Biafra War. We should elaborate specifically on those components of the novel that discuss the difficulties which women face in contemporary society, particularly where they occupy significantly less politically powerful positions both individually and collectively. Amaka, about whom her estranged husband admits earlier on in their marriage that he '[is] so proud of,'[28] finds herself faced with what is perhaps the most difficult of circumstances in an Igbo marriage - an inability to have children. Serious, as this situation could be, it is not however the catastrophe that both Katherine Frank and Oladele Taiwo make it out to be. Frank has written: 'In traditional [African] society for a woman to lack reproductive power is to lack all power, indeed to be deprived of her very identity and "raison d'être" in life.'[29] In his own astonishing reading of the situation where, among other naïve and incorrect assertions, the city of Onitsha is described as a 'village,' Taiwo notes: 'Without a child, Amaka cannot command the respect of the villagers. Nor does she have their sympathy or consideration.'[30] As we have shown earlier on in this study, a married woman's inability to bear children was so serious as to be regarded as an abrogation of her familial responsibilities. Yet, there were accepted means and ways of addressing this issue as Nwapa illustrates extensively in *Idu* and *Efuru*. Finding themselves in similar situations, Idu and Efuru, the two principal women characters respectively in the two novels, look for and 'marry women' they consider to be appropriate wives for their husbands. In so doing, each of the women ensures that the continuity of the lineages of their designated married families is maintained. In *One is Enough* this is clearly not the case. It is Obiora's mother who, without the knowledge or consent of Amaka, finds a wife for her son, arranges the marriage and delivers the package as a *fait accompli* to Amaka in the most humiliating manner. She has no recourse for redress. Obiora and his mother have made crucial decisions that impact dramatically on Amaka's life without the latter's own participation. Hence, Amaka is left with one of two choices - to accept the situation as it is, including the entry of the second wife into her home, or leave the marriage. She decides on the latter!

---

[28]*One is Enough*, p. 16.
[29]Frank, 'Women Without Men,' p. 20.
[30]Oladele Taiwo, *Female Novelists of Modern Africa* (London and Basingstoke: Macmillan, 1984), p. 65.

In turn, Amaka's mother and aunt are supporting characters for Amaka, confronting directly prevailing social practices which have become, in effect, inimical to the well-being of women. This would appear to be Nwapa's response to the changes in women's 'bargaining power,' their complementarity with men, and their overall status that have left them terribly exposed and vulnerable to the dictates of both husbands and in-laws. Additionally, through the trio characters of Amaka, her mother and aunt, Nwapa confronts the contradictions of the moral education that girls, as opposed to boys, received from missionary schools - institutions which the vast majority of Africans attended. For Nwapa, such schools decidedly left these girls 'unequipped' to cope with the demands of their own cultural mores. Reflecting on her predicament, Amaka notes that her people have always emphasised the importance of marriage ever since she could remember. But Amaka's mother and aunt no longer share this belief of her people. The aunt comments that 'what is important is not marriage as such, but children, being able to have children, being a mother.'[31] She urges Amaka to have children, to have the means to look after them properly, and then expect societal acceptance and respect as a result. Her mother teaches motherhood, self-determination, and independence from any husband almost to the detriment of marriage. Like Amaka's aunt, she urges, 'Marriage or no marriage, have children. Your children will take care of you in your old age ... As a mother you are fulfilled.'[32] Amaka's aunt's personal life, which she narrates to Amaka, is particularly illustrative and captures this apparent shift in accent in the age-old societal attitude towards marriage. She is the mother of seven children from a husband whom she dislikes from the very beginning of her marriage. After the birth of the seventh child, she refuses to have anything further to do with him sexually. To pre-empt any criticism for her action, she marries a 'sixteen year old for him,'[33] charges the new bride with *their* husband's 'welfare,' and declares that for her part she is going to develop the family business to ensure that all *their* children (wife Number 2's inclusive!) benefit from a good education and more opportunities in life. The arrangement works successfully for all concerned. This act is as ingenious as it is subversive. In one deftly planned coup, Amaka's aunt 'extracts' herself from the drudgery of an unhappy marriage to a husband who she maintains she never really loved but without abandoning the family home.[34] She retains all the natural advantages

---

[31]*One is Enough*, p. 8.
[32]Ibid., p. 11.
[33]Ibid., p. 9.
[34]Ibid., p. 8.

of being the first wife and this honorary position more than adequately helps her to address all her other responsibilities in the household. Foremost among these is of course the utilisation of the enormous wealth accruing from her business for the benefit of the family - including husband, the latter's second wife, and as it turns out subsequently, even more wives married by the man. She is thus a highly respected member of her family.

Amaka is confused at these differing scenarios put before her by her mother and aunt. Although she remains a conscientious Igbo woman, these positions are contrary to what she has been taught in school by the 'good missionaries.'[35] The missionaries have emphasised 'chastity, marriage and the home.'[36] Amaka feels that her mother is surely teaching her something else: 'Was it something different which she did not know because she went to school and was taught the tradition of white missionaries.'[37] It is not that Amaka's mother teaches promiscuity in any sense of the word. The well-being of the home, family and lineage have always been central to Igbo social norms as has been demonstrated in this study. Within this defined context therefore, the idea of promiscuity on either the part of the female or male family members becomes ludicrous. Rather, what Amaka's mother clearly abhors is a philosophy that removes from a woman her spirit of self-determination, enterprise and independence by making her weak - wholly dependent on her spouse and invariably his family, thus limiting her contributions to and status in that family. In other words, Amaka's mother rejects what in effect amounts to some exhibition of sexual modesty or propriety and a dedication to husband and home, to the extent that it jeopardises equally prized attributes in the Igbo woman's world, namely motherhood and the status of a respected, contributing member of the family. This is what Amaka's mother believes the philosophy of 'chastity, marriage and home' as taught by the missionaries, conveys, very much a reminder of the philosophy of Matron Jack, the authoritarian 'Old White Witch' in Grace Ogot's story of the same title.[38] The nurses in the story revolt against Matron Jack's insistence that they carry bedpans which the latter feels is 'part of a nurse's job ... as important as feeding or bathing a patient'[39] but which they feel is an affront to their Luo cultural sensibilities. 'Long before you came,' Monica, the nurses' spokesperson, tells Matron Jack before the outbreak of the strike, 'we agreed

---

[35]Ibid., p. 11.
[36]Ibid.
[37]Ibid.
[38]Grace Ogot, *Land Without Thunder* (Nairobi: East Africa Publishing House, 1968).
[39]Ibid., p. 9.

to nurse in this hospital on the understanding that we were not to carry bedpans. We want to be married and become mothers like any other women in the land ... no sane man will agree to marry a woman who carries a bedpan.'[40] Matron Jack is surprised at the nurses's objections who are not persuaded to change their minds – not even when she tells them that British nurses also carry bedpans as part of their work! Neither does her resort to the use of racist invectives in describing the position of the African women solve the problem. One approach that Matron Jack clearly does not embark upon is to try to understand the women's cultural objections to this sphere of the nurses's tasks however unfamiliar or disagreeable they may initially appear. It is this factor that underlines the object of contention in the story and not Ify Achufusi's flimsy dismissal of the women's protest as indicative of 'female characters [prepared to give] up their financial assets in order to ensure that they find husbands.'[41] Surely, it is the legitimate right of these women to respond to the nature of work they do based on their *own* defined interests as human beings and this would have been informed by varying criteria of considerations which would unlikely have ignored the question of culture. There is nothing objectionable, nor 'an impression of self-worthlessness' as Achufusi charges,[42] if women feel that getting involved in a particular brand of work could be inimical to their desire or goal of getting married. For the African women involved in the story, their goal of marriage is *crucially linked* to the role of being a mother, of motherhood, and the overarching impact that this has on the rest of Luo society as the leader of the nurses stresses in the quote above.

The missionaries' ethic is a European cultural chauvinist construct, and therefore from the African position it is an incapacitating philosophy because it refuses to dialogue, not to talk of understanding the Igbo/African cultural world-view which can differ or be distinct to that of Europe's. With respect specifically to what is taught to girls in school about marriage, motherhood and responsibility, the missionary philosophy misrepresents Igbo women's aspirations which emphasise the importance of *self-development* in order to achieve family cohesion. The 'chastity philosophy' robs the woman of her decisive role within marriage, subjugating her goals, indeed her female responsibilities to the will, aspirations and overall interests of her male partner. One is here reminded of a passage from Ama Ata Aidoo's *Changes: A Love*

---

[40]Ibid., p. 10.
[41]See Ify Achufusi, 'Feminist Inclinations of Flora Nwapa,' *African Literature Today*, No. 19, 1994, p. 110.
[42]Ibid.

Story on this same theme. *Changes* is a story about an African woman's quest for a wholly fulfilling relationship and her inability to come to terms with what appears to be on offer. Esi is a senior statistician with a government ministry in Accra. She divorces her husband with whom she has a child because he demands and wants too much of her time, her attention, indeed her very self! She enjoys her work tremendously - the conferences, the travels, and the overall seniority of her position. Against the advice of her mother, grandmother and best friend, Esi becomes involved with Ali. Ali is a prosperous owner of an international travel agency and husband of Fusena, both of whom have three children. Esi's friendship with Ali soon leads to marriage where she becomes the second wife. Esi imagines that as wife Number 2 her responsibilities/ commitments to her husband as well as his demands on her will be, at worst, minimal. As in the case of Amaka or Ramatoulaye (*So Long a Letter*), tradition is again transgressed. Fusena, the first wife is not involved in the marriage process, especially the key phase of selection, and Esi is here again presented as a *fait accompli*. Esi finds her role, or non-role, as Ali's wife equally unfulfilling. She is now free to travel and attend all the conferences she chooses, and to be as subsumed in her work to the degree she chooses. Yet she has no real personal life to speak of with Ali, because they are not a family in the true traditional sense of the word. She is not a part of the Ali household in the manner that Amaka's aunt's co-wife would have been. For 'in the traditional environment in which polygamous marriages flourished, happiness, like most of the good things in [African] life was not a two-person enterprise. It was the business of all parties concerned.'[43] In other words it should have included Fusena, Ali's first wife, whom Esi never even meets! The family structure of polygyny as it now operates for Esi has become heavily flawed. Consequently, holidays, family occasions, and weekends (when she is not working!) leave her feeling very lonely. Esi's daughter, much to her mother and grandmother's chagrin is effectively being raised by her in-laws from her first marriage, a fact which creates in her emotions of both relief and regret. For Esi, almost inadvertently, has selected and placed her career at the pinnacle of her many options as an African woman. The result is decidedly unfulfilling and an incapacity to manage her life develops. Esi's inability to come to terms with the balance of rich options seemingly available to her, prompts the following reflections from her which are similar to those voiced by Amaka in *One is Enough* over the latter's own 'white education':

---

[43] Aidoo, *Changes*, p. 98.

Why had they sent her to school?
What had they hoped to gain from it?
What had they hoped she would gain from it?
Who had designed the educational system that had produced her sort?
What had that person or those persons hoped to gain from it?
[A]ll this was too high a price to pay to achieve the dangerous confusion she was now in and the country was in.[44]

It is important, yet again, to return to *One is Enough* because of the underlining moral assumptions made by a number of critics on Amaka, the heroine of the novel. Whilst in Lagos, Amaka experiences a meteoric rise to material and personal success but we should note that this is not unlike the successes achieved by either Efuru or Idu even though the latter two have made theirs *in* marriage. Again, just as Efuru who is able to raise the money in marriage to pay her bride-wealth, Amaka, this time without the shared-space of a married home, pays back her bride-wealth to her husband's family as a result of her new found wealth and proceeds to create a very successful life for herself – albeit at a price. We should emphasise this contrast with Efuru because it will enable us point out the areas of mis-readings, mis-judgements, and therefore faulty conclusions that these critics have made on the career of Amaka after her arrival in Lagos. Interestingly, Achufusi cites Amaka's financial ability to return her bride-wealth to her former husband's family as the key attribute of her supposedly newly-won 'feminist ... freedom.'[45] If this is the case, then Achufusi cannot at the same time sustain the assertion that she makes in her study that in Amaka's character (after arrival in Lagos), Nwapa's 'portrayal' of women 'striving for economic independence' acquires a 'climax.'[46] On the contrary, despite the more contemporary era of the setting of *One is Enough*, there is nothing any more extraordinary that Amaka, the heroine of the novel, achieves as a successful businessperson than Efuru or Idu, both heroines in the author's earlier novels. This includes the phase of Amaka's business activity in Lagos after the breakdown of her marriage which has been the focus of controversy among critics. Efuru, in the novel of the same title by Nwapa and set in an earlier historical era, has also been responsible for paying her bride-wealth on behalf of herself and husband Adizua *in* marriage – i.e., whilst both are already married. Even though Efuru comes from a wealthy family, she establishes a

---

[44]Ibid., p. 114.
[45]Achufusi, 'Feminist Inclinations of Flora Nwapa,' p. 113.
[46]Ibid.

successful business career independent of her family whilst married which enables her not only to support her husband (who remains a not-too successful farmer) and new (extended) family but others in Ugwuta. Surely, this achievement is indicative of 'feminist ... freedom.' Similarly, Idu, the heroine in *Idu*, Nwapa's second novel, also set in an historical epoch earlier than Amaka's (*One is Enough*), is a successful businessperson *in* marriage whose income is a major source of support for the immediate and extended family alike, another achievement indicative of 'feminist ... freedom.' Despite the changed historical era of the setting of *One is Enough*, the heroine here, Amaka, is equally a successful businessperson: 'She made money.'[47] Again, just as Efuru and Idu, Amaka achieves financial success in business prior to her marriage, including participating in the 'attack trade' during the Biafra War. Whilst *in* marriage in Onitsha, she is a successful contractor 'supplying timber, sand and food' to other business enterprises.[48] Again, just as Efuru and Idu, Amaka utilises her income to support her husband (including buying him a car!) and family and the extended family. In Lagos, after she walks out of her marriage (in Onitsha), Amaka continues the trail of her financial success but now gets involved in prostitution with influential men in the state to win the contract tenders. For the first time in her long business career, Amaka 'began to see what she could do as a woman, using her bottom power, as they say in Nigeria.'[49] As a result, she is awarded several lucrative contracts including the 'construction' of an already existing wall around a military base!

Whilst Katherine Frank is very critical of Amaka's prostitution which she feels undermines the 'validity of her success,'[50] she however welcomes the heroine's decision to discontinue her marriage even though on the very dubious grounds which the critic suggests – namely, that by so doing, Amaka 'articulates a radical feminist-separatist credo.'[51] It is true that Amaka decides not to marry again after leaving Obiora but there is nothing 'radical feminist' nor 'separatist' in this position – any more than Efuru, who in an earlier generation/historical era had abandoned an 'unfulfilling' marriage and decided not to re-marry, deciding instead to dedicate herself to the worship of the lake goddess. Neither is Amaka 'radical feminist' nor 'separatist' because she rejects an offer of marriage from a reverend minister with whom she gets into a relationship and

---

[47]*One is Enough*, p. 5.
[48]Ibid., p. 4.
[49]Ibid. pp. 120 - 121.
[50]Frank, 'Women Without Men,' p. 21.
[51]Ibid., p. 22.

who is responsible for her pregnancy resulting in the birth of twins. Whilst Amaka wishes to remain single, she is emphatic of her feeling for the reverend: 'I shall forever remain grateful to him for proving to the world that I am a mother as well as a woman.'[52] On Frank's earlier questioning of the personal morality of Amaka's judgement in the pursuit of her business interests in Lagos, both Bryce-Okunlola and Stratton call for some understanding of the sociopolitical 'realities' that underpin Amaka's decisions. For Bryce-Okunlola, Amaka's judgement is dictated by the 'response to the empirical conditions of women's lives in Nigeria, an insistence on what *is*, not what ought to be' (emphasis in the original).[53] For Stratton, borrowing from Patricia Ruddy who feels that that it is 'necessity, not moral laxity, that causes Amaka to trade in sex,'[54] the prevailing Nigerian political situation has created the environment whereby Nwapa sees '[p]rostitution ... [as] a strategy women have adopted for confronting male domination'[55] or 'as a way for women to regain the freedom and power they lost under colonialism.'[56] Stratton's conclusions are most misguided as Nwapa *makes no such offer* to women. It is clear from *One is Enough* that in her decision to employ 'bottom power' to pursue the business contracts in Lagos, Amaka makes a conscious choice as the quotation above unambiguously stresses. She therefore knows what the scores are. She consciously decides which men at the strategic levers of decision making of the business award-contracting enterprise that she sleeps with to achieve the goals which she clearly sets out for herself including, for instance, the following transaction which she confides to a friend: 'I must confess to you, I have slept with the Alhaji. There is a lot to be called "Cash Madam" ... I have a site where I store timber and blocks. The Alhaji helped me buy the site. I hope to build a flat on it...'[57] Having participated in the very dangerous *afia atak* trade of the Biafra War and the very competitive business of the immediate post-Biafra War trade in Onitsha, Amaka arrives in Lagos as a very knowledgeable and mature woman and she deploys this maturity of purpose with steadfastness, if not

---

[52]*One is Enough*, p. 154.
[53]Bryce-Okunlola, 'Motherhood as a Metaphor for Creativity in Three African Women's Novels, p. 207.
[54]Quoted in Stratton, *Contemporary African Literature and the Politics of Gender*, p. 103.
[55]Ibid.
[56]Stratton, '"The Empire, Far Flung": Flora Nwapa's Critique of Colonialism,' in Umeh, ed., *Emerging Perspectives on Flora Nwapa*, p. 133.
[57]*One is Enough*, p. 68.

ruthlessness. Amaka is therefore not some naïve, impressionable woman who arrives in Lagos and is at the mercy of some vicious system she does not understand. She has choices open to her. She makes those choices and she must be held to account for these consciously made choices. Similarly, Ozoemena, a married woman and mother of two in Nwapa's 'Delinquent Adults' set in the same era as *One is Enough*, is confronted with the choices of behaviour that best appeal to her consciously designated interests following the tragic death of her husband in an automobile accident. She wants to return to study in a college but finds that the wealthy and well-connected public figure who wants to facilitate her admission wants her to sleep with him as a condition for a placement. In response, Ozoemena challenges the man: 'Why should you insult me in this way? What is my sin? Why do you want to exploit me because I lost my husband, and it would seem, have no means of livelihood[?] Haven't you a grown-up daughter? Would you like her to be thus treated if she married and lost her husband in a motor accident?'[58] After this, she storms out of the man's house. It is therefore not an effective shield, to return to Amaka, for Amaka herself nor in fact for the wider African interest for a critic to suggest that what should concern us in *One is Enough* is what is claimed to be 'what is' and 'not what ought to be' nor that Amaka's prostitution is driven by some 'necessity,' some inevitability. These critics obviously do have a very low opinion of the moral standards of both African women and men as it is unlikely that they would accept such standard for *their own* society, a point very much implied by Gay Wilentz who notes that these critics do not question 'what Amaka's success means to the growth and health of her nation.'[59] It is because of the concern for the 'growth and the health' of her people after the Biafra War that Nwapa makes scant authorial comments on Amaka's Lagos business career in the novel, but instead feels that this is a serious subject that needs a wider public debate as she states in the interview with Theodora Akachi Ezeigbo:

A woman can be virtuous and she can be assertive. She can refuse to agree to compromise with a situation or the staus quo ... *In One is Enough*, I was not out to create a role model in Amaka. I was simply creating a woman who found herself in a corrupt society and struggled

---

[58]'The Delinquent Adults,' p. 80.
[59]Gay Wilentz, 'Not Feminist but Afracentrist: Flora Nwapa and the Politics of African Cultural Production,' in Umeh, ed., *Emerging Perspectives on Flora Nwapa*, p. 159.

to exist there the way *she* thought best.[60] (emphasis added)

Language, it is acknowledged, is perhaps the most effective carrier of culture.[61] There is little wonder therefore that the tendency of the present-day Igbo elite to shed their language as a mark of 'sophistication,' a phenomenon whose genesis goes back to the missionary-led education of cultural alienation, plays havoc with the society's attempts at self determination. The theme of language and its import is one which Nwapa deals with extensively in *Women are Different.* Mbonu Ojike was a member of Nnamdi Azikiwe's cabinet, when the latter, who later became Nigeria's first president after the restoration of independence, was premier of the eastern region of the country in the 1950s. Ojike was nicknamed the 'boycott king' because he actively promoted the advancement of the Igbo language, history and civilisation as the basis for the development of Igboland whilst advocating a policy of boycotting all that was not indigenous to the society. Nwapa demonstrates the level of cultural alienation that occurs in educational institutions in Africa using the example of this great nationalist. Miss Hill, the principal of Archdeacon Crowther Memorial Girls School, invites Ojike to address her students. She believes that Ojike's philosophy of the 'preservation of the Igbo language and culture'[62] is important for the girls who, thanks to the ingrained texture of cultural alienation of the African in the school system, not surprisingly find Ojike's appearance on arrival at the school 'a bit odd' because the nationalist is dressed in Igbo attire rather than wearing 'an English suit[!]'[63] Miss Hill's positive view on an African language, coming especially from such a senior European school administrator is quite unusual as the standard practice in schools at the time is that children are barred from 'speaking in the vernacular'[64] – the 'vernacular' being the racist reference to African languages. Nwapa is of course highlighting an obvious site of contradiction in the European conquest policy on education and also hinting at the immense possibilities of change and transformation of society anticipated then on the eve of the liberation of Nigeria in the 1950s. For Nwapa, language

---

[60]Theodora Akachi Ezeigbo, 'A Chat With Flora Nwapa,' in Umeh ed., *Emerging Perspectives in Flora Nwapa*, p. 659.
[61]On this issue of language, see, for instance, Ngugi wa Thiong'o, *Decolonising the Mind: The Politics of Language in African Literature* (London: James Currey, 1982), especially ch. 1.
[62]*Women are Different*, p. 23.
[63]Ibid., p. 24.
[64]Cf. Ngugi, *Decolonising the Mind*, pp. 11 - 12.

and culture clearly evolve a sense of self, society and one's place vis à vis the remainder of humanity. Here, she obviously wades into the debate on the politics of language in post-conquest African development – interestingly, beyond the boundary of concern of African writers who have been involved in passionate exchanges on the subject since the 1962 Kampala Conference on African Literature when Obi Wali challenged African writers to employ African languages as their media of work rather than their uncritical use of European languages as the means of expression.[65] Wali had argued then that such use of European languages had 'no chance of advancing African literature and culture.'[66] Ngugi wa Thiong'o, in an apparent response to this challenge decided in the 1980s to cease writing in English and henceforth write in Gikuyu or Swahili. Nwapa would have welcomed the Ngugi declaration in the way she obviously identifies with the cultural nationalism of Ojike, but her position on the subject of language, culture and development goes beyond the restricted avenue of the Kampala debate on literature to encompass all of society – children, women, gender relations, motherhood. In other words, Nwapa's interest in language relates to its pivotal role in the development of culture as the totality of a people's identity. For, it is from this identity that evolves a vision for self and people and a framework within which this shared common vision may be achieved. In the African historical milieu, Nwapa's interest is therefore to interrogate why and how the defining features of the cultural framework of a people, like the Igbo, become threatened, and establish clearly the resulting human chaos to society. While it may appear paradoxical, Nwapa herself did not publish in Igbo, even though, as we have indicated, both *Efuru* and *Idu* read very much like literal English translations of an Igbo manuscript. Similarly, her later writings sited in Lagos and other urban areas of Nigeria incorporate the cultural/language characteristics of these settings and time periods. It is clear that Nwapa wrote in English, albeit re-fashioned to suit local cultural and historical realities, because she was very conscious of Nigeria's multinational heritage and wanted the debate on the very crucial issues raised through her writings to be all-inclusive.

The impact of a European culturally-based education on Africans as a whole and women in particular has been devastating. These very powerful European-based values have not only reinforced the myth of the 'superiority' of the European experience, but concomitantly negated the very basis of the cultural

---

[65]Ibid., p. 24.
[66]Quoted in ibid.

existence of every African woman, man and child. But the damage is not restricted to the broad population of African peoples. The position of women becomes largely irrelevant. Presently, this is relegated to a *political marginalisation never before experienced and a near-neutralisation of all structures of social change and progress developed to ensure the maintenance of women's well-being by women themselves*. In *One is Enough* and *Changes* Nwapa and Aidoo respectively demonstrate the extent of damage created by the adoption of these foreign values and the abandonment of indigenous ones. Sylvia Leith-Ross, whose study of the Igbo we discussed earlier in this research, recognises and makes reference to the displacement of these traditional norms, her distorted interpretation of the overall character of Igbo cultural history notwithstanding. Leith-Ross was unable to recognise that Igbo women did not resent 'being regarded in the light of a possession'[67] simply because they were not! They had their own systems and structures for ensuring the maintenance of balance in marital and all social relationships. Theirs was a philosophy that emphasised the predominance of children and motherhood and women's financial independence. Structures for dealing with demands in marriage and society that could directly or indirectly jeopardise these were effectively created - and, as we have shown, it worked for this society. The current tragedy of African female-male mal-relationships is contained in this observation by Leith-Ross: 'But now her attitude may no longer be satisfied. She [the Igbo woman] is being taught that Christian marriage is based on love.'[68] When Leith-Ross first encountered Igbo women, her statement regarding their lack of recognition and appreciation of their (in Leith-Ross's eyes) 'disadvantaged' position was laughable precisely because although cultural erosions were beginning to set in and consolidate, women still wielded significant degrees of autonomy. With the advent and rapid transmission of European culturally-based value systems, however, women's structures, norms and values came under attack. Zulu Sofola aptly captures the effect on African women of the contrasting worlds of the new political dispensation, in the wake of the conquest, and the previous epoch of independence: 'There was no area of human endeavour in the traditional system where the woman did not have a role to play. She was very strong and active ... in the European system there is no absolutely no place for the woman.'[69] The future now was for African women to be taught 'chastity', 'purity', 'love' and

---

[67]Leith-Ross, *African Women*, p. 125.
[68]Ibid.
[69]Adeola James, ed., *In their Own Voices: African Women Writers Talk* (London: James Currey, 1990), p. 105.

'the home' as being paramount! However, the men, for whom women were to remain 'chaste', 'pure' and 'dedicated to home and hearth', were not similarly instructed. Nwapa's *Women Are Different* is devoted in its entirety to the discussion of women's increasing loss of autonomy and status and the impact of Western value systems. The book traces the growth and development of three friends (Dora, Rose and Agnes) from their days in the mission school to adulthood, again drawing contrasts between a philosophy of life and living taught to them at school by missionaries and those of their indigenous cultural environment. While Africa's educationally-'advantaged' elite women were emerging with alienating and alienated views about their existence vis à vis the men in their society, their male counterparts were having their own structures vis à vis their women strengthened under a European World view of male-female relationships. All these occurred under the tacit acceptance by educated Africans, in particular, of the 'superiority' of this particular world-view. Not surprisingly, an exasperated Amaka's mother questions the usefulness of an education system which has failed to equip her daughter with how to deal with her life in her society. She asks: 'What were you taught in that school of yours? ... You create problems where there are none.'[70] Amaka, significantly, has no credible response to this question.

Indeed, exactly the reverse of Leith-Ross's assertion has occurred. With the marginalisation of the Igbo (African) heritage that the conquest philosophy demonises as 'primitive,' as opposed to the pragmatic adaptation/modification/development of cultural norms by a people to reflect their contemporary circumstances, which occurs in every human civilisation, African women have indeed become like chattels. As those European values of 'chastity', 'purity', 'obedience' towards husband and the 'sanctity' of home take root, Igbo women's *self- defined* philosophical world-view of the essential elements of a woman's role and responsibilities within marriage loses its focus and importance. Within this newly evolving scenario 'it seems to have been necessary for women to be swallowed up in this [process].'[71] Esi's grandmother, in her discussion with Esi over the latter's wisdom of leaving one man (her own husband) for another man (someone else's), draws a most interesting analogy between the loss of power that has occurred for women vis à vis men with that which has occurred for Africans vis à vis Europeans. With regards to women-men relationships, Esi's grandmother reflects, '[T]hey say it was not always like

---

[70]*One is Enough*, p. 11.
[71]Aidoo, *Changes*, p. 110.

this. They say that a long time back, it was different.'[72] To contemporary African society however, it now appears that '[m]en were the first gods in the universe, and they were devouring gods. The only way they could yield their best ... was if their egos were sacrificed to: regularly. The bloodier the sacrifice the better.'[73] But she continues: 'There are [also] other types of gods. No less bloody, and equally implacable. We Africans have allowed ourselves to be regularly sacrificed to the egos of the Europeans, no?'[74] Hence Ali's enraged response when Esi suggests that their marriage may be tantamount to bigamy: 'Why have we got so used to describing our cultural dynamics with the condemnatory tone of our masters' voices?'[75] – distortions within these cultural dynamics, notwithstanding! In reality it is the African family that is in danger of being devoured, and is thus imperilled. It is the African family that is being subsumed under the unquestioned racism and chauvinism of 'developmentalism' in all its ramifications as adopted by the African so-called 'middle class'. Yet it is a 'middle class' which is ill at ease with the *entire* world of their ancestors and has a somewhat tenuously-rooted base to either its cultural or even economic existence. Given the virtual collapse of the African 'nation-state' after 20 years of World Bank/International Monetary Fund neo-conquest socio-economic overseeing, this African 'middle-class' has all but in name taken flight from the continent – away to Europe and north America. It is this theme of de-accultration/alienation of the 'middle class' that Nwapa refers to in *Women are Different* when Comfort, the street-wise college-mate of three friends, comments on her reasons for attending Archdeacon Crowther Memorial Grammar School (ACMGS) in rural Elelenwa rather than the more prestigious Lagos-based Queen's College: 'I pass de entrance but my Papa say I no go go Lagos ... [M]y mama say "to go Lagos no hard, na return."'[76] In other words, the adoption of 'foreign' values, norms and mores is often quite easily acquired. The journey towards what amounts to a seduction into an alternative view of self and culture is often interesting, and at times quite delightful as the individual sheds all relationship with and responsibility to the whole. The devastation and alienation that is experienced by all parties concerned, but particularly by the individual, is often quite severe and irreparable, hence the reference to the difficulty of the return journey home - not only physically, but

---

[72]Ibid.
[73]Ibid.
[74]Ibid.
[75]Ibid., p. 90.
[76]*Women are Different*, p. 5.

also psychologically. In responding to the power shift in society which has clearly placed women at a disadvantage, women have acted to ensure their survival by making adjustments to the family structure that has at once ensured the continuity of the lineage and society as a whole, but, increasingly at the expense of the sanctity/cohesiveness of the immediate family structure which has in the past been taken for granted. *So, motherhood remains intact.* However, because of women's current insecure positions in marriage vis à vis their spouses, there is a diminished taboo about opting out of this institution to conduct (not singly, but *with the support of the extended family*) functions that previously were undertaken by father and mother as well as the extended family.

We have demonstrated throughout this study that the tenets of Igbo women's culture emphasise motherhood, self-determination and independence. Amaka's aunt in *One is Enough* summarises this: '[N]ever depend on your husband. Never slave for him. Have your own business no matter how small ... Above all ... never leave your husband.'[77] We see this philosophy reflected in Akan culture through Esi's mother and grandmother as evident in *Changes*. When Esi's grandmother establishes that Esi chooses to leave her husband Oko, not because he is violent or mean to her, but because he demands too much of her time and person, only to turn to a man who is already married, she asks, 'Leave one man, marry another. What is the difference? Besides you had a husband of your own, no?'[78] Similarly, the philosophy of independence for women is evinced in Akan culture: 'Like nearly all West African women [Fusena] had been brought up in a society that had no patience with a woman who did not work. Her husband's wealth ... was a matter of only mild importance - just something that could make life easier.'[79] Through both Nwapa's and Aidoo's work we observe how much of this philosophy has been subverted. Suddenly, the philosophy of independence gives way to 'I will encourage all my daughters to marry, just to have those three letters - M-R-S, just answer [to] MRS.'[80] This conversation occurs at Agnes's wedding between two of the wedding guests - Mama Emeka and Mama Nkem. It is Mama Emeka who believes in bearing the title MRS as an accomplishment in itself, and that this should take precedence over the education of her daughters. She will marry them off as soon as the appropriately wealthy suitors appear on the scene. Mama Emeka no longer espouses the philosophy of her ancestors. Indeed she no longer emphasises independence for

---

[77] *One is Enough*, p. 9.
[78] Aidoo, *Changes*, p. 109.
[79] Ibid., p. 67.
[80] *Women are Different*, p. 53.

her daughter through education or otherwise, but rather chooses to advise her daughters to seek out and depend on wealthy husbands. Mama Nkem, on the other hand, does not agree. This is perhaps because she lives the reality. The latter's inability to establish her own independence, at least educationally, leaves her extremely vulnerable. Mama Nkem does not have *it* - 'it' being this education/independence. '[T]hat is why Papa Nkem behaves in such an atrocious manner to me.'[81] As a result of this dependency, she is forced to tolerate his 'atrocious behaviour' because she practically reflects, 'where will I go with seven children? So I stay.'[82]

Apart from two stories in *This is Lagos* which specifically focus on the Biafra War (discussed in the previous chapter), the rest of the stories of this book demonstrate particular manifestations of the types of social and psychological alienation that Africans have assumed in their 'educated independence,' and to which the young in their societies aspire. Generally, Nwapa focuses on the cultural alienation that so easily occurs the further away from the home (philosophically speaking) that one strays. This alienation varies in manifestation and is dependent not necessarily on a physical distance from the home but rather on a psychological/philosophical dis-engagement from a cultural/indigenous understanding of the self and one's world, particularly vis à vis the multiplicity of co-existing world-views. It is a disengagement that not only causes great psychological distress to all concerned parties but also mis-directs and mis-targets the arguments around society's future development, thus, retarding societal advancement. In the story 'This is Lagos' from which the collection takes its title, the focus is the change in attitude from a communal focus to a more individualistic one, that often results when the 'town mentality' is adopted. Soha who is a considerate, helpful 20-year old woman extremely supportive of her family gets a teaching job in Lagos and leaves the village where she was born, raised and educated. She appears to settle in with her aunt, Mama Eze, very well but her attitude gradually begins to change. She begins to dissociate herself from her origins, most notably by never going home during school vacations to see her family. She makes friends, in particular a male friend whom she hides from her aunt, ensuring that the man visits only when her aunt and uncle are away. Soon she feels that a local hostel with a notorious reputation, inhabited by '[r]otten girls who will never marry'[83] is where she would prefer to live. Her aunt disapproves of this move, insisting that she will

---

[81]Ibid.
[82]Ibid.
[83]Ibid., p. 15.

inform Soha's mother of her decision before she allows it. One evening Soha turns up at her aunt and uncle's home with a man whom she claims she had married a month earlier. Additionally, she is pregnant. The family is shocked by Soha's behaviour. Soha's aunt admonishes: '[W]e don't marry like this in the place where we come from.'[84] Her neighbour, Mama Bisi, interjects, '[E]ven in the place where he comes from ... When they come to Lagos they forget their home background.'[85] And then Mama Eze captures the reasons for the abandonment of all that previously defined propriety: 'Mr Ibikunle, we don't marry like that in my home. Home people will not regard you as married. This is unheard of. *And you tell me this is what white people do*'[86] (emphasis added). 'Jide's Story' demonstrates the moral abandonment and lasciviousness of Lagos life at its height. Jide, Rose, Peju and Iyabo are all students in England who successfully complete their course of study and return home to assume various positions, mostly in the civil service. Jide marries Rose but returns to Lagos ahead of her. On the boat he meets Maria. 'She was irresistible ... All the qualities she possessed, including her make-up were all I told my wife I abhorred in women.'[87] And so begins the affair with Maria. Very soon however, Jide discovers that whilst studying in London, Marie had been committed to a psychiatric hospital following a mental breakdown. Jide learns of this in the most unsympathetic and uncaring manner from Peju, a serious alcoholic. Peju believes that 'if you have[n't] been drunk then you haven't started living. To be able to live, you have to get drunk, really drunk.'[88] Iyabo, Peju's roommate, is also constantly drunk. Yet they both 'hold very good jobs, both had cars and a string of men friends.'[89] For her constant drunken state she explains, '[S]omehow I can't help it at times. I didn't drink in England at all. I started drinking two years after my return. *Things were not as they seemed.* And now it seems as if I am beyond redemption ... I was driven to it and now I cannot stop'[90] (added emphasis). Jide himself is plagued by a different demon. He spends his evenings moving from one party to another and in the process picks up different women, even waking up on one occasion in strange surroundings. What is portrayed is a life of decadence and hedonism and all of this from a

---

[84]Ibid.
[85]Ibid.
[86]Ibid.
[87]'Jide'sStory', p. 20.
[88]Ibid., p. 22.
[89]Ibid., p. 21.
[90]Ibid., pp. 23 - 24.

young vibrant educated middle class. The image is of a society, or a component within society, terribly ill at ease with itself, a disease manifesting in varying forms of neurosis, gradually moving the society on a path of implosion and ultimate self-destruction. The evidence to date and the state of the continent unfortunately do not belie this suggestion. 'The Traveller,' another story in the collection, is about a young man called Musa whose occupation is 'work[ing] with a firm of experts.'[91] He is pompous and arrogant and assumes that Bisi, a young woman whom he meets during a brief two day stop-over in Lagos is as willing to engage in a casual sexual encounter with him as he is with her. All his efforts to seduce her are met with little or no success and Bisi poses an important question to her friend Sophia, 'Musa, what kind of man is he? And what kind of woman does he think I am?'[92] In the anonymity of the city Lagos and seemingly unfettered by a tradition that has been attacked, indeed villified as 'bush', Musa feels it is sophisticated and progressive to engage in casual sex, to embark on and engage in a physical relationship without any of the attendant responsibilities. The metaphor 'bush' is an important one in Nwapa's works, and occurs repeatedly throughout much of her writings, especially her post-Biafra War literature. Any behaviour, characteristic or opinion that is indigenous is 'bush'. Hence in 'The Traveller,' Sophia apologises that she does not drink alcohol. 'We don't drink beer here. We are bush.'[93] It is to this phenomenon that Aidoo makes reference in *Changes*: 'Like all "modern Western-educated Africans," Ali could not help it if he regularly bruised traditions and hurt people. But at least he was one of the few really sensitive ones.[94]

It is indeed ironic that Africa appears to have become a victim of 'modern Western-educated' citizens. Elsewhere in the world, education is known to be liberatory.[95] The acquisition of knowledge, the application of this knowledge for the development of one's society, the refinement of the intellect, and the capacity to generate ideas for society's advancement appear in Africa's case to act as the antithesis of its development and advancement. Hence the current estimates by Joseph Ki-Zerbo, a leading African historian, that the total number

---

[91]'The Traveller,' p. 1.
[92]Ibid., p. 8.
[93]Ibid., p. 4.
[94]Aidoo, *Changes*, p. 133.
[95]Paulo Freire, *Pedagogy of the Oppressed* (New York: The Continuum Publishing, 1970) and Ngugi wa Thiong'o, *Barrel of a Pen* (London: New Beacon Books, 1983).

of African intellectuals currently in the West is approximately 100,000,[96] underlining the flight of the so-called African 'middle class' that we referred to above. This figure constitutes the core of professional humanpower developed by the African post-conquest states in the wake of the restoration of independence. It is indeed telling that there are also about that same number of foreign workers, mostly United Nations/ voluntary/ non-governmental organisation sector currently employed in Africa at a time when 85 per cent of research on Africa is carried out outside the continent.[97] The relevance of what educators and others describe as 'Western education for Africa' must of necessity be called into question. There are however some scholars, African and European, who would disagree with this position. Adu Boahen, in editing the UNESCO series, *General History of Africa, Vol VII*, in what can only be summarised as a most incomprehensible attempt at 'scholarly objectivity' actually debates possible advantages which may have accrued to Africans after the European conquest and the introduction to Africa of 'Western education'. Following on this logic, any writer/academic who proffers to discuss in a debate or in some published work the possible 'advantages' to the Jew of Hitler's campaign of suppression and genocide against them 50 years ago or to Europeans whose lands were occupied by the Germans during the war of 1939-1945 would invariably have their political or ideological credentials sharply queried. Africa is perhaps the only part of humanity where heinous crimes committed by invaders and an occupation whose oppressive legacy still pervades can be the subject of 'polite' unproblematic intellectual discourse. Boahen's confusion is apparent. Having attested to the indisputably negative impact of the conquest on African women, he however maintains that 'in the cultural and social field, the impact of colonialism was relatively neither profound nor permanent.'[98] He continues, '[in] the rural areas ... life ran gaily on very much as before.'[99] Indeed he sees the impact of a European conquest state on women's position in society as 'regrettable,'[100] presumably to the extent that women were 'inhibited from joining most of ... the professions and job opportunities such as law, medicine, mining, etc.'[101] Boahen, in this discussion, reveals the lack of understanding and appreciation that exists amongst many

---

[96]Joseph Ki-Zerbo, 'Which Way Africa?' *Development Dialogue*, 1995:2, p. 114.
[97]Ibid.
[98]Boahen, 'Colonialism in Africa,' p. 808.
[99]Ibid.
[100]Ibid., p. 802.
[101]Ibid.

African scholars about the crucial roles women played in the conceptualisation and execution of social, spiritual, economic, political norms and values for the ordering, maintenance and advancement of society and the degree to which these were effectively destroyed. Boahen is of course not alone in this position. Ade Ajayi, another historian, maintains that the impact of colonialism on Africa did not cause any break in the 'continuity of the African experience,' hence 'the ability of Europeans to make entirely new departures in African history was limited.'[102] It is significant that the editors of the book in which Ajayi's contributing chapter appears, L.H. Gann and P.Duignan, are two of the leading proponents of the theory that the negative impact of European hegemony on Africa was 'largely minimal' as the 'overall effect' on the affairs of the continent was 'beneficial.' They state: 'the imperial system stands out as one of the most powerful engines for cultural diffusion in the history of Africa; its credit balance by far outweighs its debt account.[103] Similarly, P.C. Lloyd contends that 'Nevertheless, the difference between the condition of African society at the end of the nineteenth century and at the end of the Second World War is staggering. The colonial powers provided the infrastructure on which progress in the "independence" period has depended.'[104] Margery Perham, private secretary to Frederick Luggard who was first governor general in Nigeria also argues that 'our vanishing empire left behind it a large heritage of history which is loaded with bequests good, bad and indifferent. This neither they nor we can easily discard.'[105] The attempt here is of course a *rationalisation* by an official of a conquest regime that emerged after one of the most atrocious crimes perpetrated on humanity. Additionally, African scholarship which maintains that the encounter with European imperialism was brief ignores 400 years of slavery which had already undermined African independence and self-development prior to the Berlin conference of 1885 which formally carved up Africa among European powers. Such scholarship cannot understand, appreciate and subsequently free itself from a mind-set that continues to perpetuate Africa's non-development. Indeed, as Walter Rodney, the African Guyanese historian has argued, the European conquest of Africa

---

[102]Ade Ajayi, 'Colonialism: an episode in African history,' in L.H. Gann and P. Duignam, eds., *Colonialism in Africa, Vol 1* (Cambridge: Cambridge University Press, 1969), pp. 497 - 509.
[103]L.H. Gann and P. Duignam, *Burden of the Empire* (London: Pall Mall, 1967), p. 382.
[104]P.C. Lloyd, *Africa in Social Change* (Hammondsworth: Penguin, 1972), pp. 80 - 81.
[105]Margery Perham, *The Colonial Reckoning* (London: Collins, 1961), p. 24.

'was a one-armed bandit.'[106]

Unlike the rationalising conquest scholarship of Ajayi, Boahen, Duignan, Gann, Lloyd, Perham, etc, Rodney's conclusions no doubt inform Nwapa's works. We observe *consistently* in Nwapa's writings the detrimental impact of the European conquest in Africa, particularly with regard to the all encompassing institution of motherhood and the crucial political, socioeconomic, spiritual and philosophical roles played by women therein.

'We have our own myths, folktales and all...'

As Nwapa's writings for adults took on and confronted the racism of Western anthropological texts, her children's books also dealt with the cultural distortions confronting young African readers. She was concerned about what African children read especially the imported, largely Western written and published (children) texts which, like the adult texts in many an intellectual discipline, largely invalidated the history and cultural heritage of African people. 'When I went to the book stores, I didn't see anything that was good for my children,' Nwapa recalls.[107] Ernest Emenyonu has argued that Nwapa's desire to write for children was the 'next logical battle after the defeat of colonialism as an institution.'[108] Nwapa herself has indicated that her motivation has been to write 'good books for [her and other] growing children,'[109] indeed books reflective of her own cultural reality as a child, that launched her career in this genre. She adds

> We have our own myths, folktales and all ... We want them [children] to know about these things... If the writer can capture all these things in books, then children will read them and know about their own culture... We must make our children understand that they have a heritage and we can only do that through books.[110]

---

[106]Walter Rodney, *How Europe Underdeveloped Africa* (Dar es Salaam: Tanzania Publishing House, 1972), p. 223.

[107]Umeh, 'The Poetics of Economic Independence for Female Empowerment,' p. 666.

[108]'(Re)configurations of Child Symbolism,' in Umeh, ed., *Emerging Perspectives of Flora Nwapa*, p. 568.

[109]Umeh, 'The Poetics of Economic Independence for Female Empowerment,' p. 666.

[110]Quoted by Ezenwa-Ohaeto, 'Breaking Through: The Publishing Enterprise of Flora Nwapa,' in Umeh, ed., *Emerging Perspectives on Flora Nwapa*, pp. 193 - 194.

Nwapa's deep love for stories can perhaps be attributed to her writing career in the genre of children's stories. She traces this love to her childhood: 'As a child stories fascinated me.'[111] She also clearly attributes her knowledge of folklore to her grandmother and her (grandmother's contemporaries) with whom she spent the formative years of her life: 'There, I was able to listen to all those stories of Mammywater, Okita, and all those things. I could not help hearing those stories.'[112] It is noteworthy that Nwapa, like Chinua Achebe,[113] attributes her cultural knowledge base, and thus her writing material to her early contact with this rich cultural heritage. The onslaught on African religion by the Christian missionaries which created a dichotomy of belief-systems is clearly demonstrated in Nwapa's narration of her early years at Ugwuta. Nwapa's parents were the children of the first Christian converts in Ugwuta. She states in an interview with Sabine Jell-Bahlsen: 'We children were not allowed to do certain things, like talking about mammywater. My parents called her worship "paganism"... But then I was lucky because I went to live with my grandmother at an early age...'[114] There was undoubtedly a constant wrestling match between the retention of one's cultural groundings and essences and the adoption of Christianity, which was increasingly being associated with an educated elite. Nwapa provides an example of this rejection and even demonisation of African belief systems in her narration of the events which took place in her church following the ousting of the attacking Nigerian soldiers from Ugwuta during the Biafra War, a feat attributed to the Woman of the Lake: '[W]hen the Nigerian federal troops came from Port Harcourt crossing the lake, Ugwuta people said that it was the lake that drove the invading army away from Ugwuta. Now in church the pastor got so angry when he heard this that he did not mince words. He told Ugwuta people, "Either you are a Christian or not."'[115] Herein lies in summary one visible and tragic impact of imperialism in Africa – the very cultural base that has proved to be the literary impetus for many great African writers and which has provided them with the rich content and context of their scholarship is the unrelenting recipient of every form of demonisation, defamation, stigmatisation and invalidation.

---

[111]Sabine Jell-Bahlsen, 'An Interview with Nwapa,' in Umeh, ed., *Emerging Perspectives on Flora Nwapa*, p. 637.
[112]Ibid., p. 644.
[113]See Chinua Achebe, 'Named for Victoria, Queen of England,' in Achebe, *Hopes and Impediments,* pp. 20 - 26.
[114]Jell-Bahlsen, 'An Interview with Nwapa,' p. 644.
[115]Ibid., p. 646.

Flora Nwapa published six children's books: *Emeka-Driver's Guard*,[116] *Mammywater*,[117] *The Miracle Kittens*,[118] *The Adventures of Deke*,[119] *Journey to Space*[120] and 'The Magic Cocoyam' in *Journey to Space and Other Stories*[121] which Nwapa edited with Obiora Moneke. As in all of Nwapa's writings there are distinct themes which emerge. In this section we shall examine these themes, especially in relation to her adult themes of motherhood and familyhood as a whole. Additionally, we shall explore the degree to which comparisons exist between the child characters in her children's books and the child characters in her other works. Nwapa is certainly one of the pioneer Igbo women writers of contemporary African children's books. When asked about the feminist leanings in her writings, Nwapa had categorically denied such an orientation.[122] She claimed she wrote into her women characters only those qualities she herself had perceived in many 'ordinary' women in her society.[123] It would appear that this also was the intention behind Nwapa's children's books. Her children's books were also crafted to portray children in the 'ordinariness' of their creative and inquisitive state if correctly nurtured, guided and supported. Her stories emphasised entertainment, as well as the intellectual, moral and cultural empowerment of children within the appropriate family and cultural milieu. Furthermore, the stories contain the pivotal role played by the family in the creation of this enabling environment. As Julie Agbesiere comments on this underlining theme in Nwapa's writing, 'Family ties are very strong, especially between brothers and sisters. Together, they face and conquer the world.'[124] Additionally, Nwapa's indebtedness to her oral tradition of folklore is recognised. Agbasiere further observes: '[Nwapa] has creat[ed] a link between the oral and the written, by a blending of fantasy and realism and by striking a balance between the past and the present.'[125] Nwapa was clearly a woman who

---

[116]Flora Nwapa, *Emeka-Driver's Guard* (London: University of London, 1972).

[117]Flora Nwapa, *Mammywater* (Enugu: Flora Nwapa Books, 1979).

[118]Flora Nwapa, *The Miracle Kittens* (Enugu: Flora Nwapa Books, 1980).

[119]Flora Nwapa, *The Adventures of Deke* (Enugu: Flora Nwapa Books, 1980).

[120]Flora Nwapa, *Journey to Space* (Enugu: Flora Nwapa Books, 1980).

[121]Flora Nwapa and Obiora Moneke, ed., *Journey to Space and Other Stories* (Enugu: Flora Nwapa Books, 1980).

[122]Umeh, 'The Poetics of Economic Independence for Female Empowerment,' p. 668.

[123]Ibid., p. 669.

[124]Julie Agbasiere, 'Conquerors of the Universe: Flora Nwapa's Kiddies on the Move,' in Umeh, ed., *Emerging Perspectives on Flora Nwapa*, p. 581.

[125]Ibid., p. 580.

was very aware of and very connected with the social circumstances and ongoing mutations within her society. She reflected her knowledge of her society in her writings – both adult and children – in an attempt to generate discussion and debate on the variety of social issues therein raised. In an interview with Theodora Akachi Ezeigbo, Nwapa states: 'In Nigeria today we don't have good critics ... Good critics could give writers feedback on what people feel about their works...'[126] Nwapa's constant reflections on the changing state of society and its impact on women, men and children, and her constant attempts to 'alert' society through her writing point to a woman with a highly developed social consciousness and sense of social responsibility. That the physical quality of the works (especially as regards editing and printing) produced by her own printing press were often not of a rigorous standard should not in any way detract from the quality of the thought processes that generated these ideas and themes.

Journey to Space ostensibly appears to be a departure from Nwapa's traditional story settings, but it in fact seems to represent the merger between the traditional morals/values often portrayed in her stories and African folklore as a whole (e.g. respect for advice, the famed Igbo love of inquiry demonstrated through the famous Igbo proverb, 'those who ask questions never get lost,') and the contemporary technologically advanced age of, for instance, space travel. The story presents an appropriate setting for the young mind to begin to explore issues in a scientific realm, what Agbasiere refers to as 'scientific lore.'[127] Nwapa wrote *Journey to Space* in 1980, slightly over a decade after the historic landing on the moon by United States astronauts and may have been contributing to the amusing and fantastic discussion/debate of the landing by Nigerian children through this story.[128] As Marvie Brooks comments: 'Nwapa presents a wonderful opportunity for children and parents or teachers to explore together the issues posed by space exploration which has had tremendous

---

[126]Ezeigbo, 'A Chat With Flora Nwapa,' p. 659.
[127]Agbasiere, 'Conquerors of the Universe,' p. 577.
[128]Nwapa may have been responding to the very lively and vociferous dominant discussion about the landing on the moon both amongst adults and children at the time. One distinct theory which widely circulated among school children was that the lunar landing was associated with a major nation-wide outbreak of conjunctivitis which occurred soon after the event.

impact on youth since the 1960s.'[129] In any event, *Journey to Space* once more returns to the underlying theme of listening to one's elders. This is a story about space travel which begins for two children Eze and Ngozi in a lift one afternoon. The story opens up with a warning from a stranger to the two children: 'You children, you have been warned, don't play in the lift.'[130] They disregard the advice and find themselves hurtling through space on a journey which puts them in contact with a variety of characters with whom they explore questions pertaining to the moon. They are at last rescued by two fairies who return them to their flat with a final admonition, 'Next time don't be naughty.'[131] Even though 'Daddy Don't Strike the Match' is part of Nwapa's (adult) *Wives at War and Other Stories* collection, she raises the very important dual themes of spirituality/intuition and the voice given to children in Igbo society. The central role occupied by children in Igbo society has been discussed earlier in the study. A prescribed outcome of marriage in historical and contemporary Igboland is to raise a family. This is for the survival and continuity of the respective lineages involved. Children are nurtured from birth to develop a sense of self love/value, self assurance, and self respect all necessary prerequisites for living a responsible life as a fully contributing member of society. That children constitute much loved, much cherished and coveted members of Igboland is indisputable. It is within this environment of unquestionable love and support that Nwapa points to a significant societal deficiency and apparent contradiction in attitudes. The views of children are seen as only fit to relegate to the world of children, lacking any real contribution in the adult world and having little potential impact on the decisions of adults. Children's views are seen as 'child-like', only important in a 'childish' world, hence the process of learning and teaching is routinely unilateral, with little scope for meaningful exchange. In 'Daddy Don't Strike the Match,' Ifeoma, the youngest child in the Okeke household, is a bright, precocious child who has a highly developed sixth sense. In the world of her ancestors in *Idu* and *Efuru*, she may have been singled out for priesthood at the temple of the Woman of the Lake. In 1960s Biafra however she is a child who is constantly plagued with dreams and nightmares, speaking of the dangers around herself and family as they move from one town to the other to escape the federal Nigeria military

---

[129]Marvie Brooks, '"Either Pound in the Mortar Or Pound on the Ground": Didacticism in Flora Nwapa's Children's Books,' in Umeh, ed., *Emerging Perspectives on Flora Nwapa*, p. 619.
[130]*Journey to Space*, p. 20.
[131]Ibid.

offensive in the new republic. She gives a warning to her father's laboratory attendant that her father, Mr Okeke, should not 'strike the match' while working in his laboratory – a warning which she reiterates throughout the day, as a child would without fully understanding the significance of her words. In this story, in effect, Nwapa is conveying to her readers the reaction in the majority of people within any community to dismiss these and other similarly insightful remarks or observations made by children as 'childish play'. In this case 'the [attendant] smiled and went away, immediately forgetting the child's joke.'[132] Later, Mr Okeke strikes the dreaded match whilst in his laboratory and an explosion occurs killing him instantly.

Turning to the specifically children's *Emeka-Driver's Guard*, we are reminded of Ezeka in the adult story 'The Road to Benin,' published earlier in the *This is Lagos and Other Stories* collection. In both stories, Nwapa illustrates two important themes – the importance of education and respect for elders/family and conversely, the problems that consequently arise when parental advice is disregarded. The emphasis is however differently applied. In *Emeka-Driver's Guard*, we observe more of the role and the responsibility of the child in his/her pursuit of an education and thus an empowering and productive future. *Emeka-Driver's Guard* is the story of Emeka and Ngozi, who are twins born to a farmer and his wife in a rural Igbo village set in contemporary times. Given the age-old Igbo disquiet over twins, the parents are subjected to intense psychological pressure by the community upon the birth of Emeka and Ngozi which they perceive as a 'bad omen' amongst them: "It is a bad day when twins are born in the village."'[133] As the village gossips recall, some with evident nostalgia, the community is no longer able to utilise its usual method of rectifying such a 'problem': "In the days of our grandparents we would have let the twins die."'[134] "But those days have gone."'[135] In the meantime, the twins' parents are committed to raising their children in a perfectly normal way and do, until there is an outbreak of small pox in the village. This of course is attributed directly to the presence of the twins. To ensure the safety of the twins they are sent to live with a wealthy, caring and childless aunt in the city. The epidemic claims the lives of the twins' parents. In their new found home in the city, the dual processes of adjustment and maturation take their toll on Emeka, the male twin. He is soon caught up in the

---

[132]'Daddy Don't Strike the Match,' p. 28.
[133]*Emeka-Driver's Guard*, p. 4.
[134]Ibid.
[135]Ibid.

turbulent and incapacitating world of unruly behaviour, rebellion, truancy and non-performance. Additionally, an imbalance has occurred in the lives of the twins – the tragic loss of their parents means that the duality of male and female roles necessary (according to Igbo/African belief systems) in the raising of children is lost to a predominantly female role (i.e. the aunt) in the rearing of the children. This is obviously more problematic for the male than the female and we see the impact of this imbalance played out in the behaviour and choices which both children subsequently make.

Ngozi, the female twin, adjusts to her new life quickly and excels in school. Emeka, however, fares quite badly. The quality of Emeka's friends, his inability to see his relationship with them in its true light and thus extricate himself from its influence are perhaps singularly responsible for the subsequent choices he makes about his future. In particular the loud and aggressive Sokari emerges as an extremely bad influence on the gentler, weaker Emeka. Emeka makes several very bad decisions culminating in his decision to drop out of school and become a driver's guard. The love of his aunt notwithstanding, she is unable to provide him with the guidance/help that he needs in order to see the error of his ways and make the right choices:

> His aunt sat by him and put her arms around him.
> "Please, Emeka," she said. "Don't worry about the fees. I'll pay the fees if you go back to school and repeat the class."
> "Please, Emeka!" said Ngozi.
> "No."[136]

Emeka's emphatic refusal to heed to these words of advice puts him on course to become a driver's guard, a decision he lives to regret. But hope is never lost nor is it ever too late to reclaim an empowering heritage derived from family – parents, sister, aunt. The latter two undoubtedly serve as a positive anchor in Emeka's life. As Julie Agbasiere has observed: 'To him [Emeka] Ngozi is a symbol of affection, serenity and success. She is the type of magnet that draws him away from the wrong path. He sees his aunt as a constant reminder to go back to school.'[137] It is to them that he returns when he finally realises that his future lies in going back to the security and comfort of his home and settling down to some hard work, in spite of the humiliation to which he

---

[136]Ibid., p. 23.
[137]Agbasiere, 'Conquerors of the Universe' p. 579.

may be subjected at the hands of his school mates. In 'The Road to Benin' (*This is Lagos and Other Stories*), which we could term the adult version of this text, the emphasis is placed more on the role of the parents in creating the appropriate levels of support while establishing and ensuring adherence to expressed boundaries of behaviour and overall discipline in the home. Here, Ezeka, the eldest child of Nwanyinma and her husband, constantly tops his class and shows tremendous academic promise. His brilliant performance earns him a scholarship to college. However, in the months immediately preceding his departure for college, he becomes involved with a group of 'miscreants' who steadily lead him away from the realisation of his talent and promise. When he returns home on holiday from college he and his friends who are described with the unenviable tag of 'loafers of Onitsha'[138] embark on a series of joy rides and bar-hopping adventures which take them to several towns, eventually ending up in prison when they are apprehended in possession of 'Indian hemp' (marijuana).[139] It is clear that the problems of the family begin when the parents abdicate responsibility for their child's behaviour. The father's incapacity to assert control over his son is demonstrated in the scene in which Ezeka demands that his mother entertain him and his friends with beer. Nwanyinma, quite shocked by the request, refuses on the grounds that Ezeka is a schoolboy and furthermore the family cannot afford such luxuries. Angered, Ezeka leaves the house with his friends to go drinking elsewhere. Nwanyinma is blamed by her husband for the incident when it is recounted to him.[140] It is, however, the deteriorating behaviour of Ezeka that prompts this strong reaction from Nwanyinma who much earlier on (before he goes away to college) notices Ezeka's changing character but attempts to allay her own fears or bury her head in the sand: 'The school will take care of him. She had done her duty to her son. Now in a way she had handed over her son to the authorities in the school. It was the authority that she trusted and respected.'[141] A demonstration of the importance of parental responsibility in providing an environment which sets boundaries of behaviour, articulates high expectations for children within a loving and supportive milieu is clearly Nwapa's intention. The importance of the family and the unique though converging roles of its various members in setting the stage for the formation of character and later life success for its children is repeatedly demonstrated. In *Emeka-Driver's Guard*, this children's

---

[138]'The Road to Benin,' p. 33.
[139]Ibid., p. 39.
[140]Ibid., p. 33.
[141]'The Road to Benin,' p. 32.

version of the theme, Nwapa emphasises the responsibility of the child within this enterprise. It is Emeka who makes the choice to drop out of school and it is similarly Emeka who acquires the maturity and understanding to take the difficult decision to return home and embark on the creation of a real future for himself. These dual themes of respect for parental authority and education are recurring themes throughout Nwapa's writings.[142]

In *Mammywater* Nwapa returns to the theme of lake and deity seen in her earlier (adult) works *Efuru* and *Idu*. Helen Chukwuma has observed: 'Nwapa in [*Mammywater*] delineates the features and attributes of *uhamiri*, the goddess of the lake. These features are drawn from popular beliefs, worship and legend of the Ugwuta people.'[143] *Mammywater* is about the courage and fortitude, and once again, respect for, and attentiveness to advice, of Deke, a young boy, who goes in search of and rescues his sister, Soko, from the bottom of the lake when she is abducted by mammywater. Deke, however, rescues not only his sister but brings about the reunification of his entire family as well as a restoration of peace to the spirit world – that is between *okita*, the god of the river and *uhamiri*, the goddess of the lake – and thus his own community. The story is based in large part on dialogue generated in a series of question and answer interchanges between the story's characters or what Ifeoma Okoye refers to as Nwapa's 'use of questions and answers as a technique in story writing.'[144] Nwapa uses this style to illustrate the application of the well-known Igbo proverb, 'those who ask questions never get lost,' to the subject of child-rearing. Obviously, a people who value discussion and interrogation, this is an art which the author would appear to believe should be further encouraged in the Igbo psycho-cultural and educational environment of raising children. Deke puts this art to successful use in *Mammywater*. He is particularly precocious combining his boldness with great wisdom and humility for one so young. He asks

---

[142]When Ozoemene in 'The Delinquent Adults' (*This is Lagos*) loses her husband in a road accident, she sadly recalls the advice of many family, friends and school authorities to finish school first before getting married. The death of her husband leaves her penniless and with two children to raise. 'My Soldier Brother' (*This is Lagos*) also emphasises the value of education. Adiewere excels academically, wins a scholarship to the University of Lagos and is a source of great joy and pride to his family. Although the human wastage of war is the primary theme of this story, that of education is also significantly present. Similarly, Efuru does not listen to her father with respect to her choice of husband and ends up with an unsuitable marriage.
[143]Quoted by Agbasiere, 'Conquerors of the Universe,' p. 575.
[144]Ifeoma Okoye, 'Flora Nwapa's Legacy to Children's Literature,' in Umeh, ed., *Emerging Perspectives on Flora Nwapa*, p. 584.

Mammywater so many questions about his sister, Mammywater herself, the workings of her world, his (i.e., Deke's) status in it, and many others, that Mammywater begs for reprieve: 'Son you are too fast for me. Eat your food, we'll talk later.'[145] Yet this obvious tendency for the precocious is juxtaposed with remarkable humility and respect. When the joint purpose of the deities becomes clear, that is to decide the fate of the people of the lake whom the aggrieved *urashi* threatens to harm, Deke humbly asks for forgiveness on behalf of his people and promises to take their message to his people. He so disarms the deities that they willingly agree to all his requests: 'We are completely disarmed. We are happy that you have shown humility. But before Soko is returned to your mother, she ... must come to my home to be entertained ... and she will meet [your father] There she will meet you and Soko also. Then you will all return to your world in peace.'[146]

All through Deke's interaction with the deity he is mindful of the advice given to him. He heeds the warnings of one of the deity's wise and aged worshippers when he is specifically warned to refrain from touching the deity: '[D]on't ever touch her even if she says you can.'[147] So confronted with the situation and in response to the question posed by Mammywater :

'[W]ill you like to touch me?' Deke emphatically replies:
'No.'
'I won't hurt you,' responds Mammywater.
'No,' he reiterates.
'My clever boy, if you had touched me, you would have turned into a fish.'[148]

The theme of listening to one's elders (in other words paying attention to the advice of those concerned for one's welfare) prevalent in Nwapa's writings has already been illustrated in a number of her works. Here again in *Mammywater* it is apparent. Furthermore this intention of Nwapa to put across this message links up with the agenda of traditional Igbo folklore retold in some of Nwapa's adult books. In *Efuru* for instance, the folkstory recounted by Eneke the village storyteller revolves around the same themes.[149] The beautiful girl who disobeys

---

[145]*Mammywater*, p. 21.
[146]Ibid., p. 45.
[147]Ibid., p. 8.
[148]Ibid., p. 19.
[149]*Efuru*, pp. 105 - 111.

her mother's instructions to stay indoors is forced into marriage by a spirit. It is only through the support of one sister (*again the theme of family support is foregrounded*) that the spirit-husband is destroyed and she is able to escape the frightening prospect of life with the spirit. It is also noteworthy that the complementary nature of the sexes in Igbo society demonstrated throughout this thesis is once again given prominence in *Mammywater* in the battle between *urashi* the river god and *uhamiri*, the lake deity. The conflict between these two communities represented in the two deities – male and female – is portrayed by the author as a 'personality clash' rather than a gender war. At the centre is ego and personal aggrandizement more than anything else.[150] The resolution to this crisis is brought about, as Emenyonu aptly captures it, '[by] mutual understanding, acceptance and respectability, human qualities which have no gender.'[151] The theme of family support is also as strongly visible in the children's as in the adult text. In *Mammywater*, it is Deke who embarks on a dangerous journey into the unknown to save his sister. In *Emeka-Driver's Guard*, Ngozi proves to be an understanding and highly supportive sibling to Emeka and their aunt a very able surrogate mother. *The Adventures of Deke* is a slight variation of *Mammywater* published a year later for still younger children[152] but maintaining all the key plots and themes of earlier text as is 'Magic Cocoyam' where this time it is Kele who goes in search of his sister Lala abducted not by mammywater but the wily Mother Tortoise.[153]

As we have demonstrated, Flora Nwapa's texts for children attempted to respond to what she perceived as a serious vacuum in the children's literature of her time – the woeful failure to act as generational transmitters of culture, thereby leaving children and young adults ill-equipped to deal with the innumerable challenges of African sociopolitical existence. Perhaps, Nwapa was anticipating the impact of the current HIV/AIDS pandemic in Africa. HIV/AIDS is one of the greatest catastrophes to confront Africans in this age, particularly with regard to children and young people. The Joint United Nations Programme on HIV/AIDS (UNAIDS) currently estimates that 11.5 million Africans have died since the outbreak of the pandemic a quarter of whom have

---

[150]Emenyonu, 'Flora Nwapa's Writings for Children: Visions of Innocence and Regeneration,' in Umeh, ed., *Emerging Perspectives on Flora Nwapa*, p. 604.
[151]Ibid.
[152]Brooks, 'Either Pound in The Mortar Or Pound in The Ground,' p. 609.
[153] 'Magic Cocoyam,' p. 47.

been children.[154] Up to 23.3 million African adults and a further one million children are living with HIV/AIDS. Fifty-five per cent of these adults are women. Ten million children have lost one or both parents to HIV/AIDS, creating large numbers of street children and leaving a significant proportion of households headed by children. Nwapa would have anticipated the need to prepare adults and children alike to reassume/reinforce their age-old roles of mutual supportiveness within the extended family to meet this challenge. In the next and final chapter we shall explore the crucial role which the African family, as defined by Nwapa in her portrayal of motherhood, fatherhood and the extended family, can play in confronting and overcoming this grave emergency of the era.

---

[154]UNAIDS, *Report on the Global HIV/AIDS Epidemic* (Geneva, 1998) and UNAIDS, *Epidemiology* (Johannesburg, 30 November 1998). The rest of the statistics below have been derived from these UNAIDS references.

7
Nwapa and contemporary Africa: history as future

It is not often that one hears or reads about Africa in the West in a manner which inspires people and rekindles faith in the capacity of Africans to restore to themselves control over their own destiny, and implement, in an operative sense of the word, their own self-defined norms of human existence/co-existence and their own life opportunities. Yet, in Africa such stories abound, attested to by the capacity for daily existence and survival, often under conditions which the average Westerner could not even begin to conceptualise or fathom. And herein lies the irony which is Africa, its human resilience. In those most harrowing of African daily life experiences which often translate into Western public analysis, academic discourse, despair and fatigue over this continent, lie great opportunities to glimpse the enormous possibilities of an economic and social breakthrough for this humanity. This is based on a history, which as we have demonstrated in this study, incorporates these possibilities which can become dominantly operational when the underlying determinants of societal instability are addressed. Indeed, the very glimpses of societal possibilities demonstrate the very high probability of African peoples recapturing and reshaping their own destinies in the course of time. To the 'foreign' observer in Africa, however, the unrelenting thrust of community movement by these people towards a more humane and enduring society is often lost beneath the cascade of gruesome statistics and scenes of poverty, want and deprivation. The abuse of Africans by African leaderships is clear. The attempt at the retrieval of this loss of humanity by these peoples, especially the pivotal role women do and must increasingly play is too often indiscernible.

No greater confirmation has been given to this fact than my last three years of work as a Regional Gender Advisor on HIV/AIDS for the United Nations Development Programme in Africa. The 'popular' statistics on AIDS in Africa are fraught with numerous problems of credibility. However, these problems notwithstanding, it is safe to say that HIV and AIDS remain one of the most threatening conditions to an African capacity, described above, to recapture and reshape its own developmental ethos and direction. The complexity and degree of devastation of the virus vary from one country to another, from one region to another, indeed from one local community to another. Yet as AIDS is a global epidemic, it is safe to assume that the virus is present wherever human habitation currently exists on this extremely compact and accessible globe. Furthermore, women are disproportionately affected by this epidemic both as those infected by the virus and also as carers of those infected and affected by HIV and AIDS. We can therefore assume, that in the absence of a supportive environment that honestly and openly seeks ways of reinforcing local efforts at curbing the spread of the epidemic, those low prevalence zones may very rapidly soon disappear. So what could be construed as positive, indeed inspiring amongst this spectre of human privations? My United Nations work has exposed me to a variety of experiences where the undaunted spirit of the communities visited reconfirmed for me the legitimacy and essentiality of maintaining faith in African human resolve. These communities have been central in mitigating the impact of HIV and AIDS on their peoples through a range of activities including counselling, community and home-based care, welfare support, and income generating activities, buttressed, or not as the case may be, by the efforts of national governments. In several countries, community-based action is at the front line of the struggle against HIV and AIDS, responding to the specific needs of communities and wherever possible, playing an advocacy role for a re-evaluation of structures and systems that continue to impede societal development and therefore facilitate the easy transmission of the disease.

Grave times: confronting a serious emergency of the age

HIV/AIDS is currently Africa's most devastating emergency. The African family, by its very nature, must be centrally situated in any serious attempts to address the spread of this epidemic. We should now review those essential elements or traits which commonly feature in the structure and set up of most African families and which have been impacted most by the epidemic. Pointedly, these elements can also be instrumental in the fight against HIV/AIDS. It stands to reason that development must be perceived and approached as a whole, the actions of the totality of societal activity by its constituent parts to bring about progress. Similarly, responding to the emergency created by the epidemic is a function of the whole unit which on this occasion is the family. There must be a recognition of the roles women and men have historically played, and can once again play in the reordering of their society in times of crisis - in this case, stemming the spread of HIV/AIDS. There must also be a decisive shift in approach from addressing the subject of this emergency singly and out of context of the whole to employing a holistic approach that draws on a knowledge base predicated on both a historical and cultural understanding of the workings of African society. Africa's sociocultural institutions, particularly those that support gender relations, continue to function, albeit diminished in power. These gender-based and other pro-active indigenous social organisations and networks are the only real hope for rapidly and systematically halting the spread of HIV/AIDS in Africa at a time when most colonial/post-colonial state institutions have virtually become non-functional.

What are the key factors of the HIV/AIDS epidemic in Africa? An understanding of the nature of the epidemic is crucial to this exercise, especially the manner in which it does and potentially can impact on and challenges members of a family or community:

1. 23.3 million adult Africans and a further 1 million children are classified to be currently living with HIV/AIDS.

2. Young people are disproportionately affected by HIV/AIDS with about 50 per cent of infections occurring in people aged 15-24. Indeed sexually transmitted diseases as a whole are most common among the age group 15-24.

3. African women are disproportionately affected by the HIV epidemic, with more women than men currently being infected. Furthermore, close to four-fifths of all infected women worldwide are in Africa. More than 80 per cent of all infected women become infected through a male sex partner. Indeed the majority of infected married women have become HIV+ through (very often) their only sexual partner - their husbands.

4. It is believed that HIV/AIDS is now contributing in a major way to the increase in child mortality rates currently being experienced across Africa.

5. Life expectancy at birth for the vast majority of African countries, has, in the wake of HIV/AIDS, seen a dramatic drop.

6. Between one-third and one-half of all HIV infections in young children is

estimated to have been acquired through breast-feeding. By far the vast majority of babies in Africa are breast-fed.

7.   Death rates among adults appear to have increased dramatically in the years following the advent of HIV/AIDS in Africa, that is between the late 1980s/early 1990s. Specifically, the bulk of these deaths occur within the younger adult ages, in the prime of life.

8.   Morbidity rates, predictably, are also very high. The often long incubation period between infection and illness/death ensures that the physical effects of the infection on the individual are not immediately apparent. Once infection occurs, the individual progressively becomes subject to a host of opportunistic infections requiring medication/physical treatment, sustained care and psychosocial support.

9.   The psychological trauma of discovering that one is HIV+ and the resulting impact on self, family, and friends is enormous and often life-shattering.

10. The social ramifications of the epidemic, in an atmosphere often characterised by great ignorance and fear about the disease, means that the tendency for the abuse of individual and communal rights, the violation of legal and ethical norms of behaviour, become greatly heightened - at all levels of society.

11. Most people in Africa, young and adult, do not know about HIV or STDs, and more specifically, whether or not they are themselves infected.

12. The cost of treating HIV+ people with a course of antiretrovirals is, at current state health budgetary allocations, beyond the capacity of all African countries. Even basic health services, including the provision of essential drugs, ante-natal care, etc, are currently unavailable to the vast majority of Africa's population.

13. Health care institutions, as they currently exist in Africa, cannot solely provide the care and support required for the numbers of people now affected by HIV/AIDS.

14. There is currently minimal availability of centres for counselling and voluntary testing in all African countries, as well as detailed information about

safe feeding to pregnant women or those considering pregnancy.

15. There is currently minimal technically accurate, easily comprehensible, culturally sensitive information on HIV/AIDS available to the vast majority of Africans.

Impact: motherhood, fatherhood, familyhood

We earlier demonstrated the communal and inextricably linked nature of African family systems and how these systems constitute the very core of African social existence. We have also shown how the roles played by women and men in contemporary African society demonstrate the distortions and disequilibrium within families that occurred in the wake of Africa's conquest and occupation and the current grave crisis of the so-called nation-state. The subsequent distortions and dislocations that have occurred in African family life and which currently define African gender relations have serious repercussions for coping with the impact of the onslaught of HIV/AIDS. Yet, in spite of these distortions, there remain clearly recognisable, though latent features of Africa's past network of gender relations and social institutions in contemporary society which have not been incorporated in any meaningful way in the HIV/AIDS response within countries. Here, we shall examine how the challenges posed by the epidemic (as outlined above) presently impact upon the network of family relationships and activities. The cohesive fabric that defines and binds family life in Africa is now so stressed and pulled in virtually opposite directions as official or quasi-official attention (minimal though it is) continues to be focused on individuals or categories of individuals (e.g. women, orphans) rather than on the family - the comprehensive whole that embodies these various groups and where, we maintain, the staying capacity exists. Until that focus on attention, effort and resource is shifted by national governments from categories of individuals or newly created institutions to the *family unit and existing indigenous institutions*, little progress will continue to be made in arresting the spread of the epidemic.

Motherhood

To the vast majority of African women in contemporary society, motherhood remains the ultimate fulfillment and manifestation of being female. It is, as earlier stated, the embodiment of love, nurturing, psychological and material support. In other words, the complete propagation of the family lineage. The stresses placed on the roles embodied in motherhood are already apparent and have crucial implications for the quality of Africa's subsequent generation. As discussed, nurturing begins at birth through the close physical and emotional bond established between mother and child. One major component of this bonding process is through breast-feeding. If we consider the fact that more women are increasingly being infected with HIV and especially are more vulnerable to infection, it becomes apparent that this nurturing role and all that this entails will be affected, with grave ramifications for the subsequent generation. In a state of diminished personal health, it is apparent that the involvement of the mother in the life of the child, especially as regards its emotional and social development in the early years, will be severely curtailed. Even the process of breast-feeding, in the light of the scientific evidence available, stands threatened once there is sufficient awareness (regardless of how well-informed this awareness is) of the linkages between the mother's infected status, as assessed by her infected breast milk and general ill-health, and the child's ill-health. As HIV takes its toll on African mothers and women in general, we also witness a further strain on women caused by the pressure on them to generate material resources and contribute to the upkeep of the family at a time of massive male unemployment and general economic collapse of the 'nation-state.' Again, as the mother's health fails, or she increasingly devotes time to caring for a loved one/family member who is ill, her capacity to generate income is invariably diminished. In other words, precisely at a time when greater resources are required by the family, a woman infected by HIV finds that she is greatly limited in her capacity to fulfil one of her most fundamental roles as a mother - *to provide the required emotional and material support to her family*. The mother's traditional role as educator has already been noted. In this role, she lays the foundation in the early years of the child for the development and promotion of basic skills required for socially appropriate behaviour. The importance of this role cannot be overstressed. It helps crucially to develop the child's sense of self, worth and respect, as well as his/her connection with the family and community as a whole. The propagator of the lineage implies a womanhood with advanced managerial skills, particularly in her capacity to organise and manage the complex workings and often divergent interests of the household. The maintenance of the requisite energy demanded by such personal, family, and societal obligation or commitment, will invariably and increasingly become untenable as HIV/AIDS sets in on communities - *especially when any informed preventative action is absent at the family level.* If a mother, for instance, is expelled from her home upon becoming HIV positive (a reaction that has occurred is some cases) as a result of fear, ignorance, prejudices about the epidemic, or when the mitigating role of the extended family no longer functions, the resulting impact on the family is even more devastating. Here, two emotionally, spiritually and materially deprived households are created - the family from where the mother has been expelled, and the new family of refuge for the mother which may or may not include her children. These forms of social traumas are on the increase.

As millions of Africa's up-coming generation are raised under conditions of great economic deprivation intensified by the HIV epidemic, and further deprived of the maternal anchorage needed to cope in the circumstance, a frightening picture of a youth population with a wholly diminished capacity to extract itself from incredible levels of poverty, is steadily emerging.

Fatherhood

Fatherhood co-exists effectively and in a complementary manner with motherhood as we have stressed more than once in this study. The family, the epicentre of African social existence, could not have become such a widely acknowledged asset if the constituent members were not perceived as equal, though different contributors to the process. As in the case of motherhood, fatherhood was defined by certain distinct features, roles and responsibilities which combined with that of the mother to underscore the supportive nature of African family life. It is indeed ironical and tragically misleading that presently, in some of the literature on African gender relations, men are categorised as 'individualists who put their own desires first' in contradistinction to their women who are 'hardworking and caring with a strong orientation towards community.'[1] While African women are represented as 'hardworking and caring,' they remain nevertheless 'disempowered with little control over their social and sexual lives.'[2] Our study emphatically questions the degree to which this male/female character dichotomy, especially as it is applied to African peoples is valid. It cannot be disputed that African women have systematically and progressively lost ground in African society with regards to their socioeconomic and political status since the conquest of Africa. As they have lost out in these arena so have men simultaneously 'gained', skewing the gender balance significantly, with the resulting mono-gender (male) perspectives

---

[1]See K. Rivers and P. Aggleton, *Men and the HIV Epidemic* (New York: UNDP HIV & Development Programme 1999), p. 3.
[2]Ibid.

witnessed in virtually all spheres of the contemporary 'nation-state' society. As those institutions which promoted the social and economic independence of women came under attack and were further marginalised, society witnessed a shift in responsibility towards men as the primary provider of the family's material resources. Historically and in contemporary times, the African male's family and societal obligations, especially as a major contributor to the family's resources was and remains an established cultural ethos. Attempts at the portrayal of African men in some gender study as 'lazy' are not just 'uncomfortable' as S. C. White has asserted in a contribution to the debate,[3] but blatantly racist. Such studies demonstrate a lack of understanding of the burden of dispossesiveness that Africa has been forced to bear in its recent history and the clear challenges of reconstruction that it faces. As we have shown in this study, laziness, lack of effort, and lack of commitment to succeed, were, and are all frowned upon in the vast majority of African societies. African men continue to be judged by their capacity to ensure that, as the Yoruba say, 'shame does not befall the family.'

What impact does HIV/AIDS have on this role of fatherhood in particular and consequently the capacity of the family to withstand the impact of the epidemic? The HIV epidemic has further aggravated an already seriously undermined economic situation within African families. Individuals employed in the public and private sectors have systematically been subjected to retrenchment by employers because of ill health or 'potential' ill-health (i.e., when AIDS is suspected). This has operated largely under the guise of 'sector rationalisations' in the light of prevailing economic conditions. Indeed African men who, as we noted earlier, occupy the majority of positions within these 'nation-state'-created structures have been hardest hit by the dismal levels of economic performance in Africa in the past decades. Sector after sector has folded up - from the small scale subsistence cash crop farmer to the banker, to the civil servant. The outbreak of the HIV epidemic has served only to hasten and cement this process. The role of fatherhood, as the main provider within the family has therefore suffered greatly, as increasingly this role has become unrealised and unrealisable. Fathers also play crucial roles as educators of the children (especially male children) as they move into adolescence and beyond, as we earlier discussed. More importantly, the father, largely, sets family standards - standards of achievement, success, and standards by which the child's definition of self can coherently emerge. Indeed, the father sets

---

[3] Quoted in Rivers and Aggleton, *Men and the HIV Epidemic*, p. 3.

standards by which the very aspect of 'manhood' in that household could be judged. As earlier stated, the underlining and distinctive spirit and philosophy of African people, exemplified through the male is that their children achieve, produce, excel, survive, and in general, live and enjoy life in ways that they (the preceding generation) had not had the opportunity of experiencing. This, unfortunately, is now a prayer which, on the African scene, appears increasingly to be unanswered. In the absence of a father able to fulfil his role either as provider or educator, his ability to set the example of a model of responsibility and support towards his family is becoming highly problematic. Once again, the nature of the family legacy being handed to the subsequent generation must be called into question.

Yet, some of the examples/standards which have come to define fatherhood/ 'manhood' in recent times must be carefully examined. Power shifts and the break down of traditional norms of behaviour, especially as regards marriage, have created current situations which in the past would have been clearly unacceptable. Polygyny, an institution where the man is able to marry more than one wife at the same time, could not occur in the absence of the requisite economic resource on his part to maintain and sustain his added responsibilities towards the larger household. Furthermore, the taking of an additional wife could never occur without the involvement and consent of the existing wife/wives, and the event was always a formalised relationship – i.e., a proper marriage. When these conventions are ignored, as we have noted in *One is Enough* and *So Long A Letter*, it plunges the family into turmoil. The first wife is fully involved in the process of 'selection' of all subsequent wives to the family, underlying a very practical consideration in the process - considerations to do with, in particular, either the continuation of the lineage, health, economics, or the acquisition of greater status by the man of the house. Contemporary African society has witnessed the abuse of this institution. Not only are wives and families more often than not, not informed about these decisions by their husbands/fathers, etc., there is an associated lack of respect in this treatment which is demeaning to women, as with Amaka (*One is Enough*) and Ramatoulaye (*So Long A Letter*). Within many of these relationships, women may and do suffer from a total lack of support and even abuse. Undoubtedly, the institution of polygyny presently (whether formal or informal) has serious ramifications for addressing the HIV epidemic in Africa. First, preventative action by members of the concerned household becomes impossible if the husband/father engages in extra-marital relationships that undermine the couple's sexual health. Second, the family's capacity to plan for the future needs of members is again undermined if there is an uncertainty as regards the composition of that membership. Thirdly, and most importantly, the father's role as educator who sets, in large part, the standards of 'manhood' and fatherhood in that household, undermines the very essence of not only his own family (through the display of such levels of disrespect and abuse towards his spouse) but also that of the subsequent male generation which tend to imbibe and perpetuate such values. The importance of the father as regards the establishment of a cohesive family unit in which his responsibility to ensure the interests of the household (wife/wives and children are adequately taken care of) is undisputed. It is a requirement in Africa that a man ensures the smooth functioning of his household and societies judge a failure of this task quite harshly. This has always implied a necessary *joint partnership* between males and females in conducting what ostensibly is perceived, labelled, and accepted to be a male role, since, as we have shown, it is women who constitute the real power base in the home - implementing and managing the details. As a result of the HIV/AIDS epidemic there is now a need, more than ever before, for a re-thinking of these attitudes increasingly adopted by some men, which have resulted in enormous damage to the African family unit.

Extended familyhood

The extended family has always been, in the African context, a bedrock of social support to its members who are made up of both those related by blood and marriage. It constitutes the essential fabric which weaves together members of a family of diverse views, dispositions, and interests. This societal 'fabric' is defined by a mutual commitment to support its members in any manner required, but most notably, emotionally, physically and financially. In this manner it also acts as a form of check and balance within the family to ensure that the actions of individuals (as a result of this shared identity) remain within the boundaries of acceptable behaviour, ensuring that the well-being of the family and its individual members are not jeopardised by the actions of a few. Here family heads or the elderly are ascribed a particularly important role such as serving as arbiters of family disputes and historians of the family's past, interests and aspirations. The entire network of the extended family operates much like a welfare system or a *safety net* which provides social, emotional or material support to its members as necessary. With the advent of HIV/AIDS, this buffer zone of support has become very stretched. Increasingly, greater numbers of people call upon this support system for assistance. These calls emanate from needs as diverse as financial contributions to the numerous revenue-consuming funerals that occur in Africa, caring support for a sick member, caring for the children of people affected by HIV, and perhaps most importantly, a continued display of love, recognition, understanding and acceptance by the extended family towards members living with HIV.

HIV and society's response efforts

State services in Africa cannot solely respond effectively to the onslaught of the HIV epidemic. Rather, the role of the family must be seen as *central* in this endeavour. But what does a national HIV/AIDS response actually mean in practical terms and how can the roles of men, women and children (as outlined earlier) support these processes? We have illustrated how the African family, as a cohesive whole, has been devastated by HIV/AIDS. We have also shown that by drawing on the value systems defined and in large part retained by much of Africa, we may perhaps be tapping into the only realistic way available for preventing the continuing and uncontrollable spread of HIV. The greatest challenge to the multiplicity of players in the field of HIV in Africa (government, NGOs, UN, etc.) now lies in summoning up the commitment to focus centrally on the family by using existing structures accessed by and binding on it. AIDS practitioners would then have firmly placed decision making-power and control into the one arena in Africa where *real* decision making power exists – in the family.

With the virtual collapse of the continent's nation-state, Africa's pre-conquest indigenous sociological structures and practices currently constitute the only social institutions which are truly binding on the overwhelming majority of its people. It is what we have elsewhere referred to as 'real Africa,' somewhat removed from the structures of the state which are clearly in disarray. This distinction of the contemporary African social scene must be emphasised in order to get away from the convenient and quite often irresponsible conclusion that some commentators make by conflating the evident crisis and decay of the institutions of the African nation-state with those of indigenous Africa.[4] Such a conflation is totally invalid. On the contrary, the spectacular resilience of Africa's indigenous sociological institutions during the devastating crisis of the past decades that has gripped and all but in name strangled the nation-state, has given fresh impetus to the demands made by leading African

---

[4] See, for instance, Rivers & Aggleton, *Men and the HIV Epidemic*, Stratton, *Contemporary African Literature and the Politics of Gender*, Achufusi, 'Feminist Inclinations of Flora Nwapa,' and Umeh, 'Reintegration with the Lost Self'.

intellectuals that the foundation for the African Renaissance Project of the new millennium (the envisaged sociocultural rebirth of Africa), must be built on the people's 'real Africa'.[5] Indeed, it is to the financial/economic coffers of 'real Africa' that the 100,000 exiled African intellectuals (forced into exile due to the crisis of the nation-state and domiciled largely in North America and Europe) currently repatriate the sum of approximately £1 billion annually.[6] Essentially the fund is used to maintain the extended family (by covering, feeding, school/hospital fees and general welfare) and investing in the local economy particularly in the construction of new homes and the maintenance of existing family estates. The primary motive for this major infusion of capital from abroad stems from the fact that those concerned still imbibe one of the principal African value attributes which we examined earlier - namely, that the individual is their 'brother's/sister's keeper'. The funds just mentioned are dispatched through networks of activity and operation, many of which are often very fluid and informal, yet very tangible and employable as a route for channelling information and mobilising communities to action. Generally, this characteristic of informality, delegation and the decentralisation of decision-making and social activity typifies the workings of the institutions of indigenous Africa. With this alternative cultural framework of development and progress in place, Africa could not have been more imbued with the possibilities of escaping from the haunting quagmire of stagnation in which it currently finds itself. These indigenous institutions exist in every sphere of African societal activity. The objectives, goals, expectations and the operationalising networks of these 'home-bred' organisations differ from community to community, nation to nation, but they all broadly share those dominant characteristics we referred to above. We shall now examine one such organisation - a 'family town union'.

---

[5]Amadiume, *Reinventing Africa*.
[6]Communication (June 2000): Professor Herbert Ekwe-Ekwe. See his engaging *African Literature in Defence of History* (Dakar: African Renaissance), forthcoming October 2001.

Adu Progressive Union[7]

Background

The people of Adu or Uburu, in eastern Nigeria, live in 14 constituent villages with a total population of approximately 50,000. The headquarters of the Adu Progressive Union (APU) is situated in Uburu. It has 120 branches across Nigeria and overseas. Membership of a branch can range from one family to scores or hundreds of people, depending on the number of Uburu people living in the particular community. The APU has always existed (not necessarily under this name) in one form or another as far back as any member can remember. It is, in essence, both the main structure and process whereby the members of a community have collectively sought to address their needs over time. There is one single requirement of membership - that is s/he must be of Uburu origin or married to someone from the town. This network of individuals in turn are involved in a series of other networks, the primary one of which is their own individual family. Examples of other networks that could be found within this structure would include groups such as churchgoers, farmers and businesspersons. Meetings are held twice a month and more could be called in the event of an emergency.

Structure

There are two equal and autonomous arms of the APU - the women's and men's assemblies. Each functions independently of the other and the decisions/positions adopted by one cannot be overruled by the other. This ensures that at all times decisions have to be arrived at by consensus of the majority within both assemblies. Each assembly elects its own officials. Meetings are held bi-monthly within each wing and a joint session of the men and women assembly is held in alternate months. Meetings are held in members' houses, a deliberate policy designed to allow for a duality of functions - holding meetings/conducting official business with minimal overheads and entertainment/socialisation amongst members.

---

[7]Madam Nwaoyiri Ngwu (chair of APU Women Assembly), Madam Osunankata Okaome, Madam Adaku Ikeazu, Madam Ogonna Okonne, Mazi Agom Dibia, and Mazi Oje Nwa-Odi are gratefully acknowledged for information on the Adu Progressive Union and for their typical African warmth and hospitality during my research.

Objectives

The expressed aim of the APU is the development and advancement of Uburu and its people. This has meant that over the years, the APU has taken on a variety of tasks including building and maintaining a secondary school, local road construction/expansion, building new wards in the local hospital, building a bank, and building a post office which was then 'handed over' to the national department of communication for 'status approval'. Uburu would still be without a post office but for this APU initiative!

Activities

The APU is involved in a variety of development activities within and outside Uburu itself. These include:

1. Support to members in distress. This includes both financial assistance as well as advice.

(a) Financial
Provision of interest-free loans. As in any organisation, the financial means of the APU membership differs greatly, ranging from very wealthy businesspersons to relatively poor subsistence farmers. This implies that the degree to which individuals are able to support the union, in addition to offering skills for their collective advancement would differ. Interest-free loans are made available to members either directly from the coffers of the union, or via a member able to provide the loan. The loan is however lodged in the central pool of funds of the organisation and advanced by the APU, as an organisation to the individual as opposed to person to person.

(b) Advice
Marital advice constitutes one of the greatest service areas undertaken by the APU. Issues of support for newly-weds, family planning, children's welfare as well as infidelity, infertility, wife abuse, etc., are among the most commonly tabled for discussion and advice. The aim of the concerned wing, the women's in this case, is to resolve any difficulty being experienced by its members. This will take the form, in the first instance, of advice to the couple - singly or jointly, away from the forum of the meetings. Sanctions can however be imposed on the offending party (for example on the man in the case of establishing wife abuse) by a joint session of the women's and men's assembly.

As stated above, the goal of the APU is to resolve the problem internally so that the marriage is preserved and so that couple avoids costly litigations in state courts that hardly inspire public confidence anyway. Besides, the APU would wish to avoid the inevitable adverse publicity that would be generated in court proceedings focusing on an erring member!

2. Settlement of disputes usually involving land or other litigation. Again, members are strongly discouraged from resorting to the state judicial system and taking up legal action against a fellow member of the community unless it is completely unavoidable.

3. Infrastructural development of Uburu. Every year (usually in November/December), the APU headquarters, in consultation with its branches, draws up a detailed programme of the following year's activities with associated budgets. This can include the renovation of a school, extension of a unit in a hospital/purchase of equipment, building of sports facilities, etc. This information is sent to all branches which then proceed to levy members according to their means and willingness to contribute resources over and beyond the requested amount. It is interesting to note that there is not on record - written or orally - a case of embezzlement of local funds.

4. Social/emotional support during periods of bereavement, marriage, childbirth, etc.

5. Insurance benefits during periods of bereavement, marriage and childbirth. The monthly dues paid constitute a form of social security or insurance. The dues ensure that in the event of any of the three occasions discussed above, a lump sum is paid to the concerned family in lieu of his/her monthly payments.

6. Use of member's other professional/social networks in support of fellow members. As stated above, all members of the APU would have varying levels of access to a variety of other networks and sources of support by virtue, for instance, of their professional work and social circles of interaction. These channels are actively utilised to support the membership. For example these can be as varied as access to cheap or scarce produce, the provision of an introductory letter to a bank manager to procure services, or minimal payment for household repairs. It is perhaps worth noting that the majority of APU members are usually self employed - farmers, businesspeople, artists, artisans, etc.

HIV/AIDS connection

The scope for HIV preventative activity is enormous in this set-up, as confirmed by the chair of the APU women assembly who was interviewed for this research[8]. The following points were considered:

1. The APU annual programme of activity drawn up during the November/December general meeting should be able to incorporate HIV/AIDS activities and targets of achievement for each branch, its members, and their families.

2. The counselling role already undertaken by both the women and men assemblies could be expanded to include areas of HIV counselling in its totality, providing members with information and skills on how to address issues pertaining to this major crisis situation.

3. The insurance schemes set out to support members in times of need could be re-worked to support members/their families who become either too ill to work and/or in establishing alternative businesses.

4. The APU men and women joint sessions could prove to be invaluable forums and opportunities to address areas of gender inequity and inequality, practices that could put either men or women at risk, and mechanisms for addressing, in a realistic format, the health of the family and community as a whole.

The potential in Africa for effectively addressing the HIV/AIDS crisis within families and at community level, using existing indigenous structures, is *enormous and the examples endless.* What is needed is a programme by practitioners of HIV/AIDS to *systematically and energetically* engage these groups. Within Uburu, there exists four other key pertinent structures which could easily be incorporated in this programme:

---

[8]Madam Nwaoyiri Ngwu, Interview (Uburu, 20-24 November 1999).

Umunna

These are groups in which all members are related paternally. Within these groups, there are often subgroups which are age and gender specific. All these groups meet regularly and predate the period of conquest in Igboland.

Umunne

The *umunne* are the matrilineal equivalent of the *umunna*. These are individuals related maternally, including direct siblings, cousins, aunts, uncles, grandparents, etc. Similarly, within this group, divisions by age and gender occur. Interestingly, for the purposes of HIV/AIDS work, there are numerous occasions when the constituent units of the *umunne* and *umunna* meet as a group to address an important or crisis situation, and discuss remedial action.

Umuada

This network is one of great interest and potential to the dissemination of HIV/AIDS information primarily because it transcends geographical boundaries. The *umuada* are made up of the married and unmarried female members of a family who may live away from their communities but retain strong linkages with their community and family through these organisations. These structures are used to raise resources, provide social and psychological support to relatives, contribute to the development of their communities even if they are no longer, at least physically, a member of this (original) community. (Another important incentive to keep in touch with this community of birth is that according to the tradition, it is here and not at her husband's that the woman is buried when she dies.) Although a number of the *umuada* may have married out of their communities and consequently no longer reside there, meetings are held periodically and can be called in the event of an emergency. Such meetings would, once again, be extremely important forums for addressing issues of HIV/AIDS.

Inyom di

These are wives of the family and are therefore unrelated by blood. They are in other words in-laws. Like the *umuada*, they often traverse two families - theirs and their husbands. The interconnectedness of individuals and families is here made very evident, as is the capacity for becoming conduits of information and preventative activity to a myriad of peoples and especially family members. Finally it is perhaps important to remind ourselves that there are literally hundreds of such family/community based indigenous institutions across Africa that could and would willingly take up the core of HIV/AIDS prevention if appropriately approached and presented by its practitioners. This is of course quite apart from the innumerable NGOs that have sprung up in recent times to address various issues at community level. It cannot be overemphasised that the institutions of 'real Africa' must be central in the continent's current effort to combat the scourge of HIV/AIDs.

The challenge: Flora Nwapa in these times

It has been necessary to introduce issues of HIV/AIDS as they relate to the African family into this study. This has been embarked upon for a number of reasons. Primarily, there is a need to directly link up the overwhelming historical evidence attesting to the true roles played by African women (and men) in the development of their societies, with an HIV/AIDS solution. In so doing we hope to highlight the role that they (women and men) could and must play in dealing with one of Africa's most devastating emergencies. It is clear that the gender discourse seriously needs to be divested of its current emotive, generalised and largely uninformed characterisation, particularly in the light of 20 million infected women, men and children and millions more impacted by the 'fall out'. Additionally, there is a need to demonstrate how ahistorical theories on Africa have emerged, in a very real and dangerous sense, as the main theoretical backdrop and reference point for policy makers and programme developers on HIV/AIDS in Africa. The family, and the central role of the mother, has been selected as the focus of analysis in an attempt to stress the need for the total involvement of a powerful African institution that is central to the very existence of society. The family also constitutes the norm in society. By far the vast majority of Africans have linkages to family and family life. In so doing we have critiqued the seemingly conventional focus on Gender and HIV/AIDS discourse which revolves around 'individual risk and societal vulnerability' by highlighting presumed social phenomena 'incumbent' in a target population and how these may impact on or are being impacted on by the epidemic. In the case of Africa, the thrust of such focus is to point, for instance, to issues like wife 'inheritance' or 'disinheritance' and then evaluate or establish how these affect the spread of the epidemic. The fundamental philosophical problem with this approach is that there is a presumption about the character of the population which places the society at risk of infection. The discourse is predicated on the notion that the norms and values of the population are somewhat 'flawed,' thus support and assistance must be given to it to overcome these 'deficiencies'. Our research, on the contrary, starts from a position diametrically opposed to this premise. *We contend that the norms and values of African society are inherently valid and as such have the capacity to deal with any emergency, including HIV/AIDS.* Hence, our focus on the African family and its myriad of supportive institutions.

Besides, the social phenomena often cited as grounds for gender inequities and increased societal vulnerability in Africa at best convey the experiences of a minority of the population. It is not that these are unimportant concerns. Our position is that the war against the spread of HIV/AIDS in all its manifestations will begin to gain real momentum and indeed be won when and only when we focus on and utilise channels through which the collective experiences of Africans (women and men) are played out. Indeed how else could these important subjects of justice and equity (e.g. wife 'inheritance' by the brother of the deceased as in the case of Idu in *Idu*, wife 'disinheritance' of women – of their land and property – upon the death of the spouse, female circumcision or 'female genital mutilation') be permanently and decisively addressed except through this collective medium of family?! To put the gender discourse in perspective, it is important to understand that most African women *do not* become 'inherited' wives; most *do not* lose their homes because they are rejected by family; most *do not* undergo rituals of circumcision; most *do not* resort to sex work in exchange for money or goods or favours... It thus begs the question as to why these emerge as some of the more central issues in the discussions that affect African women whether in HIV/AIDS, gender studies/literary analysis, sociology, anthropology or development studies. Within this collective relationship/experience called family, it is important to recognise that African women have never truly been representative of the images in which they have been cast in the gender and literary discourses. To recall Abena Busia's apt observation, '[I]t should be recognised ... that the Africa being discussed ... has very little to do with *any* "Africa" Africans themselves, from whatever part of the continent might recognise as "home"' (added emphasis).[9] African women are not, have never been powerless, exploited and downtrodden, requiring external support to give direction and purpose to their being and role in society. As far as African women are

---

[9]Busia, 'Manipulating Africa,' p. 168.

concerned, 'the feminine ideal' *is categorically not* 'characterised by women's passivity, ignorance, and expectations that they will defer to men's sexual needs...'[10] Even in the light of their current political marginalisation and loss of social and economic status which we have highlighted, women remain central to the very existence and survivability of the African family and a real powerful force for mobilisation. Critically, most African women see themselves as such a force for change.

Similarly, in our understanding of the gender roles of African men, we have once again confronted and disproved stereotypes about this particular group, without minimising the gravity of the injurious behaviour (towards women and their families) in which *some* men engage. Male roles in Africa are not, and could not possibly be characterised by 'sexual prowess, multiple partnerships and control over sexual interactions...'[11] These stereotypically invented 'African men' and 'African women' need to be debunked once and for all, giving way to a more balanced, realistic and informed discourse on male and female roles in Africa with a focus on how the positive attributes of each of these roles can be harnessed in combating the spread of this epidemic. The 'conventional' discourse on gender has in fact had important ramifications for the manner in which practitioners have approached the mobilisation of the community. Because this discourse has hitherto been predicated on the negative stereotypes and faulty extrapolations and generalisations about society, rather than the use of centuries of tried and tested value systems, structures and processes that have been the mainstay of African society, practitioners of HIV have tended to be extremely prescriptive in dealing with communities. Thus, communities are not meaningfully engaged in dialogue about how they can, given the strengths of their own human resource, protect themselves and their families from the epidemic. Rather, they are presented with a list of 'Dos' and 'Don'ts' about their behaviour - most pointedly, sexual behaviour, cultural traditions and belief systems. As cultural beliefs are deeply rooted in society, this prescriptive approach serves only to further alienate these communities, and, more ominously, present HIV as some intractable problem. We have demonstrated that there is an existing African social, economic and political framework for addressing the ramifications of HIV on the family and thus on society. One of the greatest challenges facing all HIV/AIDS practitioners is a genuine and

---

[10]See UNAIDS Technical Update, *Gender and HIV/AIDS* (Geneva, September 1997), p. 4. See also Stratton, *Contemporary African Literature and the Politics of Gender*, p. 103.

[11]UNAIDS Technical Update, *Gender and HIV/AIDS*, p. 4.

courageous shift in perspective and resource that allows for the hub of HIV activity to rightly relocate to the nerve centre of Africa's social existence - *the family and the community as represented through the multiplicity of institutions that have evolved in its support.*

In the light of our discussion, the treasures of Africa, rather than the diamonds, oil, gold and other material resources bandied around in developmental parlance are African peoples, typically represented in units of families that inhabit the continent, the majority of whom are women. Flora Nwapa's position, as demonstrated throughout her writings, consistently shows the immeasurable role women have played, as women in their own right, in the construction and development of their societies. The women encountered during my United Nations work follow in the traditions of Efuru and Idu in their industriousness and ability to establish autonomous structures to address society's problems. These women do not necessarily consult the male population in developing their response to a perceived societal problem, and their activities are not hostile to the interests of other members of society. Quite clearly, they are responding to a serious societal emergency that is affecting the health, socio-economic and indeed survival status of their societies. As with Efuru and Idu their activities complement those of men and other interests in society. In contrast, the United Nations mainstream and other IMF/World Bank-driven assumptions on development in Africa currently are derived from a Western intellectual tradition which has, in effect, hardly acknowledged the African heritage of the Efurus and Idus. Within this 'new' model or tradition women do and have always occupied a subordinate role as we have shown in this study. Nwapa illustrates the loss of power and status that have occurred for Igbo women, women's reactions to and responses to these losses of autonomy and the subsequent distortions of these roles which we currently witness in society. From Nwapa's classical works, *Idu* and *Efuru*, we get a feel for the crucial role women have played as mothers, educators, providers, and overall architects of their own society. In Nwapa's Biafra War literature we again have insight into the enormous contributions of Igbo women to the social, economic and spiritual continuity of society in the midst of this human tragedy. Nwapa's post-war literature accomplishes two important functions. First, it manages to convey the degree and seriousness of the erosion of women's societal rights and responsibilities and the institutions created to safeguard these. Secondly, it clearly illuminates the vast potentiality, nay societal obligation, women have to recapture their legacy as architectural partners in the reconstruction of the nation, if an Igbo world-view of society is to predominate. Nwapa's writings are vindicated by historical and sociological fact about both the roles and status of women in the pre-European conquest state and their positions subsequently, especially as regards their political and economic marginalisation. Furthermore what her writings have clarified which the main corpus of contemporary historical and sociological discourses have as yet not seriously addressed, are the undaunted efforts adopted by Igbo women to survive what amounts to an onslaught, while attempting to minimise losses to both their individual and institutional autonomy, in all spheres of human interaction. In the remainder of this study, we shall, drawing once again on Nwapa's writings, suggest how she would have seen women positioned in this particular epoch, working to recapture their legacy fully in order to rescue a clearly dysfunctional society. We shall examine the key roles consistently attributed to Igbo women by Nwapa with a view to identifying possible ways forward for this humanity.

Motherhood - restated

As stated elsewhere in this study, motherhood for Nwapa includes not solely a woman's capacity to conceive and deliver a child, but an overarching philosophical institution that at once incorporates a woman's familial and communal responsibility and the organic cultural sensibility of the people. Motherhood for Nwapa, we have demonstrated, is the embodiment of love, nurturing, wisdom or temperance (constantly acting as a mediating voice of reason in the home and community) and strength - an enduring but extremely purposeful capacity that emphasises a definitive element of selflessness without at all being disinterested in the well being and advancement of the self. Indeed we are able to discern three broad concepts of Nwapa's definition of motherhood. First, there is the physical process of childbirth which is felt by Igbo women to represent an extremely important definition of their femaleness or womanness - the capacity to deliver a child into the particular lineage and society as a whole. Along with this process is the mother's ability to provide appropriate nurturing and caring for the child, using all personal, familial and societal resources available. Second is an inherent often minimised (in contemporary society) individualised and collective role of supervision and guidance to the community and in particular its children, in effect the subsequent generation of society's citizens. This component of mothering embodies the collective responsibility of women (including those who have not borne children) to steer society's growth, through its youth in a particular direction and according to prescribed norms and values as defined by the overall society. The third clearly discernible theme which runs though Nwapa's concept of motherhood is closely linked with the second - the element of individual and communal responsibility. However, it is the spiritual component of society that is here emphasised. Mothering incorporates an intuitive appreciation for and responsibility to infuse in society's offspring a spiritual base that honours and reaffirms the sanctity of all life, in all its dimensions, and consequently the social responsibility society's members must have for one another. This then is the basis upon which the monumental task of motherhood operated in Igboland prior to the European conquest. It remains a legacy that has for too long been confined to Africa's historical past, falling far below its potential in its capacity to impact upon the development of contemporary society. Vestiges of this legacy clearly exist within not only this society but Africa as a whole, but sadly it is greatly diminished.

To further illustrate the lost opportunities to impact their society that have occurred for Igbo women we shall compare two distinctly different mothering roles and historical era in Nwapa's writings - Efuru and Idu on the one hand, and the women in Nwapa's later works including Rose, Agnes and Dora in *Women are Different* (women immediately preceding Nigeria's liberation from British rule), Kate in *Never Again* (the Biafra War period), and Amaka in *One is Enough* (in the post-Biafra War era). Each of these periods we will observe marks a progressive shift for women away from the roles defined above. That is, a role of active co-participant in defining the modality of society's operation, through both the articulation as well as the practical demonstration of the spiritual, the humane, the loving, the compassionate, the just face of society; characteristics which most of humanity would accept are critical in defining and directing every aspect of human economic, political and social advancement. It is therefore of little surprise that as society has become more skewed, more marginalising and therefore distorted in its perspective, the ugliness (the fear, the terrible conflicts and loss of life, the despair, the desperation, the injustice) in society has occurred increasingly as the collective influence of women has diminished. The most discernible difference between characters Efuru, Idu and Ojiugo as women of an earlier historical epoch, and the remainder of Nwapa's women in the novelist's later works, is the sense of worth and esteem in which the former women hold and are held by their societies. Both *Efuru* and *Idu* are replete with instances that demonstrate that Efuru, Idu and Ojiugo are women of considerable standing in society. The humility of these women, despite their societal reputability, remains prominently intact, demonstrating the correspondingly high levels of esteem to which the women equally hold members of their own community.

Efuru is consistently and tirelessly available to members of her community for advice and direct assistance. Her influence and assistance in arranging for Nnona to have an operation at the general hospital is greatly appreciated by the patient and her family alike. From Nnona's daughter, 'Efuru...[t]hank you very much...We have no words to thank you.'[12] Efuru has gone about securing help for Nnoni with resolute purpose and determination and has succeeded. Similarly Ojiugo is a woman of standing in the town. 'She was prosperous, had a lot of will power and was very generous.'[13] Idu's magnanimity is also a source of comment in the town, including her influence, in this regard on her husband Adiewere. 'Idu is a good woman...Adiewere was not all that magnanimous when he married Idu. Now the two of them are about the kindest couple I know in this town.'[14] Kindness, compassion and the observance of the old adage about being one's brother's/sister's keeper are hallmarks of these three women's characters and behaviour. They clearly see themselves as having a communal/social responsibility to respond to the needs of the people of their society, either through the mobilisation of collective action or in the provision of individual financial and emotional support, depending on the nature of the need. In other words, these women exhibit the highest standards of public conduct and possess both a social conscience and a sense of social responsibility in addressing the needs of their society, most especially given their relatively privileged positions. Efuru is the epitome of *communal motherhood*. She demonstrates through her actions all those components of motherhood earlier discussed - love, compassion, nurturer, provider, educator, and, to borrow a most apt phrase from Nah Dove's recent study on African mothers, the 'determinant of the fruition of [society's] future potential.'[15] Her home is the centre of congregation, especially by children, where they daily partake of Efuru's generosity in the form of meals and story-telling. Efuru, commenting on their timely arrival at her home at meal times, states, 'These children are just in time. The way they time themselves is admirable. If you have a late lunch, they are sure to be there to have it with you. If you have an early lunch it suits them best...'[16] Similarly it is at Efuru's house that Eneke, town story teller, conducts his regular sessions of local narrative. These are not merely gatherings for entertainment but opportunities for moral instruction. Not only do the stories themselves contain in-built lessons of

---

[12]*Efuru*, p. 132.

[13]*Idu*, p. 35.

[14]Ibid., pp. 2 - 3.

[15]Nah Dove, *Afrikan Mothers: Bearers of Culture, Markers of Social Change* (New York: State University of New York, 1998), p. 234.

[16]*Efuru*, p. 100.

morality and social behaviour, but the children's presence in Efuru's home affords opportunities of direct instruction about behaviour and conduct, as the example of Oputa reveals.[17] Oputa is one of the five children who arrives, uninvited, at Efuru's house for lunch. Oputa tries to prevent another of the children from eating, claiming that on the previous day he had not shared food given to the group with him. Efuru gently admonishes the young boy in an attempt to curb any leanings towards selfishness, even at such a tender age. Efuru's incapacity to fulfil the physical component of motherhood does not preclude her involvement in other areas. She is undoubtedly a *mother* in the most important sense of the word as defined in Nwapa's world. She is caring and generous, bright, hard working with a strong sense of natural justice and social responsibility. Indeed she is acutely aware of the responsibilities which her privileged position places on her and she easily rises to the occasion. It would appear that in Efuru's world wealth and social standing grow in direct proportion to one's sense of responsibility to one's community.

In Idu, we see the same sort of sense of social responsibility for the community. Idu is filled with compassion for Uberife, a mother whose son displays symptoms of mental illness, and decides to visit her to see what can be done to assist her. This is in spite of Nwasobi's (her friend) concern about both the enormity and sensitivity of this mission. Uberife is highly honoured by Idu's visit and offer of help: 'Idu you have come to my house today. This year will be good for me. I am honoured today. Please wait for me to bring a mat that befits you.'[18] Indeed it is Idu's social standing in society that gives impetus to her level of magnanimity and social concern. Like Efuru she is acutely aware of duty to family and community, that wealth must be shared by the entire society, and the responsibility which wealth and achievement (in particular) place on a person. In Nwapa's subsequent works, especially *One is Enough*, *Wives at War* and *Women are Different* we see a *decided shift* in the focus of mothering. The three phases discernible in Nwapa's earlier writings remain visible but with some components assuming much greater prominence than others. Communal responsibility and the provision of guidance for society's young is greatly diminished, giving way to a much more focused emphasis directly on the welfare of the individual and the individual's family. This is not to suggest that the sense of community and the assumption of responsibility for the other has evaporated in its entirety. Rather, through Nwapa's later writings, we witness

---

[17]Ibid., p. 101.
[18]*Idu*, p. 120.

a diminishing emphasis on this particular component of mothering. Hence Amaka accumulates great wealth in Lagos, and these resources fail to impact on her community in any meaningful way beyond helping individual friends and the personal acquisition of yet more houses and cars! Through her remarkable business acumen, Dora, in *Women are Different* also accumulates a fortune. But this has no useful impact either on her own community or indeed her own immediately family in the form of her daughter for whom the wealth is clearly a corrupting influence. Indeed in all subsequent characters we fail to see the interest in and commitment to the community which we see in Nwapa's earlier characters in *Idu* and *Efuru*. There is no real sense of social responsibility and that tenet of pre-conquest Igbo, indeed African cultural life and philosophical thought of being one's sister's/brother's keeper, has become increasingly marginalised both in its importance and application in society. The loss of Igbo women's autonomy and their efforts to respond to and cope with this loss have not occurred without some major cost to society. Herein lies the tragedy of contemporary Africa and the crux of Africa's problem. African philosophical and cultural systems have failed to make the leap from an *independent* or pre-European conquest society into contemporary settings, contemporary world-views/perspectives and contemporary social mores. This has occurred as a result of the continuing devaluation of African culture. With the European conquest of Africa, Igbo and indeed other cultural systems became stifled and were no longer in a position to develop and advance on their own terms. *Rather these cultures were now responding to the diktat of the conquest.* It cannot be overstressed that the European conquest robbed African peoples of the opportunity of their own continuing cultural development primarily in accordance with the logic of their own societies. What we have in contemporary Africa are caricatures of European cultural thought and institutions. It is this fact that Nwapa recognises and demonstrates in her writings. It is this unique insight into the near asphyxiation of Igbo culture, especially as it has impacted on women in post-conquest Igboland, that is Nwapa's greatest achievement and undoubtedly her triumph. Nwapa demonstrates the consequences of the degradation of Igbo indigenous systems and beliefs, tracing the transition of society from independent pre-conquest times where we witness the existence of an ingrained social conscience and sense of collective responsibility as demonstrated in *Efuru* and *Idu*, to the resulting total social disarray which defines contemporary society, the unfortunate recipient of decades of first conquest and occupation, and then dubious developmentalism. In recognising the immense contributions of Igbo women to the evolution of their societies as we have demonstrated in this study, they must, once again, recapture the moral, spiritual, political and economic ethos and power upon which their societies were built and flourished for centuries, thus taking the lead in the *re-birth* of Africa ... Renaissance Africa.

Selected bibliography

Work by Flora Nwapa

Novels
Efuru, London: Heinemann Education Books, 1978.
Idu, Oxford: Heinemann International, 1970.
One Is Enough, Enugu: Tana, 1981.
Never Again, Enugu: Tana, 1975.

Short Stories
'The Campaigner,' in Chinua Achebe, et al, *The Insider: Stories of War and Peace from Nigeria*, Enugu: Nwankwo-Ifejiaka, 1971.
This is Lagos and Other Stories, Enugu: Nwankwo-Ifejiaka, 1971.
Wives at War and Other Stories, Enugu: Tana, 1980.

Poetry
Cassava Song and Rice Song, Enugu: Tana, 1986.

Essays
'Women in Politics,' *Presence Africaine*, 141, 1, 1978.
'Nigeria – The Woman as a writer,' *Realities*, 1, 1985.
'Priestesses and Power Among the Riverine Igbo,' in Flora Edouwaye S. Kaplan, ed., *Queens, Queen Mothers, Priestesses, and Power: Case Studies in African Gender*, New York: New York Academy of Sciences, 1997.
'Women and Creative Writing in Africa,' in Obioma Nnaemeka, ed., *Sisterhood, Feminisms, and Power*, Trenton: Africa World, 1998.
'Writing and Publishing for Children in Africa – A Personal Account,' in Raoul Grandqvist and Jurgen Martini, *Preserving the Landscape of the Imagination: Children's Literature in Africa*, Amsterdam/Atlanta: Editions Rodopi, 1997.

Children
Emeka-Drive's Guard, London: University of London, 1972.
Mammywater, Enugu: Flora Nwapa Books, 1979.
The Miracle Kittens, Enugu: Flora Nwapa Books, 1980.

The Adventures of Deke, Enugu: Flora Nwapa Books, 1980.

Journey to Space, Enugu: Flora Nwapa Books, 1980.

'The Magic Cocoyam,' in Flora Nwapa and Obiora Moneke, ed., *Journey to Space and Other Stories*, Enugu: Flora Nwapa Books, 1980.

Historical and literary criticism & other works

Abubakr, Rashidah Ismaili, 'The Emergence of Mariama Ba,' in Abdulrazak Gurnah, ed., *Essays on African Writing*, Oxford: Heinemann Educational, 1993.

Achebe, Chinua, 'Igbo's Road to Recovery,' *Tell*, Lagos, 27 December 1999.

Achebe, Chinua, 'Words of Anxious Love,' *The Guardian*, London, 7 May 1992.

Achebe, Chinua, *African Trilogy*, London: Pan Books/William Heinneman: 1988.

Achebe, Chinua, *Hopes and Impediments*, Oxford: Heinemann International, 1988.

Achebe, Chinua 'Chi in Igbo Cosmology,' in Achebe, *Morning yet on Creation Day*, London: Heinemann Education Books, 1975.

Achebe, Chinua, 'Girls at War,' in Achebe, *Girls at War and Other Stories*, London: Heinemann Educational Books, 1972.

Achebe, Chinua et al, *The Insider: Stories of War and Peace from Nigeria*, Enugu: Nwankwo-Ifejiaka, 1971.

Achufusi, Ify 'Feminist Inclinations of Flora Nwapa,' *African Literature Today*, No. 19, 1994.

Afigbo, A.E., 'Women in Nigerian History,' in Martin Ijere, *Women in Nigerian Economy*, Enugu: Acena Publishers, 1991.

Afigbo, A.E., 'Women as a Factor in Development,' in Martin Ijere, *Women in Nigerian Economy*, Enugu: Acena Publishers, 1991.

Agbasiere, Julie 'Conquerors of the Universe: Flora Nwapa's Kiddies on the Move,' in Marie Umeh, ed., *Emerging Perspectives on Flora Nwapa: Critical and Theoretical Essays*, Trenton and Asmara: Africa World, 1998.

Aidoo, Ama Ata, *Changes: A Love Story*, London: Women, 1993.

Ajayi, Ade, 'Colonialism: an episode in African history,' in L.H. Gann and P. Duignam, eds., *Colonialsm in Africa, Vol 1*, Cambridge: Cambridge University, 1969.

Ake, Claude, *A Political Economy of Africa*, Harlow: Longman, 1981.

Amadiume, Ifi, *Male Daughters, Female Husbands: Gender and Sex in an*

African Society, London: Zed books, 1987.

Amadiume, Ifi, *Reinventing Africa*, London & New York: Zed Books, 1998.

Amuta, Chidi, *The Theory of African Literature*, London and New Jersey: Zed Books and Institute for African Alternatives, 1989.

Andrade, Susan, 'Rewriting history, motherhood, and rebellion: naming an African women's literary tradition,' *Research in African Literatures*, 1990.

Ani, Mariama, Yurugu: *An African-Centered Critique of European Cultural Thought and Behavior*, Trenton: Africa World, 1994.

Anyanwu, U.D., 'Gender Question in Igbo Politics,' in U.D.Anyanmu and J.U. Aguwa, eds., *The Igbo and the tradition of Politics*, Enugu: Fourth Dimension, 1993.

Ardner, Shirley, ed., *Defining Females: The Nature of Women in Society*, London: Croom Helm, 1978.

Asante, Molefi Kete, Kemet, *Afrocentricity and Knowledge* Trenton: Africa World, 1990.

Azodo, Ada Uzoamaka, '*Efuru* and *Idu*: Rejecting Women's Subjugation,' in Umeh, ed., *Emerging Perspectives on Flora Nwapa*, Trenton and Asmara: Africa World, 1998.

Bâ, Mariama, *So Long a Letter*, London: Heinemann, 1981.

Bala, Sasi, 'Heroines of Flora Nwapa,' *Commonwealth Fiction, Vol. II*, 1988.

Banyiwa-Horne, Naana, 'African Womanhood: The Constrasting Perspectives of Flora Nwapa's *Efuru* and Elechi Amadi's *The Concubine*,' in Carole Boyce Davies and Anne Adams Graves, *Ngambika: Studies of Women in African Literature*, Trenton: Africa World, 1986.

Barthes, Roland, *Writing Degree Zero*, London: Cape, 1967.

Bascom, William & Melville Herskovitz, eds., *Creativity and Change in African Cultures*, Chicago & London: University of Chicago, 1959.

Bazin, Nancy Topping, 'Weight of Custom, Signs of Change: Feminism in the Literature of African Women,' *World Literature Written in English*, 25, 2, 1985.

Berrian, Brenda, 'The Reinvention of Women through Conversations and Humour in Flora Nwapa's *One Is Enough*,' *Research in African Literatures*, 26, 2, 1995.

Boahen, Adu, 'Colonialism in Afria: its impact and significance' in Boahen, ed., *General History of Africa: Vol VII*, London/California/Paris: Heinemann and the University of California and UNESCO, 1985.

Boateng, Felix, 'African Traditional Education: A Tool for Integenerational Communication,' In Molefi Kete Asante and Kariamu Welsh Asante, eds., *African Culture*, Trenton: African World, 1990.

Boehmer, Elleke, 'Stories of Women and Mothers: Gender and Nationalism in the Early Fiction of Flora Nwapa,' in Susheila Nasta, ed., *Motherlands*, London: Women's, 1991.

Booth, James, *Writers and Politics in Nigeria*, London: Hodder and Stoughton, 1981.

Brecht, Bertolt, 'Popularity and Realism,' in E. Bloch et al, *Aesthetics and Politics*, London: Verso, 1980

Brooks, Marvie, '"Either Pound in the Mortar Or Pound on the Ground": Didacticism in Flora Nwapa's Children's Books,' in Umeh, ed., *Emerging Perspectives on Flora Nwapa*, Trenton and Asmara: Africa World, 1998.

Brown, Lloyd, 'The African Woman as Writer,' *Canadian Journal of African Studies*, 9, 3, 1975.

Bryce-Okunlola, Jane, 'Motherhood as Metaphor for Creativity in Three African Women's Novels: Flora Nwapa, Rebeka Njau and Bessie Head,' in Susheila Nasta, ed., *Motherlands*, London: Women's, 1991.

Busia, Abena, 'Manipulating Africa: the buccaneer as "liberator" in contemporary fiction,' in David Dabydeen, ed., *The black presence in English literature*, Manchester: Manchester University, 1985.

Carovano, K, 'More than Mothers and Whores: Redefining the AIDS Prevention Needs of Women,' *International Journal of Health Services*, Vol. 21, 1992.

Carlston,Kenneth, S., *Social Theory and African Tribal Organizations*, Urbana: University of Illinois, 1968.

Carruthers, Jacob, 'Black Intellectuals and the Crisis in Black Education,' in Mwalimu Shujaa, ed., *Too Much Schooling, Too Little Education*, Trenton: African World, 1994.

Cheikh Anta Diop, *Cultural Unity of Black Africa*, London: Karnak House, 1989.

Chikwe, Kema, *Women and New Orientation: A Profile of Igbo Women in History*, Owerri: Prime Time, 1994.

'Children Under Arms,' *The Economist*, London, 10 July 1999

Chinweizu, Onwuchekwa Jemie and Ihechukwu Madubuike, *Toward the Decolonization of African Literature*, Enugu: Fourth Dimension, 1980.

Chukukere, Gloria Chineze, *Gender Voices and Choices: Redefining Women in Contemporary African Fiction*, Enugu: Fourth Dimension, 1995.

Chukukere, Gloria Chineze, 'Images of Women in Contemporary Afrian Fiction.' In Chukukere, ed., *Introducing Readings in the Humanities and Social Sciences*, Onitsha: University Publishing, 1988.

Chukwuma, Helen, *Feminism in African Literature: Essays on Criticism*, Lagos: New Generation, 1994.

Chukwuma, Helen, 'Aspects of Style in Igbo Oral Literature,' in Chukukere, ed., *Introductory Readings in the Humanities and Social Sciences*, Onitsha: University Publishing, 1988.

Conde, Maryse, 'Three Female writers in Modern Africa: Flora Nwapa, Ama Ata Aidoo and Grace Ogot,' *Presence Africaine*, 82, 2, 1972.

Davies, Carole Boyce, 'Motherhood in the Works of Male and Female Igbo Writers: Achebe, Emecheta, Nwapa and Nzekwu,' in Carole Boyce Davies and Anne Adams Graves, eds., *Ngambika: Studies of Women in African Literature*, Trenton: Africa World, 1986.

Diallo, Alpha Boubacar, 'Maternal Mortality in Senegal - Implications for Africa,' *African Peoples Review*, Vol. VI, No. 2, May-August 1997.

Diop, Cheikh Anta, in Carlos Moore, 'Conversations with Cheikh Anta Diop,' *Presence Africaine*, Nos. 3/4, 1993.

Diop, Cheikh Anta, *Civilization or Barbarism*, New York: Lawrence Hill Books, 1991.

Diop, Cheikh Anta, *Cultural Unity of Black Africa*, London: Karnak House, 1989.

Dove, Nah, *Afrikan Mothers: Bearers of Culture, Makers of Social Change*, New York: State University of New York, 1998.

Dudley, Billy, *Instability and Political Order*, Ibadan: Ibadan University, 1973.

Ebogu, Afam, 'Igbo Sense of Tragedy: A Thematic Feature of the Achebe School,' *Literary Half-Yearly*, 24, 1, 1983.

'Eight countries, one destiny,' *Newsweek*, New York, 15 November 1999.

Ejizu, Christopher, *Ofo: Igbo Ritual Symbol*, Enugu: Fourth Dimension, 1986.

Ekejibua, F.E., 'Omu Okwei: The Merchant Queen of Ossomari,' *Nigerian Magazine*, No. 90, 1996.

Eko, Ebele, et al, Flora Nwapa, *Critical Perspectives*, Calabar: University of Calabar, 1997.

Ekwe-Ekwe, Herbert, *Africa 2001: The State, Human Rights and the People*, Reading: International Institute for African Research, 1993.

Ekwe-Ekwe, Herbert, *Issues in Nigerian Politics Since the Fall of the Second Republic*, Lampeter: Mellen, 1991.

Ekwe-Ekwe, Herbert, *The Biafra War, Nigeria and the Aftermath*, Lewiston & Lampeter: Mellen, 1990.

Ekwe-Ekwe, Herbert, *Conflict and Intervention in Africa*, London and Basingstoke: Macmillan, 1990.

Ekwensi, Cyprian, *Survive the Peace*, London: Heinemann, 1976.

Emecheta,Buchi, *The Joys of Motherhood*, New York: George Braziller, 1979.

Emecheta, Buchi, *Destination Biafra*, London: Allison & Busby, 1982.

Emenyonu, Ernest, 'Who does Flora Nwapa write for?' *African Literature Today*, No. 7, 1978.

Emenyonu, Ernest, '(Re)configurations of Child Symbolism,' in Umeh, ed., *Emerging Perspectives on Flora Nwapa*, Trenton and Asmara: Africa World, 1998.

Evans-Pritchard, E.E., *The Position of Women in Primitive Societies and Other Essays*, London: Faber and Faber, 1965.

Ezeigbo, Theodara Akachi, 'A Chat With Flora Nwapa,' in Umeh, ed., *Emerging Perspectives on Flora Nwapa*, Trenton and Asmara: Africa World, 1998.

Ezeigbo, Theodara Akachi, 'Myth, History, Culture and Igbo Womanhood in Flora Nwapa's Novels,' in Umeh, ed., *Emerging Perspectives on Flora Nwapa*, Trenton and Asmara: Africa World, 1998.

Ezeigbo, Theodora Akachi, 'Traditional Women's Institutions in Igbo Society: Implications for the Igbo Female Writer,' *African Languages and Culture*, Vol. 3, No. 2, 1990.

Ezekwugo, Christopher, *Chi: The True God in Igbo Religion*, Alwaye: Pontifical Institute of Philosophy and Theology, 1987.

Ezenwa-Ohaeto, 'Breaking Through: The Publishing Enterprise of Flora Nwapa,' in Umeh, ed., *Emerging Perspectives on Flora Nwapa*, Trenton and Asmara: Africa World, 1998.

Ezenwa-Ohaeto, Chinua Achebe, *The Life*, Oxford: James Currey, 1997.

Feldman, D.A. ed., *Global AIDS Policy*, Connecticut: Bergin & Garvey, 1994.

Fido, Elaine Savory, 'Okigbo's *Labyrinths* and the Context of Igbo Attitudes to the Female Principle,' in Davies and Graves, eds, *Ngambika: Studies of Women in African Literature*, Trenton: Africa World, 1986.

Finer, S.E., *The Man on Horseback*, London: Pall Mall, 1962.

Fortes, Meyers, *Oedipus and Job in West African Religion*, Cambridge: Cambridge University, 1959.

Frank, Kathleen 'Women Without Men: The Feminist Novel in Africa,' *African Literature Today*, No. 15, 1987.

Freire, Paulo, *Pedagogy of the Oppressed*, New York: The Continuum Publishing, 1970.

Friedl, Ernestine, *Women and Men: An Anthropologist's View*, Stanford: Holt, Rinehart & Winston, 1975

Gerber, Mercella, 'Psycho-Motor Development of African Children,' *Journal of Social Psychology*, Vol. 47, 1958.

Gibbs, James, ed., *Handbook for African Writers*, Oxford: Hans Zell Publishers, 1986.

Gurnah, Abdulrazak, 'Introduction,' in Gurnah, ed., *Essays on African Writing:*

A Re-evaluation, Oxford: Heinemann International, 1993.

Hakim, N.J, and E.G. Bay, eds., *Women in Africa*, Stanford: Stanford University, 1976.

Huntington, Samuel, *Political Order in a Changing Society*, New Haven: Yale University, 1968.

Ike, Chukwuemeka, 'Forward,' in Marie Umeh, ed., *Emerging Perspectives on Flora Nwapa: Critical and Theoretical Essays*, Trenton and Asmara: African World, 1998.

Ike, Chukwuemeka, *Sunset at Dawn*, London: Fontana, 1976.

Ikonne, Chidi, 'The Folk Roots of Flora Nwapa's Early Novels,' *African Literature Today*, No. 18, 1992.

'IMF Says sorry to Africa,' *West Africa*, London: 31 January - 6 February 2000.

Innes, Lynn and Caroline Rooney, 'African Writing and Gender,' in Mpalive-Hangson, Msiska and Paul Hy, eds., *Writing and Africa*, London: Addison Wesley Longman , 1997.

Innes, C.L., 'Virgin Territories and Motherlands: Colonial and Nationalist Representations of Africa and Ireland,' *Feminist Review*, No. 47, Summer 1991.

Innes, C.L., *Chinua Achebe*, Cambridge: Cambridge University, 1990.

Innes, C. L, & Lindfors, Bernth, eds., *Critical Perspectives on Chinua Achebe*, London: Heinemann Educational Books, 1979.

Iroh, Eddie, *Forty-Eight Guns for the General*, London: Heinemann, 1972.

Isichie, Elizabeth, *The Ibo People and the Europeans*, London: Faber and Faber, 1973.

James Adeola, ed., *In their Own Voices: African Women Writers Talk*, London: James Currey, 1990.

James, Adeola, 'Review of *An Introduction to the African Novel* by Eustace Palmer,' *African Literature Today*, 7, 1975.

James, Adeola, '*Idu*: Flora Nwapa,' *African Literature Today*, 5, 1971.

James, Wendy, 'Matrifocus on African Women,' in Shelley Ardner, ed., *Defining Females: The Nature of Women in Society*, London: Croom Helm. 1978

Jell-Bahlsen, Sabine, 'An Interview with Nwapa,' in Umeh, ed., *Emerging Perspectives on Flora Nwapa*, Trenton and Asmara: Africa World, 1998.

Jones, Eldred, 'Locale and Universe,' *Journal of Commonwealth Literature*, 3, 1967.

Kalu, Ogbu 'Ethical Values In Igbo Tradition of Politics,' in Anyanwu and Aguwa, eds., *The Igbo and the Tradition of Politics*, Enugu: Fourth Dimension, 1993.

Ki-Zerbo, Joseph, 'Which Way Africa?' *Development Dialogue*, No. 2, 1995.

Larson, Charles, *The Emergence of African Fiction*, London and Basingstoke: Macmillan, 1978.

Laurence, Margaret, *Long Drums and Cannons*, London and Basingstoke: Macmillan, 1968.

Lebeuf, Annie, 'The role of women in the political organizations of African societies,' in Denise Paulme, ed., *Women of Tropical Africa*, Berkeley: University of California, 1963.

Leith-Ross, Sylvie, *African Women: A Study of the Ibo*, London: Routledge and Kegan Paul, 1939.

Lindfords, Bernth, 'Achebe's Followers,' *Revue de Litterature Comparee*, 48, 3, 4, 1974.

Lloyd, P. C., *Africa in Social Change*, Harmondsworth: Penguin, 1972.

Lukacs, Georg, *The Meaning of Contemporary Realism*, London: Merlin, 1963.

Madubuike, Ihechukwu, *The Senegalese Novel*, Washington: Three Continents, 1983.

Mahood, M.M., *The Colonial Encounter*, London: Rex Collins, 1977.

Mba, Nina, *Nigerian Women Mobilized*, Berkeley: University of California, 1982.

Mezu, S.O., *Behind the Rising Sun*, London: Heinneman, 1972.

Mojola, Yemi, 'The Works of Flora Nwapa, in Henrietta Otokunefor and Obiageli Nwodo, eds., *Nigerian Female Writers*, Lagos: Malthouse, 1989.

Mojola, Yemi, 'Flora Nwapa,' Yemi Ogunbiyi, ed., *Perspectives on Nigerian Literature: 1700 to the Present, Vol. Two*, Lagos: Guardian Books, 1988.

Mohanty, Chandra, 'Under Western Eyes: Feminist Scholarship and Colonial Discourses,' *Feminist Review*, No. 30, 1988.

Moore, Carlos, 'Conversations with Cheikh Anta Diop,' *Presence Africaine*, Nos. 3/4, 1993.

Moore, Gerald, *African Literature and the Universities*, Ibadan: Ibadan University, 1965.

Moore, Gerald, *Seven African Writers*, London: Oxford University, 1962.

Morrison, Toni, *Playing in the Dark*, London and Basingstoke: Pan Books, 1993.

Nasta, Susheila ed., *Motherlands*, London: Women's, 1991.

Ngugi wa Thiong'o, *Barrel of a Pen*, London: New Beacon Books, 1983.

Ngugi wa Thiong'o, *Decolonisnig the Mind: The Politics of Language in African Literature*, London: James Currey, 1982.

Ngugi wa Thiong'o, *Devil on the Cross*, London: Heinemann, 1982.

Ngugi wa Thiong'o, *Petals of Blood*, London: Heinemann, 1977.

Ngugi wa Thiong'o, *The River Between*, London: Heinemann Education Books, 1965.

Ngugi wa Thiong'o, *Weep, Not Child*, London: Heinemann Education Books,

1964.

Njoku, Theresa, 'The Mythic World in Flora Nwapa's Early Novels,' in Umeh, *Emerging Perspectives on Nwapa*, Trenton and Asmara: Africa World, 1998.

Nwankwo, Chimalum, 'The Lake Goddess: The Roots of Nwapa's Word,' in Marie Umeh, ed., *Emerging Perspectives on Flora Nwapa*, Trenton: Africa World, 1998.

Nwankwo, Chimalum, 'The Igbo Word in Flora Nwapa's Craft,' *Research in African Literatures*, 26, 2, 1995.

Nwana, Pita, *Omenuko*, London: Longman, 1933.

Nwoga, Donatus, *The Supreme God As Stranger in Igbo Religious Thought*, Ekwereazu: Hawk, 1984.

Nwoga, Donatus, 'The Chi, Individualism and Igbo Religion: A Comment,' *Conch*, 3, 2, 1971.

Nzekwu, Onuora, *Highlife for Lizards*, London: Hutchinson, 1965.

Nzimiro, Ikenna, *Studies in Ibo Political Systems*, London: Frank Cass, 1972.

Obiechina, Emmanuel, *Culture, Tradition and Society in the West African Novel*, Cambridge: Cambridge University, 1975.

Ogot, Grace, *Land Without Thunder*, Nairobi: East Africa Publishing House, 1968.

Ogu, J.N., 'Creativity and Children's Literature,' in Chidi Ikonne, Emelia Oko and Peter Onwudnjo, eds., *Children and Literature in Africa*, Ibadan: Heinemann, 1992.

Ogundipe-Leslie, Omolara, 'African Women, Culture and Another Development,' *Journal of African Marxists*, February 1984.

Ohadike, Don, *Anioma*, Athens: Ohio University, 1994.

Okereke, Grace Eche, 'Children in Nigerian Feminist Novel,' in Ikonne, Oko and Onwudinjo, eds., *Children and Literature in Africa*, Ibadan: Heinemann, 1992.

Okigbo, Christopher, *Labyrinths*, London: Heinemann Education Books, 1971.

Okonjo, Kamene, 'The dual-sex political system in operation: Igbo women and community politics in Midwestern Nigeria,' in N.J. Hakim and E.G. Bay, eds., *Women in Africa*, Stanford: Stanford University, 1976.

Okonkwo, Juliet, 'Adam and Eve: Igbo Marriage in the Nigerian Novel,' *Conch*, 3, 1971.

Okpewho, Isidore, *The Last Duty*, London: Longman, 1976.

Okoye, Ifeoma, 'Flora Nwapa's Legacy to Children's Literature,' in Umeh, ed., *Emerging Perspectives on Flora Nwapa*, Trenton: Africa World, 1998.

Omotoso, Kole, *The Combat*, London: Heinemann, 1972.

Oppong,, Christine, ed., *Female and Male in West Africa*, London: George Allen,

1983

Osai, G.K., *The African: His Antecedent, His Genius, and His Destiny*, New Hyde Park: University Books, 1971.

Otokunefor, Henrietta and Obiageli Nwodo, eds., *Nigerian Female Writers*, Lagos: Malthouse, 1989.

Ottenberg, Phoebe, 'The Position of Women among the Afikpo Ibo' in William Bascom & Melville Herskovitz, ed., *Creativity and Change in African Cultures*, Chicago & London: University of Chicago, 1959.

Palmer, Eustace, 'Elechi Amadi & Flora Nwapa,' *African Literature Today*, 1, 1968.

Paulme, Denise ed., *Women of Tropical Africa*, Berkeley: University of California, 1963.

Perham, Margery, *The Colonial Reckoning*, London: Collins, 1961.

Phillips, Mellanie, 'Women behaving disgracefully,' *The Sunday Times*, London, 12 October 1999.

Reisman, Paul, *Freedom in Fulani Social Life*, Chicago: University of Chicago, 1977.

Rodney, Walter, *How Europe Underdeveloped Africa*, Dar es Salaam: Tanzania Publishing House, 1972.

Rosaldo M.Z. and Lamphere, L. ed., *Women, Culture and Society* Stanford: Stanford University, 1974.

Rwabukwali C, et al., 'Culture, Sexual Behavior, and Attitudes Towards Condom Use Among Baganda Women,' in D.A. Feldman, ed., *Global AIDS Policy*, Connecticut: Bergin & Garvey, 1994.

Schipper, Mineke, 'Mother Africa on a pedestal: the male heritage in African literature and criticism,' *African Literature Today*, 15, 1987.

Sembene, Ousmane, *Xala*, London: Heinemann, 1976.

Sesay, Kadiatu, 'Ekwensi and Okpewho on the Nigerian Civil War,' *Africa Literature Today*, No. 9. 1978.

Shujaa, Mwalimu, ed., *Too Much Schooling, Too Little Education*, Trenton: African World, 1994.

Sofola, J.A. *African Culture and the African Personality*, Ibadan: African Resources, 1973.

Spivak, Gayatri Chakravorty, *In Other Worlds: Essays in Cultural Politics*, New York: Methuen, 1987.

Steady, Filomina Chioma, *The Black Women Crossculturally*, Cambridge: Schenkman, 1981.

Stratton, Florence, '"The Empire, Far Flung": Flora Nwapa's Critique of Colonialism,' in Umeh, ed., *Emerging Perspectives on Flora Nwapa*, Trenton and Asmara: Africa World, 1998.

Stratton, Florence, *Contemporary African Literature and the Politics of Gender*, London and New York: Routledge, 1994.

Sudarkasa, Niara, 'The "Status of Women" in Indigenous African Societies,' in Ralyn Terborg-Penn et al, *Women in Africa and the African Diaspora*, Washington: Howard University, 1987.

Taiwo, Oladele, *Female Novelists of Modern Africa*, London and Basingstoke: Macmillan, 1984.

Terborg-Penn, Ralyn, et al, *Women in Africa and the African Diaspora*, Washington: Howard University, 1987.

The Report of the South Commission, *The Challenge to the South*, Oxford: Oxford University 1992.

T'Shaka, Oba, *Return to the African Mother Principle of Male and Female Equality: Vol I*, Oakland: Pan Afrikan, 1995.

Uchendu, Victor, *The Igbo of Southeast Nigeria*, New York: Holt, 1965.

Umeh, Marie, 'Introduction: Historicizing Flora Nwapa,' in Umeh, ed., *Emerging Perspectives on Flora Nwapa*, Trenton and Asmara: Africa World, 1998.

Umeh, Marie, 'The Poetics of Economic Independence for Female Empowerment: An Interview With Flora Nwapa,' in Umeh, ed., *Emerging Perspectives on Flora Nwapa*, Trenton and Asmara: Africa World, 1998.

Umeh, Marie 'Reintegration With The Lost Self: A Study of Buchi Emecheta's *Double Yoke*,' in Carole Boyce Davies and Anne Adams Graves, eds., *Ngambika: Studies of Women in African Literature*, Trenton: Africa World, 1986.

UNAIDS, *Gender and HIV/AIDS: Taking stock of research and programmes*, Geneva, March 1999.

UNAIDS, *Report on the Global HIV/AIDS Epidemic*, Geneva, 1998.

UNAIDS, *Epidemiology*, Johannesburg, 30 November 1998.

Van Allen, Judith, '"Sitting on a Man": Colonialism and the Lost Political Institutions of Igbo Women,' in Sharon Tiffany, ed., *Women and Society*, Montreal: Eden, 1979.

Van Sertima, Ivan, 'Evidence for an African Presence in Pre-Columbian America,' in Van Sertima, ed., *African Presence in Early America*, New Brunswick and London: Transaction Publishers, 1992.

Wilentz, Gay, 'Not Feminist but Afracentrist: Flora Nwapa and the Politics of African Cultural Production,' in Umeh, ed., *Emerging Perspectives on Flora Nwapa*, Trenton and Asmara: Africa World, 1998.

Wilentz, Gay, *Binding Cultures* Bloomington & Indianapolis: Indiana University, 1992.

Woodson, C.G., *The Miseducation of the Negro*, Washington: Associated Publishers, 1969.

Young, Robert, *Colonial Desire: Hybridity in Theory, Culture and Race*, London: Routledge, 1995.

Index